ANATOMY OF ABUNDANCE™

A CONSCIOUS GUIDE TO CREATING PROSPERITY IN ALL ASPECTS OF LIFE

Email: patrina@patrinawisdom.com

Website: www.PatrinaWisdom.com.

ISBN # (paperback) 979-8-218-34105-3

ISBN # (Kindle) 979-8-218-34106-0

Hybrid Publishing by Action Takers Publishing™

Dedication

This book is dedicated to every woman out there who has ever grappled with the weight of not feeling that they are "enough." To the women who have wrestled with self-esteem, battled with body image, and found themselves ensnared in the never-ending cycle of comparison, this dedication is for you. It is for those who have grappled with the shadows of their past experiences and traumas, and who have faced fear head-on, refusing to let it shackle them to a life of limitation.

To the women who have nodded "yes" when their hearts were screaming "no," who have spent their lives feeling silenced, functioning as peacekeepers, and maintaining the façade of the "good girl" image—this dedication celebrates your journey toward reclaiming your voice.

To those remarkable women who have discovered the courage to shatter the chains of others' expectations, societal norms, and the control of anyone other than themselves—your strength is both inspiring and powerful. To all the courageous women who have stared down adversity and refused to be defined by it, this dedication is a tribute to your strength and resilience.

This book is a tribute to the women who have boldly refused to be consumed by the relentless hustle culture, recognizing the boundless reservoir of divine feminine energy that flows within them.

To the women who have chosen not to settle for mediocrity and, against all odds, have resolved to create prosperity and wealth in every facet of their lives.

In the pages of this book, we celebrate your unwavering determination to rise above limitations, embrace the abundance that is your birthright, and embody the radiance of your true self. Let it be a testament to your indomitable spirit, your limitless potential, and your unwavering commitment to creating a life of profound abundance.

With unwavering admiration and belief in your limitless potential, Patrina Wisdom

Acknowledgments

No matter how turbulent the journey, I am profoundly grateful for every step of it. Each moment has been a unique thread in the tapestry of my life, weaving together the relationships, the pain, the adventures, and the invaluable lessons that have shaped my path.

I extend my heartfelt gratitude to my perfectly imperfect parents who, through their love and guidance, have nurtured me into becoming the strong, resilient woman I am today. Your unwavering support and enduring lessons have been my foundation.

I am deeply thankful for my co-creative relationship with Spirit, which has led me on this incredible journey of discovery and self-realization. The work that I've been directed to bring forth has been both a privilege and a calling, and I cherish every moment of it.

To the outstanding experts and collaborators who enthusiastically joined me on this beautiful book project, I offer my sincerest appreciation. Your wisdom, dedication, and willingness to co-create have immeasurably enriched the pages of this book.

My heartfelt thanks goes to my spouse, who has been both the sounding board for my wildest ideas and the unwavering shoulder to lean on during moments of uncertainty and self-doubt. Your steadfast support has been my rock.

To my children, I extend my gratitude for your boundless patience and understanding as I've journeyed, sometimes far from home, to serve a higher purpose. Your grace and love inspire me daily.

In this collective tapestry of gratitude, each thread represents a unique and cherished relationship. To all those who have touched my life, whether mentioned here or not, thank you for being a part of this incredible journey.

With profound appreciation and love, Patrina Wisdom

Introduction

Welcome to the pages of *"Anatomy of Abundance™: A Holistic Guide to Creating Prosperity in All Aspects of Life."* I invite you to step into a journey that's far more than just reading another book; it's a transformative roadmap crafted upon the powerful foundation of my "Anatomy Of Abundance™ Framework." If utilized with intention, it can absolutely change the trajectory of your life.

In this extraordinary collaboration, we've partnered with 16 remarkable experts and co-authors. These exceptional minds come bearing not just their specialized expertise but also their deeply personal stories and data, all to provide you with a multi-dimensional approach to creating abundance in your life.

Within these chapters, you'll embark on an exploration that fuses spiritual principles, practical strategies, and timeless wisdom. It's a journey that will lead you toward the manifestation of true abundance, not as an abstract concept, but as a vibrant reality in every facet of your life.

Imagine opening a treasure trove filled with insights and strategies poised to reshape your mindset, elevate your actions, and empower you to craft a life of pure abundance. This is precisely what awaits you within these pages.

By reading this book, you're setting out on a profound journey of growth, purpose, and fulfillment. A journey that promises to be truly life-changing. So, get ready to embrace this holistic guide, for it will illuminate the path toward prosperity in all aspects of your life.

With gratitude for your trust in our collective wisdom and anticipation of the transformation ahead, Patrina Wisdom and our exceptional team of co-authors.

About Author Patrina Wisdom

Abundance Activator & Strategist | Best Selling Author | TEDX Speaker | Living Room Wisdom Podcast Host | Creator of the Anatomy Of Abundance™ Framework | Founder of Pure Abundance Retreat™

https://patrinawisdom.com/

Patrina Wisdom is the CEO and visionary leader of Pure Abundance Inc, abundance activator & strategist, best-selling author, TEDx speaker, podcast host, and founder of the Anatomy Of Abundance™ Framework and Pure Abundance Retreat™. She is committed to guiding women in overcoming generational patterns of struggle, scarcity, and fear and embodying a life of pure abundance.

In 2009, Patrina's husband of 20 years lost his life by suicide. On the same day, she found out she was pregnant with her fourth child. After processing this devastating tragedy, Patrina took her personal story and decades of experience as an entrepreneur and fearless business leader and began the process of creating her company, Pure Abundance, Inc., and Anatomy Of Abundance™ Framework. With a background as a certified life coach, yoga instructor, and NLP practitioner, along with over 20 years of experience as a licensed financial educator and broker, Patrina brings a holistic approach to helping women break free from generational cycles of struggle, fear, and scarcity with a range of programming and luxe retreat experiences designed to help women embrace their personal power and align with their true purpose.

A Word from Your Guide, Patrina Wisdom

If there's one thing I've learned in this journey we call life, it's that true abundance is not defined by the hand we're dealt, but by the choices we make and the actions we take. Just like you, I've traversed the winding paths of existence, seeking to understand the art of crafting abundance in every aspect of life.

I wasn't born into privilege. As an African American woman and the only child born to a 16-year-old single mother, I wasn't handed the manual on how to manifest abundance, nor did I have the luxury of witnessing its embodiment in my early years. My life has been a tapestry woven with diverse experiences, some breathtakingly beautiful, while others were profoundly challenging.

Personal development has always been 'my thing.' In fact, I started my journey of self-discovery at 13 years old, fresh out of grammar school and entering into middle school. For as long as I can remember I've absorbed all I could learn about self-esteem, transformation, … anything that would move me closer to knowing who I am and who I was to become.

And, I believe that my commitment to healing and growing saved my life.

My passion for personal development equipped me to move through many life-altering experiences, including the pain of my first heartbreak, disappointment, molestation, date rape, financial hardship, divorce, the challenges of single parenting, and countless other traumas. I not only made it through all of these experiences but I came through it all with a pretty good sense of self.

My inner work would be tested on the fateful day of January 6th, 2009, a day that forever altered the course of my life. It began like any other day, little did I know that it would soon become a turning point filled with heartache, challenges, and an unexpected path to even deeper self-discovery.

This was the morning that my husband of over two decades—my best friend—my lover and father to my three children—dressed in his suit and tie (as usual), grabbed his briefcase, told us he loves us, and kissed us goodbye, fully aware that this would be the last time.

In the ensuing 24 hours, my husband inexplicably disappeared, and after numerous unresponsive calls and texts, I received a heart-wrenching call from the police, confirming the devastating news that my husband had taken his own life.

I was heartbroken and felt completely blindsided by the news! My husband's sudden disappearance and subsequent discovery of his suicide plunged me into a cycle of profound grief, confusion, and responsibility. If that wasn't enough, in the midst of this turmoil, I discovered I was pregnant with our fourth child, adding a bittersweet layer to an already overwhelming experience.

Overnight, I found myself thrust into roles I had never anticipated—a single mother, the primary breadwinner, and the steward of our finances, and financial business. The weight of those roles was accompanied by self-doubt, fear, and uncertainty. I was forced to confront my own insecurities and embrace a new identity.

Managing the finances was a daunting challenge. Despite my husband's efforts to educate me about financial matters, I felt ill-equipped to navigate this realm. Overnight, I became the beneficiary of a large sum of money from life insurance, providing some financial relief but also a deep sense of responsibility that I had never faced before.

In the days, months, and years following his passing, I prioritized caring for others while neglecting my own well-being. I ensured my children received therapy and support, worked diligently to uphold my husband's reputation and legacy, and extended myself to friends, clients, and family. However, this devotion distracted me from dealing with my grief and masked a crumbling sense of self-worth that was intricately tied to my experience.

I had lost not only my partner but also my sense of safety, and my sense of self. I began stumbling through life, numbing my pain with reckless behaviors like alcohol, shopping, sex, and other vises. I felt like a fish out of water, operating on autopilot while suppressing my grief and feelings of displacement. I kept myself so busy taking care of others, and being what they needed or expected me to be, that aside from a few rumblings in the middle of the night alone in my room, I didn't create space to honor my own pain.

In 2013, a shift occurred. I awakened to the realization that I had been running from the pain and avoiding my true healing. The grief had lingered, and I had been living in the space in between. It was time to face things head on and dive back into a journey of self-rediscovery.

By confronting the void that I had been trying to fill with distractions. The pain, the grief, and the roles I had played for so long were acknowledged. I realized that by embracing my pain, I could transform it into strength. It was a pivotal moment of clarity and acceptance.

My journey from tragedy to triumph involved a process of letting go. I shed the old identity that had been intertwined with my husband's beliefs, familial and societal expectations, and patriarchal bullshit, and I began to rebuild a sense of being self grounded in my own worth and desires. I made the pain "my bitch," and the wounds of the past became stepping stones toward a brighter future.

The chapter of my life that started with heartbreak had transformed into a story of resilience, self-discovery, victorhood, and empowerment. Through pain, I uncovered purpose. Through loss, I found strength. Through adversity, I discovered my own capacity to rise.

So, from the ashes of my grief, a phoenix of empowerment emerged. Like you, the journey was not without challenges. It was a journey of healing, and as a result, it re-defined my sense of purpose. As the pages of my story turned, I learned that transformation is not only possible but essential.

In many ways, I am a reflection of you, and with the cards that life has dealt me, I could have easily chosen to create my future story from a place of scarcity.

However, I made a pivotal decision, a decision that has been the cornerstone of my life ever since—I chose to create my life from unconditional love and abundance instead of responding from a place of scarcity and fear. I opted to shape my existence from a perspective of boundless opportunity and unwavering faith.

In this book, I aim to share not only my personal discoveries but also the framework that was birthed from my journey.

It is my profound honor to present to you the "Anatomy Of Abundance™ Framework"—a distillation of wisdom and insights gathered from my own life and the lives of the experts and authors I've chosen to create this incredible work with.

Within these pages, you'll discover a guide that transcends the boundaries of mere survival and catapults you into the realm of thriving. It is my hope that the insights and principles shared here will serve as beacons of light, illuminating your path toward prosperity in all areas of your life.

Together, we will unlock the secrets of abundance and prosperity, and through shared wisdom, transcend the limitations that life may have imposed upon us.

Table of Contents:

TABLE OF CONTENTS:

CHAPTER 1

Are You Creating from a Place of Scarcity or Abundance?

Abundance is your birthright.

~Patrina Wisdom

In the pursuit of our dreams and goals, it's important to reflect on the mindset from which we approach our endeavors. Are we creating from a place of scarcity or abundance? The answer to this question can have a profound impact on our success, fulfillment, and overall well-being. In this chapter, we will explore the concepts of scarcity and abundance mindsets, their characteristics, and how they shape our creative journeys.

A scarcity mindset is rooted in the belief that there is a limited supply of resources, opportunities, and success. Those who operate from a place of scarcity often view the world as a zero-sum game, one in which one person's gain is another's loss. This mindset is characterized by fear, anxiety, and a constant worry about not having enough. It leads to a sense of competition, comparison, and a tendency to hoard resources.

When we create from a place of scarcity, our actions and decisions are driven by a fear of lack. We may hold back on pursuing our dreams because we believe there won't be enough for us or that we will miss out on opportunities. We may hesitate to take risks, fearing failure and its potential consequences. This scarcity mindset can limit our potential, stifle our creativity, and prevent us from fully realizing our aspirations.

On the other hand, an abundance mindset is grounded in the belief that there is an infinite supply of resources, opportunities, and success available to us. Those who embrace an abundance mindset see the world as abundant and full of possibilities. They understand that one person's success does not diminish their own chances of success; instead, it inspires and opens doors for others.

Creating from a place of abundance means recognizing that there is enough for everyone and that opportunities are abundant. It involves approaching our endeavors with a sense of gratitude, optimism, and possibility. When we create from abundance, we are more likely to take risks, embrace challenges, and persist in the face of setbacks. We trust that the universe will provide what we need and that there is always more to be gained.

So, how can we shift from scarcity to abundance in our creative journeys? It starts with awareness and self-reflection. Recognize the scarcity-based thoughts and beliefs that may be holding you back. Challenge these limiting beliefs and replace them with empowering ones. Cultivate gratitude for what you already have and celebrate the successes of others. Surround yourself with a supportive community that embraces abundance and encourages growth.

Practicing mindfulness and abundance affirmations can also help rewire our thinking patterns. By consciously choosing thoughts and words that affirm abundance, we train our minds to see and attract more opportunities. Visualize your desired outcomes as if they have already been achieved, and let go of attachment to specific outcomes, trusting that the universe will guide you towards what is meant for you.

Creating from a place of abundance is not just about material gain; it's about embracing a mindset that acknowledges the vast possibilities and potential within us and in the world around us. It's about aligning our thoughts, actions, and intentions with the energy of abundance and trust in the process.

Remember, you have the innate ability to create a life of abundance and bring your dreams to fruition. It all begins with the mindset from which you choose to create.

CHAPTER 2

Embracing the Beauty of Duality

Success is not the key to happiness. Happiness is the key to
success. If you love what you are doing,
you will be successful.
~Albert Schweitzer

Amidst the ever-changing landscape of life, I find it imperative to explore a concept that has been weighing on my mind during the creation of this book on abundance—the profound idea of embracing and living within duality.

In the intricate journey of life, we frequently encounter situations, emotions, and experiences that appear to exist in stark contrast to one another. Light and dark, joy and sorrow, success and failure—these dualities are an intrinsic part of our human experience. Yet, rather than perceiving them as opposing forces, I have come to believe that embracing and harmonizing these dualities can lead to a more profound and fulfilling existence.

The acceptance of duality begins with acknowledging that life is an ongoing interplay of opposites. Just as the tides rise and fall, our lives also ebb and flow between these dualistic states. During moments of happiness, it is crucial to remember that periods of sadness may follow, and vice versa. Instead of resisting these fluctuations, we can learn to navigate them with grace, recognizing that both the crests and troughs contribute to our growth and resilience.

Living in duality also invites us to recognize the multifaceted nature of our own selves. Within each of us resides aspects of both light and shadow, strengths and weaknesses, moments of clarity and confusion. It is in the integration of these contrasting elements that we unearth our true authenticity. By accepting our flaws alongside our virtues, we cultivate a more genuine and holistic self-image, nurturing self-compassion and self-acceptance.

Furthermore, embracing duality can enrich our relationships and interactions with others. Every person we encounter brings their own unique blend of qualities, experiences, and perspectives. Rather than passing judgment based on a solitary facet, we can learn to appreciate the complexity and depth that each individual contributes to our lives. This not only fosters empathy but also opens doors to more profound connections.

In the grand tapestry of existence, duality is not a flaw but a remarkable feature. It serves as a reminder of the richness and diversity that life offers. It encourages exploration, elevation, and evolution. It imparts the wisdom that balance and harmony can be discovered within the most seemingly contradictory circumstances.

As you navigate the pages of this book, I invite you to consider how embracing duality can pave the way for a life filled with more ease and flow. After all, your current reality and your future are intricately shaped by every thought, belief, and action you undertake daily. Just Imagine the incredible benefits that will come as you begin constructing your life on the bedrock of an abundance mindset.

The creation of abundance is a continuous journey, one that I've discovered can foster a deeper understanding of ourselves, our relationships, and the world that envelops us.

CHAPTER 3

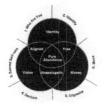

Illuminating Blind Spots—Navigating the Path to Abundance

"The only thing worse than being blind is having sight but no vision."

~Helen Keller

In the pursuit of abundance, one of the most significant obstacles we face is the presence of blind spots. These are the hidden barriers, beliefs, and biases that lurk beneath the surface of our consciousness, obstructing our path to growth and prosperity. This chapter delves into how this book and the Anatomy Of Abundance™ Framework are invaluable tools for identifying and overcoming these blind spots, illuminating the way to a life of abundance.

The Challenge of Blind Spots

Blind spots are tricky because, by definition, we are unaware of them. They are like hidden potholes on the road of life, causing us to stumble and divert us from our intended path. These can manifest as limiting beliefs about money, relationships, or self-worth, often stemming from past experiences of cultural, religious, gender specific, or societal conditioning.

The Role of Self-Reflection

Self-reflection is the first step in identifying blind spots. This book encourages you to embark on an introspective journey, to question your beliefs, and to examine your past experiences. It provides exercises and prompts to facilitate this process, helping you shine a light on those areas where you may be holding yourself back.

The Anatomy Of Abundance™ Framework as a Mirror

The Anatomy Of Abundance™ Framework serves as a mirror, reflecting back to you the areas in your life where abundance may be obstructed. It provides a structured approach to examining your mindset, values, relationships, and actions. By following the framework, you gain insight into where your blind spots may lie.

The Power of Guidance

Sometimes, blind spots are so deeply ingrained that we need external guidance to uncover them. This is where coaches, mentors, or therapists can be invaluable. The framework encourages seeking the support of experts who can provide a fresh perspective and tools to help you navigate these uncharted territories.

Building Awareness and Resilience

Identifying blind spots is not enough; the key is to build awareness and resilience. This book equips you with tools and practices to develop mindfulness, emotional intelligence, and self-compassion. These tools enable you to recognize when you're operating from a blind spot and to respond with greater awareness and intention.

Community Support

Surrounding yourself with a community that values personal growth and abundance can also aid in blind spot identification. In a supportive community, individuals can provide valuable feedback and insights, helping you see aspects of yourself that you may have overlooked. As you read this book, you've gained access to a global community of empowered leaders, particularly focused on embracing and supporting you as you move forward on your transformative journey.

The Continuous Journey

It's important to recognize that the journey of identifying and moving through blind spots is ongoing. As you grow and evolve, new blind spots may surface. The Anatomy Of Abundance™ Framework and the resources in this book are not just tools for a one-time fix; they are companions for your lifelong journey of self-discovery and growth.

The Transformational Power of Awareness

By shedding light on your blind spots, you empower yourself to make conscious choices and align your actions with your true desires. This book and the Anatomy Of Abundance™ Framework are your guides on this transformative journey. Together, they provide the map and the lantern to navigate the terrain of your inner world, illuminating the path to a life of abundance, purpose, and fulfillment.

CHAPTER 4

From Scarcity to Abundance: A Romanian Odyssey

by Izabela Hamilton

To my beloved son, Ezekiel L Hamilton, every word in this chapter whispers of the love and boundless inspiration you bring into my life. This chapter, a narrative of our intertwined lives and a tribute to love, resilience, and abundance, is devotedly dedicated to you. I love you!

Introduction: Between Two Worlds

In the heart of Romania, where ancient forests whisper tales of old and cobblestone streets echo with memories, I began my dance with life. It was a dance of contrasts, the mesmerizing beauty of my homeland against the palpable weight of limited horizons. Have you ever felt the tug of dreams that seem just out of reach? That was my reality, where aspirations often felt like distant stars, beautiful but elusive.

Yet, amidst this backdrop, a quiet voice within spoke of a different tune, one of abundance and boundless possibilities. It whispered of a land far away, where dreams weren't just admired from afar but lived and breathed. With a mix of trepidation and excitement, armed with a few borrowed dollars in my pocket and a reservoir of hope, I set my sights on the USA. But what awaited wasn't just a change of address; it was a profound transformation of my soul.

This isn't merely a tale of miles traveled or dollars earned. It's a journey from a world of 'not enough' to one where the heart and soul know no bounds. As you delve into my story, I invite you to reflect on your own dance with life. Could there be an untapped reservoir of abundance within you, waiting to be discovered?

1. Early Life in Romania

The church bell's chime, a familiar yet distant echo, signaled another day's end in my quaint Romanian town. Those cobblestone streets, once charming, now felt like a confining maze, trapping me in a world I yearned to escape. Amidst the laughter of children and the comforting aroma of freshly baked bread, a longing for something more, something beyond the horizon, cast a shadow over my heart. My soul craved a world not yet here, and it would be years before I understood the power of creating my own reality.

In the soft glow of my room, daydreams of a life unbound by tradition and expectations would envelop me. My mind, a vessel of burgeoning questions and dreams, wandered through the possibilities of a different life. A life where dreams shaped reality, where a young girl like me could dare to envision a future larger than life. Romania, with its rich history and vibrant culture, was embedded in my soul, yet an undeniable voice calling for more constantly whispered in my ear. Questions of identity and place, born in my childhood, now grew into a powerful force, propelling me towards something new.

Books became my escape, tales of brave souls and grand adventures were my solace. Each story whispered assurances that the voice urging me to leap into the unknown, to embrace a new world, was right. In the quiet of my room, a dream of America took root. A simple, bright white house with a bunk bed, a symbol of something more, something new, became my nightly vision. And so, with a heart teetering between fear and excitement, I began a journey that would take me from Romania's familiar streets to America's bustling avenues, a journey of self-discovery, challenges, triumphs, and rebirth. In the embrace of my early years, amidst the scarcity of communist Romania, seeds of perseverance, dreams, and authenticity were sown. Christmas, especially Saint Nicholas Eve, was a beacon in those times, teaching me early lessons about scarcity, preservation, and the small joys that could be found even in the most trying times. Memories of waiting in long queues for basic essentials, of storing water for the inevitable times it would be shut off, painted my childhood in hues of scarcity and resilience. Growing up in the 1980s, under Ceaușescu's regime, and through the 1989 revolution, I witnessed a nation's struggle and transformation, which mirrored my own evolving dreams and resilient spirit. Amidst the national upheaval, my dreams took flight, nurtured by the resilient Romanian spirit that whispered tales of distant lands and possibilities.

Responsibility found me early. With my parents working late, ensuring my siblings were safe and fed often fell on me. A vivid, painful memory of my sister Roxy's sledding accident, her face marred by a deep, fearsome wound, was a harsh awakening to life's cruel unpredictability. It was a different pain than the collective sorrow of communal hardship, a personal, piercing anguish that solidified a vow within me to shield my family always. It stoked the fires of determination to escape Romania and lead my family to a haven where safety and abundance were more than fleeting dreams.

2. The Catalyst for Change

From the very beginning, even as a child, there was a restless spirit within me. I felt as though I was born with a heart that beat to a different rhythm, one that resonated with places and possibilities far beyond the narrow streets of my hometown in Romania. The city, with its familiar faces and age-old routines, felt both comforting and confining. Each day, I'd watch the people around me, their lives a testament to resilience and endurance. But beneath their stoic exteriors, I sensed dreams deferred and hopes buried deep.

Money, or the lack thereof, was the ever-present specter in our lives. It dictated choices, silenced desires, and cast long shadows over our simplest joys. I remember the muted longing in my mother's eyes when I'd ask for something as trivial as a new shirt or a bottle of perfume. The gentle rebuke, reminding me of our financial realities, became a refrain I knew all too well. The sight of my parents, wearied by relentless work and constant worry, was a daily reminder of the life we were ensnared in.

As I blossomed into adulthood at 18, I was fueled by a mix of hope and desperation. I believed that a job, any job, could be the key to easing our burdens. But the world outside wasn't kind. Each rejection, each closed door, seemed to echo the same refrain: too young, unknown lineage, a 'nobody.' It was a bitter pill to swallow. How could I be a 'nobody' when every fiber of my being screamed otherwise? I felt a profound connection to the universe, a sense that I was part of something much larger than my humble origins.

This growing chasm between who I was and how the world perceived me became unbearable. The dream of escape, of finding a place where I would be recognized for my essence and not just my background, consumed me. I envisioned a paradise where my worth wasn't tied to my past but to the promise of what I could become. With each passing day, the winds of change grew stronger, beckoning me toward a destiny I felt was rightfully mine. It wasn't just about leaving; it was about finding a place where my spirit could truly soar.

Amidst the struggles and yearnings of my youth in Romania, a seed was planted within me—a seed that would later blossom into my understanding of true abundance. While the world around me equated abundance with material wealth, I began to sense that there was more to it. The richness I sought wasn't just about monetary prosperity but a deeper, more profound wealth of experience, relationships, and inner contentment. I realized that abundance wasn't just about having more but about seeing more, feeling more, and being more.

As I navigated the challenges of my early years, this budding understanding of abundance became my compass. Instead of viewing life through the lens of scarcity, where every opportunity seemed like a fleeting mirage, I started to see the boundless potential in every moment. I began to understand that celebrating the successes of others didn't diminish my own journey but enriched it. This shift in perspective wasn't about denying the hardships I faced but was about recognizing them as stepping stones, each one leading me closer to a life of true fulfillment.

This journey towards cultivating an abundance mindset wasn't without its challenges. It meant unlearning many of the beliefs ingrained in me from my surroundings and society at large. But as I grew, both in age and in understanding, I realized that the true essence of abundance lay not in the possessions one amassed but in the moments of connection, the joy of giving, and the pursuit of purpose. It was a revelation that would guide my steps, pushing me not just to seek a better life but a richer, more meaningful one.

In the cozy embrace of my childhood home, Christian Orthodox traditions gently wove themselves into the fabric of our daily lives. While we weren't devout in the conventional sense, Sundays occasionally found us in the hallowed halls of our local church, and Easter and Christmas were sacrosanct. But my memories of confession are tinged with unease. The priest's stern warnings about sin and its consequences cast a shadow over my young heart, making the church feel less like a sanctuary and more like a place of judgment. Gradually, I found myself distancing from its stone walls and echoing hymns.

Yet, it was my grandmothers who introduced me to a more intimate, personal form of spirituality. They taught me the art of prayer—not as a ritual, but as a heartfelt conversation with the Divine. Their words, whispered in the quiet corners of our home, became my spiritual anchor. Even now, with the tapestry of knowledge and understanding I've gathered over the years, their prayers resonate deeply within me, timeless and comforting. They're like cherished heirlooms, passed down through generations, offering protection and solace.

Life, in its playful way, began to show me signs of this greater force. I recall a day, tinged with the impatience of youth when my mother's request to do laundry clashed with my plans with friends. As if in response to my silent plea, the laundry machine mysteriously malfunctioned. It was one of many little 'coincidences' that seemed to dance around me. The universe, it appeared, had a way of listening, of responding to my unspoken wishes, be they trivial or profound. And while I assure you, I never intended for the laundry machine to break, it was hard to ignore the feeling that something bigger was at play.

3. The Leap of Faith: Moving to the USA

On a crisp winter night, the world blanketed in a fresh layer of snow, I made my way home from an evening class. At 20, life hadn't quite unfolded the way I'd envisioned. The college I had aspired to remained a distant dream, and though I had found work, love, and friendship, the confines of my hometown seemed to tighten around me with each passing day. My father's unspoken disappointment, a silent specter, often lingered in the air. But that night, as snowflakes playfully kissed my face, a glimmer of hope appeared in the most unexpected of places.

Through the gentle snowstorm, a note pinned to a lamppost caught my eye. Drawn by an inexplicable curiosity, I approached and read: "Do you want to move to America? Call this number." Heart racing, I snatched the note and sprinted home, the weight of its potential promise propelling me forward. Could this be real? A call confirmed the legitimacy of the agency behind the note, but there was a catch—the cost of participation equaled a year's salary in Romania. That familiar sinking feeling returned, my dreams once again tethered to the ever-elusive concept of money. Would the specter of scarcity forever haunt me? Yet, in a twist of fate, my father managed to secure a loan, and just like that, the distant dream of America was within reach.

Tears blurred my vision as I bid farewell to my family, the land of my birth, and the memories of my youth. At 21, with a heart full of hope and a suitcase filled with dreams, I stepped onto American soil. The challenges were immediate—the language barrier, the cultural nuances, and yes, the overly sweet food. But as I settled into a house filled with unfamiliar faces, my host family for the year, I realized that this was the beginning of a new chapter, one where dreams could, and would, come true.

With a single $100 bill my whole net worth, which I half-jokingly considered framing instead of spending, I was ready to dive headfirst into the American dream. Or, at the very least, get a taste of that famous American pie. My first call home was a whirlwind of emotions as I recounted my maiden flight. While everyone else on the plane seemed to be seasoned travelers, casually flipping through magazines or dozing off, I was the wide-eyed newbie, gripping the armrests and hoping my face wasn't as green as I felt. Touching down in America, I half-expected to see streets paved with gold. I would've dropped to the ground and kissed it, if not for the lingering queasiness from the journey. Ah, New York, where even the air smelled like dreams and deep-fried food!

That initial euphoria, however, was short-lived. The reality of being a 21-year-old in a foreign land quickly set in. I imagined myself as a modern-day superhero, ready to take on any challenge. Instead, I felt more like a toddler in oversized shoes, stumbling at every step. The lessons came thick and fast. Want respect? Speak up! Need a break?

Speak up! Tired of feeling like a human machine, working around the clock? You guessed it—speak up! It was here, amidst the hustle and bustle of American life, that I learned the art of setting boundaries.

But it wasn't all life lessons and growing pains. There were moments of pure, unadulterated hilarity. Like the time I tried to order a 'large' coffee and was handed a container that looked more like a bucket. Or my first encounter with a peanut butter and jelly sandwich—why were these two things together? And then there was the time I got lost in a supermarket, wandering the aisles and marveling at the sheer variety of potato chips on offer. Every day brought its own set of challenges, but also its own set of chuckles. As I navigated this new world, with its quirks and its lessons, I realized that while I might've been far from home, I was right where I needed to be.

The art of saying, "No," when necessary and, "Yes," when desired was a dance I was still mastering, a rhythm I was still finding. But as I began to grasp this, other lessons queued up, waiting for their turn in the spotlight. The seeds of belief and determination, sown during those initial days, began to sprout. With one dream realized, it was time to chase the next. Staying legally in this land of dreams and bringing my parents over became my new mission. I leaned into my tried-and-true method: visualization. The contours of this new dream began to take shape in my mind's eye, even though its realization was still years away. But I was equipped with a newfound belief, a conviction that seemed to stem from sheer necessity. It was a do-or-die situation, and I was all in.

This unwavering focus wasn't new to me. I recalled a pivotal moment from my younger days when I had applied to a prestigious high school in my city. The director, in a bid to gauge my alternatives, had inquired about my second and third choices. My father's response still echoed in my ears, "We only have one option. We're getting in. No backup needed." It was a lesson in single-minded determination, a testament to the power of zeroing in on a goal with unyielding focus. These early teachings, once dormant, began to resurface, guiding me through the maze of my American journey.

The path ahead was filled with challenges, but also brimming with potential. Every hurdle was a lesson in disguise, every setback a stepping stone. The blend of my Romanian roots and my American aspirations created a unique tapestry of experiences. As I navigated this new chapter, I was fueled by the memories of the past and the dreams of the future, ready to embrace whatever lay ahead.

4. Spiritual awakening

The tapestry of my life in the U.S. began to take on the vibrant hues I had once only imagined. The white house with the bunk bed, which I had shared with you at the outset of my tale, was my first American abode. It was only after I moved out that the realization hit me like a bolt of lightning: this was the very house I had visualized during those cold Romanian nights. The universe, it seemed, was leaving breadcrumbs, guiding me along a path I had unknowingly charted. While challenges were aplenty, my dreams were manifesting one by one, as if being ticked off an ethereal checklist.

However, my ascent to millionaire status was nothing short of serendipitous. With my family by my side and a child to call my own, the world felt like a vast playground. I was conjuring abundance, seemingly from thin air. But with every accomplishment, a nagging question arose: what force was orchestrating this symphony of successes? While I had mastered the art of business and communication, the weight of my achievements began to bear down on me. How was it that I had amassed so much, yet felt so profoundly hollow? This paradox led to an egoic crisis, sidelining me for a year. The more I questioned my dreams and visions, the deeper I sank into a quagmire of self-doubt. The persona of Izabela, the go-getter who had defied the odds, achieved so much, and built a life many could only dream of, suddenly felt like a beautifully crafted mask.

Peeling back the layers, I began to introspect. The many avatars of Izabela—the e-commerce maven, the doting mother, the loyal friend, the enigmatic stranger—all began to blur. A profound realization dawned upon me: while money could offer comfort, it wasn't the elixir of happiness. My dreams of becoming a billionaire persisted, but I understood that true abundance lay not in material wealth, but in the richness of the soul.

The glitz and glamor of success, while intoxicating, often cast shadows that only a few talk about. As my life in America progressed, the external milestones I achieved began to feel increasingly hollow. The deeper I delved into my accomplishments, the more I found myself questioning the very essence of life. What was my true purpose? Beyond the accolades and the material gains, what were the values that truly defined me? And amidst the cacophony of societal expectations, what were my heart's genuine desires?

This internal churning wasn't without its consequences. As I evolved and began to seek deeper meanings, I noticed a gradual distancing from many friends. It wasn't out of malice or any overt conflict, but our paths, values, and conversations began to diverge. The adage, "It's lonely at the top," took on a painfully real dimension for me. The houses, the lavish parties, and the so-called 'high life' often echoed with a silence that was both profound and deafening. The very success I had once yearned for became a gilded cage, isolating me from genuine connections.

It was during this period of introspection and solitude that I turned to spirituality. Not as a refuge, but as a means to understand the grand tapestry of life. The teachings I encountered spoke of a universe far more intricate and interconnected than I had ever imagined. I began to see myself not as a solitary entity chasing individual dreams, but as a part of a cosmic dance, where every being had a role to play. This shift in perspective was transformative. My priorities began to change. Instead of seeking external validation, I yearned for inner peace. Instead of accumulating wealth, I sought experiences that enriched the soul. And in this spiritual awakening, I found a compass that didn't point to the north, but to the true essence of my being.

5. Reflection

Throughout my journey, from the nostalgic streets of Romania to the bustling avenues of America, the lessons I've gleaned have been both profound and transformative. One of the most pivotal realizations was understanding that our mindset, more than our circumstances, shapes our reality. While external factors play a role, it's our internal narrative that truly dictates life's trajectory.

Action Step: Begin each day with a positive affirmation. Tell yourself, "Something wonderful is happening to me today," and truly believe in the power of these words. Over time, this simple practice can shift your mindset from one of limitation to one of boundless potential.

Another invaluable lesson was the importance of resilience and adaptability. Life is unpredictable, filled with highs and lows. However, it's not the challenges we face that define us, but how we respond to them. Embracing change, learning from failures, and persistently pursuing our goals, even when the path is strewn with obstacles, is the key to true success.

Action Step: Whenever faced with a setback, instead of asking, "Why me?" Change the question: "What can I learn from this?" This shift in perspective transforms challenges into opportunities for growth.

Lastly, the essence of true abundance lies not in material accumulation but in the richness of experiences, relationships, and personal growth. While material success can provide comfort, it's the spiritual and emotional wealth that brings genuine fulfillment.

<u>Action Step</u>: Dedicate time each week to self-reflection. Journal your thoughts, express gratitude for the small joys, and set intentions that align with your true desires. This practice not only grounds you but also helps in aligning your actions with your higher purpose.

From the dimly lit classrooms of Romania, where winter's chill was both outside and in, to the sprawling landscapes of America, my journey has been one of metamorphosis. Born into a world where scarcity was not just a concept but a lived reality, I navigated through life's labyrinth, often with no more than hope as my compass. But as the chapters of my story unfolded, I discovered that true abundance isn't measured by what we possess, but by how we perceive.

To you, dear reader, who might find echoes of your own story in mine, know this: the journey from scarcity to abundance is as internal as it is external. It's about recognizing that even in moments of lack, there is an inherent abundance of spirit, resilience, and potential within you. Challenges, while daunting, are also the crucibles that forge our strength and character. Embrace them, learn from them, and let them guide you toward your own transformation.

In conclusion, life, with all its twists and turns, is a canvas of limitless possibilities. When we shift our perspective from one of scarcity to one of abundance, we don't just change our reality; we change our world. The universe is vast, and its treasures, both material and spiritual, are waiting to be discovered. With an abundant mindset, every sunrise brings a promise, every challenge becomes an opportunity, and every dream is just a heartbeat away from reality.

Izabela Hamilton

Izabela Hamilton, with a decade of Amazon expertise, is the dynamo behind RankBell and Ink of Genius. RankBell, birthed from her drive to aid others in financial success, has propelled thousands of Amazon brands to soaring sales figures. Her publishing company, Ink of Genius, embodies her belief in the power of storytelling, providing a platform for individuals to share their mouth-watering narratives and leave a lasting legacy for future generations, a testament to her adeptness honed over the years on Amazon.

Hamilton's life philosophy is rooted in spirituality and the idea of creating one's reality. This spiritual ethos fuels her daily quest for self-improvement, reflected in her ventures aiming at bettering services and adding value for clients.

Besides being a successful entrepreneur, Hamilton is an international speaker and transformational mentor, sharing her insights to inspire and aid others on their self-improvement journey. As a dedicated mother,

her life is a blend of personal and professional endeavors, all infused with a touch of spirituality and an unwavering drive for excellence.

In essence, Izabela Hamilton's journey from Romania to become a pivotal figure in the Amazon marketplace, alongside her roles as a mentor, speaker, and mother, showcases a life lived in the relentless pursuit of growth, self-betterment, and altruism. Her narrative is not just a business success story, but a life imbued with a spirit of continuous learning and a heartfelt desire to make a positive impact on others' lives.

Connect with Izabela at www.inkofgenius.com.

CHAPTER 5

The Power of Forgiveness

by Priscilla Melekhshalom-Kashani

I want to dedicate this chapter to my parents who sacrificed
everything so that I could have the life that I have now.
To my husband and kids—thank you for believing in me
every step of the way.
To my teachers—thank you for being a shining light in my
life and a source of inspiration.

Have you ever found yourself trapped in the relentless grip of negative emotions, imprisoned by the hurt and anger inflicted by someone else's actions? Have you pondered the profound meaning of forgiveness and wondered why it holds such significance in the tapestry of our lives? Let us draw inspiration from the wisdom of Nelson Mandela, a man who walked a path filled with adversity and emerged as a symbol of hope and resilience. He once articulated:

As I walked out the door toward the gate that would lead to my freedom, I knew if I didn't leave my bitterness and hatred behind, I would still be in jail.
~Nelson Mandela

These words resonate with truth, serving as a reminder that forgiveness is a journey inward—a process that transcends forgiveness and invites us to liberate ourselves from the suffocating chains of resentment and anger.

Forgiveness has an immediate, profound impact on our emotions. Grudges and anger function as heavy chains that imprison us, hindering our happiness and inner peace. But forgiveness provides the key to unlocking these chains, allowing us to release emotional baggage and experience true emotional freedom. As we forgive, we feel lighter, as if a heavy weight has been lifted from our shoulders. In the pages that unfold, we shall navigate the intricate pathway to forgiveness. We shall unravel its layers and decode its mysteries. We shall delve into the essence of what forgiveness truly means, exploring its many dimensions and unveiling the healing potential it carries within. We shall contemplate why forgiveness occupies such a hallowed place in our human experience, and how its significance echoes through the corridors of our emotional and spiritual well-being.

Through the eyes of forgiveness, we shall witness the emergence of emotional freedom—a liberation from the shackles of bitterness and resentment that can weigh down even the mightiest of souls. We shall uncover the value of empowerment, recognizing that forgiveness is not an act of weakness but a testament to our inner strength. And we shall open our minds to the idea that forgiveness holds the key to doors that swing wide to blessings we may have never imagined, including the realm of financial abundance.

This journey can change how we relate to others, ourselves, and the world. It's a path to freedom, empowerment, and boundless blessings for those willing to forgive.

What Does Forgiveness Mean?

To begin our transformative journey of forgiveness, we must first grasp its intricate meaning. Forgiveness, often misinterpreted as a simple pardon for wrongdoings, is far deeper. It's a multidimensional concept encompassing both outward actions and profound inner transformation. At its core, forgiveness entails a tremendous shift in our perspective and emotional state. It's about consciously releasing the threads of negative emotions that tie us to past hurts. When we forgive, we choose to let go of our emotional baggage, freeing ourselves from the past's shackles. Forgiveness isn't solely about the one who wronged us; it's an act of self-liberation. It's a deliberate choice to shed the weight of anger, resentment, and pain that burdens our hearts and souls. We untangle the intricate web of negative emotions that constrain us.

The expectation of outcomes can sometimes trap us in a cycle of anger or resentment. It's important to understand that not everyone follows the same path of spiritual growth that we do. Realizing that we can change no one except ourselves and focusing on our personal growth brings out our strength and capability to move forward independently of others.

It's crucial to understand that establishing healthy boundaries doesn't require negative emotions; it can stem from inner strength. We can create boundaries for well-being and self-protection when empowered, not just when angry or resentful.

The great sage, Hillel, once expressed:

If I'm not for myself, who will be for me?
But if I'm only for myself, who am I?
And if not now, when?
~Hillel Ethics of Our Fathers Chapter 1:14

Forgiveness is complex; it doesn't condone actions but grants emotional freedom. While acknowledging victimization, it rejects victimhood. It doesn't mean enduring further abuse; instead, forgiveness establishes strong boundaries for self-preservation and empowerment. By setting clear boundaries, we protect ourselves and assert that we deserve respect, kindness, and fairness.

Forgiving can be tough due to complex emotional factors. Some fear delving into emotional pain, using negative emotions as shields against further hurt. Self-worth issues fuel self-punishment and resentment.

Holding onto anger and resentment may seem like maintaining control, but it harms us subconsciously. Fear of loneliness or uncertainty about life without the other person can contribute to clinging to negative emotions. True forgiveness means sincerely wishing for their happiness, not finding joy in their suffering.

Subconscious guilt or shame can lead to holding onto anger, creating a barrier or separation. Even in indirect connections, negative emotions persist as constant reminders of pain. Ongoing mental repetition keeps these emotions alive, disrupting our lives. Confronting deeply ingrained negative beliefs is daunting, but letting go is essential for our well-being.

The fear of confronting deeply ingrained negative beliefs, lurking just beneath our consciousness, can keep us anchored to our negative emotions. It's often easier to cling to what is familiar than to face these core beliefs head-on.

There's also the desire to change others or make them understand the depth of our suffering, which can lead us to hold onto anger and resentment. When we let go of wanting the other person to change then we give ourselves a chance to forgive the other person.

Why Is Forgiveness Important?

Forgiveness is not merely a virtue or a moral obligation, but a profoundly potent healing elixir that has the potential to mend the deepest of emotional wounds.

At its core, forgiveness serves as a powerful antidote to the toxic emotions of resentment and anger. When we harbor these emotions, we unwittingly burden ourselves with a heavy load, one that exerts a relentless toll on our overall well-being.

Forgiveness paves the path to inner peace. We find ourselves standing in the calm of a newfound serenity, where the noise of anger and bitterness has given way to a profound stillness. This inner peace is not passive; it is a wellspring of resilience and strength, nurturing our ability to navigate life's challenges with grace and harmony.

Forgiveness is a potent source of empowerment. When we forgive, we assert our authority over our own emotions and responses. We recognize that we have the power to choose our emotional state and our reactions to external events. In this realization, we unearth a wellspring of strength and resilience that empowers us to overcome adversity and transcend our circumstances.

Forgiveness also leads us to the doorstep of abundance. It is not merely a coincidence that as we release the heavy burden of negative emotions, we create space for positivity and blessings to flow into our lives. Our energy shifts from one of constriction to one of expansion, aligning us with the abundant flow of the universe. Doors that were once closed swing open, revealing opportunities and possibilities we may have never imagined.

The Old Testament transmits a deep concept: that whatever energetically belongs to us will inevitably return to us and can never be canceled or taken away. When someone steals our money, it triggers intense emotions such as anger, frustration, and sadness. However, beneath these emotions lies a deep-seated fear—the fear of never being able to recover the stolen money.

To heal from this experience, it's crucial to address both the immediate emotional turmoil and the underlying beliefs and fears. Removing these negative emotions and beliefs is a vital part of the healing process. It involves acknowledging that the monetary loss, while distressing, does not define your ability to generate income or rebuild your financial security.

This pivotal biblical commandment encapsulates forgiveness:

You shall not take vengeance or bear a grudge against
any of your people, but you shall love your neighbor as
yourself: I am the Lord. ~Leviticus 19:18

This verse emphasizes the divine directive to abstain from seeking revenge and nurturing grudges. It calls for extending love and understanding to fellow human beings, reflecting forgiveness's divine nature.

The word "selach" or "salah" mentioned repeatedly in the Old Testament symbolizes forbearance, pardon, and forgiveness. This verse delves into the depth of this concept:

Keeping mercy for thousands, forgiving iniquity and
transgression and sin, and that will by no means clear the
guilty, visiting the iniquity of the fathers upon the children,
and upon the children's children, unto the third and the
fourth generation. ~Exodus 34:7

Forgiveness extends to addressing sins that hinder our closeness to the Divine. These can manifest as negative emotions and deep-seated beliefs that we hold onto. When left unaddressed, they can be passed down through generations, affecting not only us but also our descendants. It is imperative to correct and elevate these aspects, bridging any gap that exists between us and the Creator to prevent this transfer of negativity.

In families with a history of trauma, such as Holocaust survivors, the transgenerational spread of negative emotions and beliefs is a significant phenomenon. The emotional scars of survivors can be passed on to their children and subsequent generations. This highlights our collective duty and responsibility to take every possible measure to eliminate these negativities. Various mechanisms such as parenting styles and epigenetics contribute to this transmission of negative emotions and beliefs. Understanding this process is essential to breaking the cycle of inherited pain and fostering resilience and emotional well-being in future generations. It underscores the need to address and heal these deep emotional wounds at the individual, family, and community levels, particularly in traumatic histories.

The Positives of Forgiving and Insights from My Healing Practice

When we forgive, we are not merely doing an act of grace and kindness, we are bringing positive transformation into our lives and unlocking a multitude of blessings that extend far beyond the act of absolving others.

Forgiveness showcases our inner strength and resilience, affirming that we are survivors, not victims. It empowers us to choose our responses to life's challenges, infusing renewed vigor and confidence. This transformative force shifts our focus from scarcity to abundance, from victimhood to empowerment, creating space for positivity and blessings. Emotional freedom aligns with the abundant flow of the universe, unveiling opportunities and blessings once concealed.

Forgiveness has the remarkable capacity to mend fractured relationships. It is a bridge that connects individuals who were once estranged by hurt and anger. When we forgive, we open the door to reconciliation and healing.

The benefits of forgiveness extend beyond the realm of emotions and touch our physical well-being. Individuals who practice forgiveness often experience lower stress levels, reduced blood pressure, fewer headaches, and improved overall health. This connection between emotional well-being and physical health underscores the profound impact that forgiveness can have on our holistic well-being.

Real-life examples vividly demonstrate forgiveness's transformative power, alleviating the burdens of hatred and resentment across various life aspects. In my practice, Shalom Energy Healing, I apply these insights to guide my clients through forgiveness, facilitating profound shifts. Through spiritual healing, my clients transform their mindsets, unlocking their gifts and capabilities. The work I do at Shalom Energy Healing encompasses breathwork, meditation, spiritual healing, Kabbalistic Astrology, Kabbalistic Numerology, and other healing methodologies. The shared stories of my clients are not theoretical but authentic accounts of significant life changes through forgiveness, grounding my work in impactful experiences. These narratives testify to the value of forgiveness in promoting emotional well-being and abundance.

A female client of mine, divorced for over eight or nine years, was very resentful toward her ex-husband. Every word she spoke about him was filled with bitterness and anger, as she felt he had shattered her life. This deep-seated hatred and sense of unfair treatment had kept her from moving forward, leaving her unable to pursue new relationships, marriage, or the prospect of having children. However, after she embarked on the journey of forgiveness, a transformation occurred. Her emotional freedom allowed her to step into the realm of dating and embrace new relationships. This powerful shift highlights how forgiveness can take apart emotional barriers and usher in opportunities for growth and connection.

One of my male clients was unemployed for several years despite being skilled and he faced the risk of losing everything. His job search was unsuccessful, and he relied on financial assistance from his mother. Exploring his troubled childhood with his mother, where she treated him negatively, revealed his subconscious patterns of punishing her for her poor treatment of him. Through meditation and healing sessions, I guided him to forgive his mother, release pent-up anger, and appreciate the lessons learned. The transformation was profound—he found a rewarding job within a month, not just changing his career but liberating him from emotional burdens, allowing him to embrace his true potential and achieve financial abundance.

Another example with a male client, facing a prolonged and challenging divorce with unresolved financial matters, who harbored intense anger toward the lawyers and bitterness about losing money to his ex-wife. Through the process of forgiveness, he forgave the lawyers first, then extended forgiveness to his ex-wife through meditation and discussions. During this transformational journey guided by a Higher Power, he shed tears, recognizing valuable lessons and gaining courage. Approaching his ex-wife from a place of newfound understanding, he suggested mediation instead of lawyers, which she finally agreed to after being approached many times. This resulted in a financial settlement within two weeks.

A story with a female client who had been battling infertility and had severe back issues and negative experiences with doctors carried a considerable burden of fear and resentment toward the medical system. These negative emotions caused her to fear a recurrence of back problems and a lack of confidence in medical interventions, which prevented her from becoming pregnant. Through a process that involved clearing these fears and resentments while fostering faith in a Higher Power, she found the inner peace and guidance required to locate the right doctor. She regained her calm and renewed her faith in God. This transformation paved the way for her to achieve pregnancy with ease.

In another compelling story, a woman in her late 50s suffered severe shoulder pain for two years despite seeking help from various healthcare professionals. Upon investigating, I discovered a connection between the onset of her pain and the reappearance of her father's Alzheimer's. She had moved in to care for him but felt overwhelmed and unsupported by her siblings. Exploring her past, I uncovered a pattern of overwhelming responsibilities from childhood. Addressing the need for forgiveness through meditation and self-reflection, she forgave both her mother, who had been a tough disciplinarian during her childhood, and her siblings. The release of emotional burdens resulted in the complete disappearance of her shoulder pain, leading to a significant improvement in her overall well-being. This case highlights the profound impact of forgiveness on emotional and physical health.

These stories emphasize a fundamental truth: we cannot change anybody else but ourselves. This serves as a powerful reminder of the transformative force that forgiveness carries. Forgiveness releases us from emotional burdens, paving the way for positive change in our lives. Forgiveness leads to new relationships, the resolution of legal disputes, and improvements in physical and emotional well-being. These examples vividly illustrate the connection between forgiveness and abundance, well-being, and new opportunities.

The Process of Forgiving

The journey of forgiveness is a deeply introspective and transformative process, comprising several essential steps. It's a path that requires patience, courage, and a willingness to confront our innermost emotions and beliefs. Here, we explore these steps, each contributing to the profound journey of forgiveness.

In the forgiveness process, the initial step is to ask God for genuine assistance and guidance. Approach this step with sincerity and say, "I really want to forgive and let go of my negative emotions, but I don't know how. Please guide me." It's essential to emphasize the intensity of your desire to forgive. The stronger your desire, the more motivated you become to take the necessary mental and emotional steps toward forgiveness. Your desire fuels the commitment to the forgiveness process and drives you to do the inner work needed to achieve it.

The next step involves acknowledging and fully embracing our pain. This is an act of self-compassion that allows us to grieve the hurt we've endured. Find a quiet place, connect with nature, or use soothing music to help you access your emotions. Here, you may cry, express your frustrations, and release your anguish.

Next, turn to a higher power and earnestly request the courage to confront the truth. This surrender can offer the strength and clarity necessary to navigate the intricate terrain of forgiveness.

Many of us tend to define ourselves by our titles, reputation, or our good name. However, it's essential to recognize that this is merely our ego identity, and our soul encompasses so much more. When we've been hurt by someone who may have damaged our reputation or good name, letting go of our ego identity and understanding the enormity of our soul can pave the way for forgiveness. No one can truly harm the essence of our soul.

Another valuable step in the forgiveness process is journaling. I encourage individuals to write down their emotions, experiences, and the lessons they've learned along their forgiveness journey. This practice allows them to witness their transformation and growth on paper, providing a tangible record of their progress and healing.

Forgiveness can stir intense and overwhelming emotions. It's essential to remember that our emotions don't define us entirely; our true self, our soul, is more expansive than our fleeing emotional states. Viewing our feelings from a detached perspective, much like a ship captain steering through turbulent waters, helps us recognize their transitory nature. This perspective helps us become stronger and more emotionally aware, allowing us to approach forgiveness with purpose and kindness, even when our emotions are fluctuating.

Seek to understand the reasons behind the person's hurtful actions, not to excuse them but to grasp the conditions that led to their behavior, fostering empathy. Exploring their past, especially any adversity or hardship can reveal the origins of their actions.

Consciously shedding negative beliefs, such as the fear of irreparable loss, relieves emotional burdens and propels us forward. Accepting that we can't change others brings peace. Forgiveness, though it may seem vulnerable, is a sign of strength as we prevent past manipulation from repeating.

Focus on the lessons learned from the hurtful experience. Every challenge is an opportunity for growth, contributing to our evolution. By embracing these lessons, we move beyond the role of a victim and become a more empowered version of ourselves.

One crucial step on the path to forgiveness involves addressing the negative belief that often impedes our ability to forgive. This belief revolves around our inability to envision a bright future for ourselves without the presence of those who have caused us pain. This inability to see a positive future is often rooted in the deep emotional wounds we carry. To make progress in the forgiveness journey, it's important that we change our belief system to be able to envision a brighter future.

Lastly, remember that forgiveness extends not only to others but also to us. Frequently, we carry self-blame or regret for our actions or choices. Self-forgiveness is crucial in our journey towards healing and wholeness.

These steps form a tapestry of healing and growth, guiding us toward emotional freedom, empowerment, and forgiveness—a powerful testament to our inner strength and capacity for compassion. Embracing forgiveness, we embark on a journey of self-discovery and liberation, freeing ourselves from the burdens of the past and opening the door to a brighter future.

The Role of Meditation and Breath Work

In the journey of forgiveness, we encounter moments when the chaotic currents of emotions threaten to overwhelm us. It is during these challenging times that the ancient practices of meditation and breathwork emerge as guiding lights, helping us navigate the path of forgiveness. Meditation is a timeless practice that turns us inward, inviting exploration of our consciousness and connection with inner stillness. It provides a sacred space to observe thoughts and emotions with detached awareness, cultivating mindfulness—full presence in the moment without judgment. This practice unlocks our inner wisdom, serving as an inner compass for forgiveness and inner peace. Through deep reflection in meditation, we access intuition and find the strength to forgive. Breathwork, connecting us to life's rhythm, is a powerful practice bridging the conscious and unconscious. By controlling our breath, we release negative emotions and energetic blockages hindering forgiveness. Additionally, intentional breathing serves as a tool to clear energy blockages, particularly beneficial for physical manifestations of emotional pain, like tension in the shoulders or chest.

Incorporating meditation and breathwork into our forgiveness journey is not only a means to facilitate emotional release and clarity but also a profound act of self-care. These practices offer us the tools to navigate the inner landscape of forgiveness with grace and resilience.

In our pursuit of happiness, we seek more than possessions—we want inner joy and peace. Spiritual richness, found in qualities like gratitude and love, goes beyond material wealth, providing purpose and happiness. Letting go of negative feelings through forgiveness allows positive emotions to thrive.

Forgiveness is the key to spiritual abundance, aligning us with life's flow and unlocking blessings. It resolves conflicts, promotes inner peace, and enhances our sense of interconnectedness, deepening our purpose in the larger tapestry of life. Embracing forgiveness liberates us from the past, ushering in a life of joy, peace, and purpose.

In the complex tapestry of forgiveness, a profound shift in perspective can change how we perceive those who have hurt us. It's the recognition that the person who caused our pain might be a divine teacher, imparting a crucial lesson. Every challenge and wound becomes an opportunity for growth and transformation, orchestrated by a higher force.

When someone hurts us, seeing it as a lesson from the Divine offers a chance for personal growth. Embracing the wisdom in each experience breaks the cycle of recurring patterns, providing valuable insights. For example, betrayal can teach us about intuition and healthy boundaries, freeing us from distrust and deepening our understanding of self-preservation in relationships.

Acknowledging the Divine's lessons empowers us to move from victimhood to strength. Compassion for those who hurt us arises from understanding their journeys of learning and change.

Embracing these lessons aligns us with a higher purpose, infusing life with meaning and fostering trust in our journey's unfolding, even in adversity. Challenges, though painful, serve a purpose in our spiritual and personal evolution.

Forgiveness of Self

In the intricate world of forgiveness, self-forgiveness is often overlooked but equally essential. It's the key to breaking down self-doubt and negativity. We tend to be our harshest critics, creating inner judgment, blame, and guilt. Self-forgiveness dismantles these walls, acknowledging our imperfections and the human experience of making mistakes. It releases guilt and shame, fostering self-acceptance, self-worth, and personal growth.

Self-blame and self-criticism lead to self-sabotage. Self-forgiveness breaks these cycles, enabling healthier choices and positive self-beliefs. It's an ongoing journey of self-compassion, acknowledging our humanity, and unconditionally loving and accepting ourselves. Self-forgiveness liberates the past's grip on our present and future, leading to profound healing and personal growth.

The Sacred Journey of Forgiveness

Forgiveness is a sacred journey of self-discovery and healing, allowing us to transcend our past and elevate our consciousness. It is the crucible for transformation, shedding layers of pain and bitterness. Forgiveness positively impacts our vibrational frequency, shifting us from constriction to expansion, making us magnets for synchronicity and opportunities.

Choosing forgiveness is a testament to our strength and courage. It liberates us, unlocking a life of purpose, joy, and peace. Embracing forgiveness is an affirmation of our commitment to well-being and personal growth. It's an act of self-love, freeing us from the past and opening doors to limitless possibilities. It leads us to a life resonating with the abundance of the universe.

Priscilla Melekhshalom-Kashani

Priscilla Melekhshalom-Kashani's journey into the world of healing has been a lifelong commitment sparked by her desire to make a positive impact on the world. Her journey began early, fueled by a deep passion for healing and dedicated pursuit of personal transformation.

Over more than a decade, Priscilla engaged in extensive studies in spirituality, Kabbalah, and various healing modalities. This deep exploration equipped her with the knowledge and courage to make a significant shift from her career in accounting. She courageously embraced her true calling as a professional healer and coach, solidifying her commitment along the way as she overcame her health issues and coped with the loss of close family members.

Priscilla Melekhshalom-Kashani holds certifications in Theta Healing®, Conscious Parenting Method™ Coaching, and Kabbalistic Astrology & Numerology. Her approach to healing draws from an integrated fusion of various methodologies, including evidence-based techniques such as meditation, breathwork, energy healing, coaching, and the profound insights of spiritual healing, and Kabbalistic Astrology and Numerology.

Priscilla's holistic approach goes beyond personal healing, integrating spirituality and healing modalities with Conscious Parenting Method™ Coaching.

Her unwavering dedication to healing and her compassionate heart make Priscilla a skilled and caring healer, committed to guiding you on a journey of personal transformation and enhancing your capacity for wholeness, ultimately enabling you to lead a happier and more fulfilling life.

Connect with Priscilla at https://shalomenergyhealing.com.

The Anatomy Of Abundance™ Framework

"The journey of a thousand miles begins with one step."

~Lao Tzu

In the quest for a life brimming with prosperity, it's often said that abundance is not just about money, but about a holistic, all-encompassing wealth that encompasses every aspect of our existence. In this chapter, we delve into the foundational concept of the "Anatomy Of Abundance™ Framework," a comprehensive approach designed to activate abundance in every facet of your life.

The Genesis of the Anatomy Of Abundance™ Framework

Developed by our founder, Patrina Wisdom, the Anatomy Of Abundance™ Framework is the culmination of years of introspection, exploration, and the unwavering belief that true abundance can be achieved by anyone, regardless of their starting point in life. It's a dynamic and transformative system that amalgamates mindset upgrades, spiritual principles, the psychology of money, and an intentional roadmap for action.

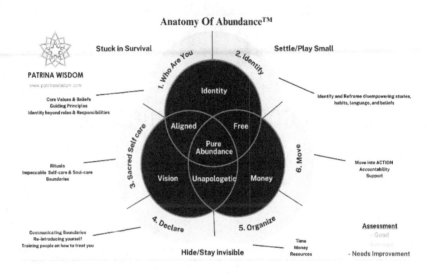

A Multifaceted Roadmap

At its core, the Anatomy Of Abundance™ Framework provides you with a structured roadmap that guides you towards the manifestation of abundance. This roadmap is not a one-size-fits-all solution but a multifaceted approach that accommodates your unique journey. Let's dive into its vital components:

Mindset Upgrades: One of the foundational stones of abundance is your mindset. We'll explore how shifting your beliefs, perspectives, and attitudes can profoundly impact your ability to attract and retain abundance in your life.

Spiritual Principles: Abundance is not merely a material concept; it's deeply intertwined with spiritual principles. We'll delve into how aligning your spiritual beliefs with your aspirations can supercharge your journey toward abundance.

The Psychology of Money: Money: Understanding the psychology behind money can be the key to unlocking financial success. We'll examine how your relationship with money affects your abundance journey and how to reshape this relationship for the better.

Intentional Roadmap for Action: Theory alone cannot bring abundance into your life. You need an actionable plan. The Anatomy Of Abundance™ Framework offers a step-by-step roadmap designed to help you put your intentions into practice. This includes financial education and strategic planning tailored to your unique financial goals.

The Ultimate Aim: Pure Abundance

The ultimate goal of the Anatomy Of Abundance™ Framework is to activate and manifest abundance in all aspects of your life. We believe that a life of Pure Abundance empowers you to be aligned, unapologetic, and free.

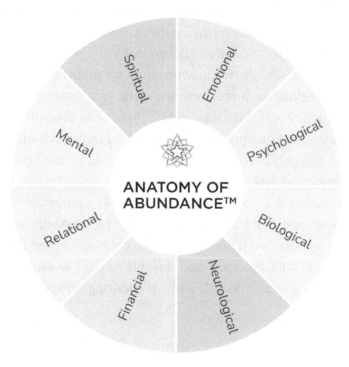

Aligned: To be aligned, you must possess a strong and unwavering identity. Without a clear sense of self, you may find yourself settling for less and playing small. You might even unknowingly shape-shift to fit into other people's expectations or projections of who you should be.

Unapologetic: Being unapologetic requires a vision. Without vision, you may develop a tendency to hide or lurk in the shadows. You will lack the motivation to take risks or put yourself out there. A compelling vision propels you forward, urging you to embrace your true self and your purpose in life.

Free: True freedom is the culmination of three critical elements: mastery over oneself, the ability to command one's time, and financial autonomy. To be truly free is to possess the sovereignty to shape your destiny, to allocate your hours in pursuit of your passions and purpose, and to have the means to fuel your aspirations without constraints. It's the harmonious orchestration of these three pillars that empowers individuals to navigate life on their terms, unburdened by the limitations that often shackle us to a state of dependency and restraint.

In the pursuit of a life rich in abundance, we often discover that time and money are our most precious resources. Yet, paradoxically, those who have money may lack time, while those with time often struggle with money. The Anatomy Of Abundance™ Framework offers a path where you can obtain both—the time to savor life's moments and the financial means to make those moments truly extraordinary.

This framework is more than just a guide; it's a philosophy, a way of life, and a promise that you can create a life of Pure Abundance. In the following chapters, we'll dive deeper into each step of the framework, equipping you with the tools and insights needed to embark on this transformative journey towards a life of enduring prosperity.

C H A P T E R   7

Step 1—Who Are You?

The privilege of a lifetime is to become who you truly are.

~Carl Jung

In the quest for abundance and self-realization, there comes a pivotal moment of reckoning—a moment when you pause, look within, and ask, "Who am I?" This question transcends the labels society has bestowed upon you, the roles you play, and the expectations others have of you. It delves into the very essence of your being, exploring the depths of your identity, your core values, desires, strengths, and weaknesses.

Peeling Away the Layers

Unraveling the true self is akin to peeling away layers of an onion. Each layer represents a facet of your identity, but it's not until you reach the core that you discover your authentic self. This core is where your essence resides, unencumbered by external influences or societal constructs. It's the place where your most profound desires and genuine strengths are nurtured, and where your weaknesses, if acknowledged, become opportunities for growth.

Detachment from Expectations

To embark on this journey of self-discovery, one must first detach themselves from the expectations of others. Society often tries to mold us into predefined roles—the good girl, the responsible mom, the high-achieving professional. While these roles may be part of who you are, they do not define your entirety.

The Influence of Roles

Roles serve a purpose, and they can bring fulfillment, but they should not overshadow your authentic self. For instance, you may excel in your career, but that alone does not define your identity. You might be a dedicated mom, but motherhood alone is not your sole identity. Beneath these roles, there is a unique individual, waiting to be expressed, recognized and celebrated.

The Power of Core Values

At the heart of discovering your authentic self are your core values. These are the principles and beliefs that define your character and the principles that guide your decisions. They are the compass that keeps you true to yourself. Identifying and embracing your core values is a fundamental step in understanding who you are beyond societal expectations.

Desires and Dreams

Your desires and dreams are like stars in the night sky, guiding your journey through life. They represent your deepest yearnings and aspirations. Often, these desires are buried beneath the weight of responsibilities and the noise of everyday life. It's in reconnecting with these desires that you uncover a profound sense of purpose.

Strengths and Weaknesses

Acknowledging your strengths empowers you to leverage them to their full potential. These are the qualities that make you exceptional and unique. Conversely, recognizing your weaknesses is equally important. They are not flaws but opportunities for growth. Embracing both your strengths and weaknesses, the duality is integral to your journey toward self-discovery. In my experience, it's more effective to invest your time in leveraging your strengths and surrounding yourself with individuals who excel in the areas where you may not.

Embodying Your Truth Unapologetically

To embrace the higher law of self-realization, you must shed the layers of conformity and step into the truth of who you are unapologetically. It's a transformative process, one that requires courage, self-compassion, and the willingness to shed the identities that no longer serve you. You can no longer go along to get along. The world needs visionary leaders to light the way forward.

By uncovering and embodying your truth, you align yourself with the higher law of authenticity, and in doing so, you pave the way for a life that is not only abundant but profoundly fulfilling.

Explore These Questions:

1. Who am I, and what are the inherent personality traits I possessed as a child?
2. What are my three most prominent core values? For instance, these could be values such as integrity, compassion, and creativity.
3. What were my childhood passions, and what activities brought me joy during that time? For example, were you passionate about painting, playing musical instruments, or exploring nature?

4. What are three expectations that I have of myself that are not serving me?
5. What are three expectations that others have of me that are not serving me?

Unmasking Your Authentic Self

by Patrina Wisdom

"When we are not in our self-authority we lean
toward recklessness.
We abandon our sense of worth. Under-estimate our value,
and feel disconnected from all that we are.
But, when anchored in the power of self-authority,
we consider, discern, and make choices that are in
alignment centered and in harmony with
our heart and our mind and our spirit."
~Patrina Wisdom

In a world where we often play different roles and wear masks to conform to societal norms and expectations, it's easy to lose sight of who we truly are. Have you ever felt like you're living someone else's life, following a script that doesn't align with your heart's desires? You're not alone. This chapter, "Unmasking Your Authentic

Self," is your first step in a profound journey of self-discovery and transformation. It's about peeling back those layers of conformity and revealing the beautiful, authentic you that's been hidden beneath.

The Masks We Wear

We all wear masks in life. These masks often act as defense mechanisms, developed to protect us from judgment, pain, or rejection. Think of the tough guy or girl mask—someone who appears fearless but is often sensitive deep down. Perhaps you've worn the "people pleaser" mask, always putting others' needs before your own, or the "successful professional" mask, hiding behind titles and achievements. These masks might have served a purpose in the past, but they can limit your authenticity and growth.

The Impact of Hiding Your True Self

Hiding behind masks can lead to various challenges. Loose boundaries are often the result of not knowing who you truly are. You might say "yes" when you mean "no," leading to burnout and frustration. There's a common pattern of seeking approval and putting others' feelings or well-being above your own. In relationships, these patterns can cause strain, as you're not authentically connecting with others. In your quest for financial prosperity, these masks can limit your success, preventing you from pursuing your true passions.

How has not living in self-authority robbed you of the confidence, relationship, and/or financial abundance that you deserve?

I started my personal development journey at 13 years old, fresh out of grammar school and entering middle school. For as long as I can remember I've absorbed all I could learn about self-esteem, transformation, … anything that would move me closer to knowing who I am and who I can become.

And, I believe this study saved my life.

You see, at a very early age, I'd already come face to face with a life filled with all kinds of experiences. Some of them are incredible, and some of them are not so great.

My passion for personal development prepared me for these experiences. It prepared me for the pain of my first heartbreak, disappointment, molestation, rape, devastating personal loss, financial hardship, divorce, single parenting, and many other traumas.'

I not only made it through all of these experiences but I came through it all with a pretty good sense of self.

That was until the fateful day on January 6th, 2009. It started like any other day. My husband, three kids, and I woke up, had breakfast, prepared for our day, and around 8a.m. said our "I love you's" to my husband Alex and kissed him goodbye as he left for work.

As I floated through my day full of excitement and anticipation for my husband's return home I thought it was weird that he had not called, texted, or checked in, but I just assumed he was busy. Then when the clock struck 10 p.m., 11 p.m., and then midnight and I still hadn't heard from him, I knew that something was wrong.

After a sleepless night of worry, fear, and confusion, I was blindsided by an early morning call from the police department and a voice on the other end of the phone telling me that my husband's body was found in the desert, he had died from suicide, and that I needed to come and identify his body.

My heart sank to my feet because on the same day that my husband went missing, I also found out that I was pregnant with my (our) fourth child and I was excited to share the news with him.

In one day my world was turned upside down and would be forever changed. Overnight, I found myself as a single mother, head of household, I stepped into the role of primary breadwinner and inherited our financial business.

I felt abandoned, scared, alone, unsafe, and unworthy. I had feelings of self-doubt, and I did not necessarily trust myself because I had spent so many years hiding behind my husband, and relying on him to lead the family and show me the way. But I refused to play the victim. On the contrary, I was committed to becoming a victor over my situation and turning my tragedy into triumph.

I was especially nervous about having to manage the finances. As an only child of a teenage single mother, we never had money growing up, and although my husband and I had managed to do well for ourselves, I had never been in the position that I had found myself in; breadwinner and steward of the finances. I always had part-time businesses and contributed to the household but I had never been the sole provider and I never had the responsibility of managing money and paying the bills.

Overnight, I came into a large amount of life insurance money and while it was a beautiful gift that allowed me the time and space to find my way, the responsibility of it frightened the hell out of me.

Despite my insecurity about managing this money, I was grateful that my husband loved his family so much that he made sure we would be taken care of in his absence. He forced me to learn how money works and made sure that I understood financial concepts, but knowing concepts is very different from applying them.

I spent the first two years after his passing taking care of everyone else (mentally, spiritually, and financially). I made sure that my kids got the therapy and healing that they needed. I took time to make sure that our families were okay. I took care of my husband's friends, clients, and teammates, and even took over our financial business for two years in an effort to continue my husband's legacy, avoid disappointing others, and making everyone around me proud.

All good things, if my own self-worth wasn't tied to it.

My life had been turned upside down and I lost all sense of self because my entire identity had been wrapped up in my roles within the

54

life I'd built with my husband. And then he was gone. He was my best friend, my protector, my provider, my lover, my everything.

My heart was broken and I was wandering around like a fish out of water, trying to figure it all out. No intention, no vision for what I wanted to create, and no degree or skills to fall back on. I was numb and on automatic. I put my feelings of grief, fear, and displacement on a shelf to focus on everyone and everything else and to distract myself from the pain. I was in the space in between my YES and my NO.

As a result, I became reckless. My sense of self-worth was stripped away by my experience and the pain was so unbearable that I would do almost anything to numb the pain or fill the void. Some of my favorite antidotes were alcohol, shopping, traveling, and sex.

It wasn't until early 2013 after finally taking time to deal and heal from pain that things shifted for me. I woke up one morning and I was complete. Complete with the grief. Complete with numbing. Complete with the roles I'd played out for so many years. Complete with all of it!

I knew that I no longer wanted to be in Las Vegas, I no longer wanted to play it safe, and I no longer wanted to run my husband's financial business, it was time to go. I was a HELL NO to staying in these roles and a HELL YES to creating a new life.

After a process of re-engaging my personal development and spiritual practices, I finally developed the courage to stand on my own two feet. So after almost four years of living by default, and letting other people's expectations guide my life, I made the tough decision to leave the financial business that my late husband and I spent over a decade building (despite my belief in what we did for families and being a beneficiary of what we did), sold my 6,000 sq. foot house and most of our belongings, and moved myself and my four kids from Las Vegas, where I had the support of my family and friends, to San Diego where I knew nothing and no one.

It was time for me to grow up and step fully into my Self-Authority. I knew that moving away was an opportunity for me to rediscover myself, access and develop my inner strength, and recreate my life on my terms. So despite my feelings of fear and uncertainty, and people thinking I was losing my mind, I took the leap.

Within my first two years in San Diego, I attracted an incredible community of friends, successfully grew my business in personal development, began homeschooling my kids, wrote a Best Selling book called, *"Motherhoods Not For Punks,"* and had proved to myself that I could take ownership of all of my experiences and use them to fuel the creation of a life filled with Pure Abundance! A journey that has beautifully supported me in fulfilling my mission to lead, empower, and inspire other women to do the same.

New awareness flooded in ...

Self-authority is not given, it's earned. It's something you grow into and develop over time. It's the deepest and truest form of confidence and trust in oneself that is strengthened or diminished with every decision you make.

Each time you honor your YES or your NO you are gaining self-authority. When you are in your self-authority you feel a sense of safety, you feel confident, connected, and in integrity.

Not only can you recognize and receive opportunities, but you begin magnetizing them. You feel limitless and in flow which is a result of functioning in your highest state of being. In return, you experience a sense of purpose and fulfillment, natural joy, and become an inspiration to those around you.

Reconnecting with Your Authentic Self

So, how do you begin the process of unmasking your authentic self? It starts with asking better questions.

What do you want in life?
What fulfills you in a relationship or career?
What unique gifts can you share with the world?

And on the flip side …

What are the areas of your life that no longer feel aligned?

Where have your boundaries become loose or non-existent?

What roles are you playing in life that no longer serve you?

What is not changing or shifting these things costing you (money, time, self-respect, energy)?

Are you willing to do the work and give yourself the same time, attention, and compassion that you give to your job, relationships, or children?

Letting Go and Finding Your Authentic Self

To unmask your authentic self, you must be honest with yourself about who you are, what you need, and what you want. This involves connecting with your vulnerability and rediscovering the optimism and openness of a child, coupled with the intuition and insight of an adult. It's about embracing your true self and living in alignment with your authentic essence.

The Higher Laws That Make Up Who You Are

The "higher laws of who you are" often refer to the fundamental principles or truths about your authentic self. These higher laws encompass the idea that you are more than your external roles, titles, and societal expectations. They pertain to:

Authenticity: Being true to yourself and not compromising your values, beliefs, or desires to conform to others' expectations or societal norms.

Self-Awareness: Understanding your inner thoughts, emotions, and beliefs and using this knowledge to make conscious choices aligned with your true self.

Purpose: Discovering your unique life purpose and aligning your actions and decisions with this purpose, leading to a more fulfilling and meaningful life.

Self-Love: Cultivating a deep sense of love and acceptance for yourself, recognizing your worthiness and deserving of happiness and abundance.

Abundance Mindset: Embracing the belief that there is an abundance of opportunities, resources, and love available to you, and letting go of scarcity and lack-oriented thinking.

Intuition: Trusting your inner wisdom and intuition to guide your decisions, as your authentic self often communicates through gut feelings and inner knowing.

Boundaries: Setting healthy boundaries in your life to protect your well-being and maintain authenticity in your interactions with others.

Vulnerability: Being open to exposing your true self, fears, and insecurities to others, fostering deeper and more authentic connections.

Empowerment: Realizing that you have the power to shape your life and that you are not a victim of circumstances or external forces.

Living in Alignment: Aligning your actions, relationships, and choices with your authentic self, which results in a life that feels more meaningful, fulfilling, and abundant.

In essence, the higher laws of who you are reflect the path to living a life that is deeply aligned with your true self, allowing you to experience more joy, love, and abundance.

Unveiling the Lurking Blocks to Currency Flow

Currency, in its various forms, plays a significant role in the symphony of life's abundance. Whether it's the financial resources that fuel our aspirations, the energy we exchange in relationships, or the creativity that drives innovation, currency flow is essential. However, this chapter isn't just about money; it's about understanding and navigating the obstacles that can impede the flow of various forms of currency in your life.

The Flow of Abundance: A Natural State

Picture a pristine river meandering through a lush forest. The water flows effortlessly, nourishing the flora and fauna along its path. Birds sing merrily, fish swim gracefully, and the forest teems with vitality. This serene scene illustrates the natural flow of abundance. Just as the river sustains life along its course, the continuous flow of currency, in all its forms, is meant to nurture your existence.

When you embrace and align with the truth of who you are, and use it as a foundation for creating your life, life harmoniously meets you to create holistic currency flow.

Obstacles to the Flow: Hidden Undercurrents

Life, however, isn't always this idyllic river. It's complex, and sometimes, the currents of abundance are obstructed by hidden undercurrents. These impediments, while not always visible, can be powerful, and they often operate beneath the surface of your conscious awareness.

So let's embark on an expedition into the depths of your life's river. Let's shine a light on those hidden obstacles that might be impeding the smooth flow of currency, whether it's money, love, energy, or creativity.

Shedding Light On Hidden Blockages:

To uncover hidden blockages, we must first recognize that our lives often contain invisible impediments to the smooth flow of currency. These barriers, although concealed beneath the surface, are capable of causing significant disruptions and limiting the realization of our abundance.

Limiting Beliefs:

One of the most potent yet concealed obstacles is the set of limiting beliefs we hold. These notions often lurk in the shadows, like specters haunting our financial and emotional landscapes. Thoughts like, "I'm not good enough," "I don't deserve this," or "Money is the root of all evil," can quietly sabotage our progress. Unearthing and confronting these limiting beliefs is essential to removing the barriers to currency flow.

In a world where we're constantly bombarded with messages and expectations, it's no surprise that we sometimes internalize detrimental beliefs about ourselves and our worth. They act like weeds in the garden of our consciousness, choking the life out of our dreams and desires. But remember, these beliefs are not truths; they are stories we've adopted over time.

Fear and Scarcity:

Fear and scarcity are two interlinked emotions that can severely hinder the movement of currency in our lives. Fear, whether it's fear of change, fear of failure, or fear of success, can paralyze us and prevent us from making the necessary leaps toward abundance. Scarcity, on the other hand, fosters a mindset of insufficiency, where we believe there's never enough to go around. Together, these emotions erect walls around our lives, restricting the flow of abundance.

Imagine fear as a dam, blocking the river of abundance. Behind that dam, there's a reservoir of untapped potential waiting to be released. The flow is restricted because of apprehensions and hesitations. To break the dam, you must confront your fears and let the abundance flow freely.

Scarcity, the belief that there's a limited supply of abundance in the world, can be likened to a constriction in the riverbed. It narrows the flow and creates turbulence. To overcome this scarcity mindset, you must widen the riverbed of your belief system, understanding that abundance is not a finite resource.

The Power of Self-Awareness:

Before we can dismantle these hidden blocks, we must first become acutely aware of their existence. Self-awareness is the light that reveals the lurking shadows of our psyche. By introspectively investigating our thoughts, emotions, and beliefs, we can shine a beacon on these hidden blockages and initiate their dissolution.

Begin this process by keeping a journal. Record your thoughts, emotions, and reactions. This will help you spot patterns and identify areas where limiting beliefs and fears are most influential. Also, practice mindfulness and meditation to observe your inner world without judgment.

Rewriting Your Money Story:

One potent approach to overcoming these blockages is to rewrite your money story. Often, the narratives we've developed around money and abundance are heavily influenced by our past experiences, societal conditioning, and inherited belief systems. By revisiting and revising these stories, we can open doors to abundance where they were previously locked.

Start by considering the financial stories you've heard throughout your life. How have they influenced your beliefs about money? Were you told that "money doesn't grow on trees" or that "rich people are greedy?" Recognize how these stories have shaped your relationship with money and decide how to rewrite them. Create new stories that align with the abundance you desire.

Fostering a Mindset of Plenty:

Embracing a mindset of abundance is essential to shatter the shackles of fear and scarcity. When we adopt a perspective of plenty, we acknowledge that there's enough for everyone, and our success doesn't diminish the opportunities available to others. Abundance is not a finite resource; it's a boundless flow of energy, creativity, and wealth that expands as we embrace it.

To foster this mindset, practice gratitude daily. Recognize the abundance that already exists in your life. Start small: appreciate a beautiful sunrise, a tasty meal, or a kind word from a friend. This gradually shifts your perspective towards abundance and away from scarcity.

In the pursuit of authentic abundance, it is imperative to confront and dissolve the hidden blocks that obstruct the flow of currency, whether it's financial wealth, love, energy, or creativity. By uncovering limiting beliefs, conquering fear and scarcity, fostering self-awareness, and embracing a mindset of plenty, we can finally remove the veil that has obscured our path to genuine abundance.

As a result of doing "the work," I have fully embraced divine feminine power and have used it to claim my space, own my unique voice, and hold lovingly firm boundaries. I live my life by design and enjoy the freedom, abundance of love and connection, fulfillment, and prosperity that comes with just BEING me.

"Unmasking Your Authentic Self" is a pivotal chapter in your journey to living an abundant life. By letting go of the masks and embracing your true self, you unlock the door to a life filled with love, joy, fulfillment, and prosperity. Your authenticity is your superpower, and the world is waiting for you to shine as your genuine self.

In the chapters that follow, we'll delve deeper into how living authentically can transform your relationships, career, financial abundance, and overall well-being. But first, let's take that first courageous step—unmasking your authentic self.

Patrina Wisdom

Patrina Wisdom is the visionary CEO of Pure Abundance Inc., abundance activator & strategist, best-selling author, TEDx speaker, podcast host, and founder of the Anatomy Of Abundance™ Framework and Pure Abundance Retreat™.

After processing the sudden death of her husband of 20 years, who committed suicide in 2009, and finding out the same day that she was pregnant with her fourth child, Patrina took her personal story and decades of experience as an entrepreneur and fearless business leader and began the process of creating her company and the Anatomy Of Abundance™ Framework to offer a range of programming and luxe retreat experiences designed to help women break free from the generational cycles of struggle, fear, and scarcity, and guide them into a life of embodied abundance.

Patrina's expertise has been featured in a variety of international publications. With a background as a certified life coach, yoga instructor, and NLP practitioner, along with over 20 years of experience as a licensed financial educator and broker, Patrina brings a holistic approach to helping women. Her remarkable ability to connect with audiences and convey complex ideas in a clear and engaging manner leaves a deep and lasting impact on listeners and motivates them to take action and make positive changes in their lives.

Connect with Patrina at https://patrinawisdom.com/.

Design Over Destiny

by Brandi Daniels

This chapter is dedicated to my hero, my muse, and my soul mate—my mom. You believe in me no matter what, and your unconditional love is always my true north home. I love you forever, thank you.

On the evening of January 3, 1987, an American Businessman by the name of Alan Robert Krakower found himself alone in Ibiza, where, in a supremely frustrated state, he encountered the 'Voice.' The Voice said: "Are you ready to work?" And for eight days and eight nights (without eating, sleeping, or drinking) he worked, transcribing in detail what is now known as The Human Design System. This experience was said to have been terrifying and painful for him. Thirty-four years later, I would encounter Human Design and went on to have an equally painful and terrifying experience that would (re)shape my life.

Although I never had the pleasure of meeting Ra Ura Hu (the name he was later known as) before he passed, our paths are similar even down to our design. We're both Splenic Manifestors who have felt in our souls that we'd found our purpose through Human Design. More importantly, we have seen the value in using Human Design to help transform our own lives and the lives of others.

Now this chapter is not just about finding your purpose but discovering who you are at your core. It is about finding what you want, how to align to those energies, calling them in, and living the abundant, authentic life YOU KNOW you were placed here to experience.

So let's start at the beginning, what is Human Design, and why does it exist?

What is Human Design?

Human Design is a field of study that combines ancient wisdom with modern technology to create a truly unique system of personal growth. Pulling from Astrology, The IChing, the Hindu Chakra System, and Quantum Physics—The Human Design System allows people to explore their unique energetic blueprint and to better understand how they interact with the world around them.

By understanding your type (the energy you came here with) and purpose (the energy you get to align with), you can make better decisions in life based on what truly feels aligned and in flow for you.

The "Human Design Bodygraph," is the most important tool used in Human Design. It's a visual representation that helps you understand yourself better by analyzing your body's energy centers (or chakras).

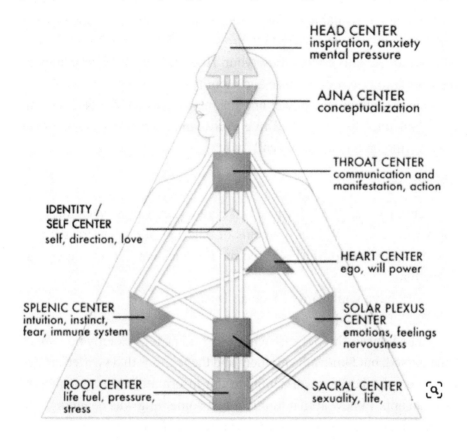

Human Design exists to show us areas where we can find more balance, as well as where potential challenges might arise if we don't pay attention to our individual needs. With this information in hand, individuals can better understand their strengths and weaknesses, so they can start living based on what resonates with them rather than just following societal norms or trends.

Where woo meets science ~

Let's get one thing clear, YOUR unique energetic blueprint, known as your Human Design, comprises 64 Gates. These Gates govern the energy readily available to you—your innate talents and superpowers. They are intricately linked to your very DNA, the 64 codons that form your genetic code. Thus, your Human Design is an authentic representation of your essence and identity.

Once you know the power and magnetism you hold, you'll be able to go out into the world and live in a manner of being unstoppable, unwavering, and unapologetically you.

My Story ~

On February 22, 2022, I arrived in Hawaii on a mini vacation/work trip with a friend. Within moments of entering our home for the next few days, my friend Marlys asked me the question that would change everything.

"Girl, have you heard of Human Design?"

"No," I responded.

To be honest, I'm not sure what was said next or exactly how much time passed, but I know the moment and the feelings that swirled around me when she began to disseminate the information she downloaded from an app. I knew at that moment that something was changing.

She began to tell me things about myself that she could not have known, from ticks and triggers to behavioral patterns, thoughts, and generational traumas. She told me about the challenges I have faced and those I might face in the future if certain changes or awareness aren't brought to the surface.

For the first time, I understood why things like innovation, autonomy, and peace were so important to me. She explained why and how I keep bumping up against burnout and how my expectations of others can be harmful in relationships. She showed me, in my Design,

68

why I had to make all the mistakes and do the crazy things I did in my youth and how that wisdom will all be beneficial in the future. I learned that my nickname "Community Connector," was more than a nickname, but a true representation of who I am and what I'm meant to contribute and do in this life.

I learned that the pain, challenges, stress, and tension I might experience are actually meant for something much greater and are going to be used to serve others on a higher level.

But most of all, I learned that I am not broken, I am not missing crucial important elements, and I am not behind nor am I not ready. I am perfectly complete and my only job, or mission in this life, is to realize that. To surrender and use my God-given gifts to create the impact I know I'm meant to deliver in this lifetime.

For the first time, I felt seen.

Conditioning ~

As my friend read my Design to me, I realized that a lot of things I believed to be true were stories, or worse they weren't even my beliefs. They were just things I picked up along the way.

You see, I believe that in order for you to live the life of your dreams, you have to know what you want so you can align yourself with it. Before you can dive further into this book and start your journey of the *Anatomy of Abundance*, your journey starts within you. Knowing from the starting gate **WHO YOU ARE DESIGNED TO BE, What gifts you naturally came here with, and the Wisdom you are here to learn and share.** These will set you up for true success on your journey.

So, what stops us?

The question of all questions, the answer is simple. Conditioning. I will explain the three most common types of conditioning here:

1. The stories you tell yourself about money, your weight, your profession, and your relationships; this is *societal conditioning.*
2. The internal traumas (even the ones you're not entirely aware of) and the wounds you carry, (although you were never personally inflicted); this is *generational conditioning.*
3. The global beliefs you carry and choose not to question; this is *homogenous conditioning.*

Conditioning has become the cornerstone of our lives, it acts like a virus infecting us on a cellular level. Moving or stalling our bodies, turning common sense into chaos, and forging us on paths that in our heart of hearts, we do not want to take.

Conditioning has been sold to us as a way to keep us safe, but really it stifles our souls and keeps us from utter happiness. So how do we rid ourselves of this?

First, understand what type of conditioning is driving you (see the three types listed above) and decipher what is really beneficial and resourceful and what is not. But let's begin at the beginning—sometimes just understanding Your Type is a great place to begin self-inquiry.

I invite you to grab your Human Design chart, if you haven't pulled it already, simply visit my website to download it for free - https://www.livingyourhd.com.

Know Your Type ~

In Human Design there are five possible types or classifications of Aura. In foundational Human Design readings, we always start by explaining to you which Aura Type you are.

Generator (approximately. 38% of the world's population)

Manifesting Generator (approximately. 32% of the world's population)

Projector (approximately. 20% of the world's population)

Manifestor (approximately. 8% of the world's population)

Reflector (approx. 1% of the world's population)

DECONSTRUCTING YOUR HUMAN DESIGN CHART

1. TYPES

THERE ARE CURRENTLY 5 TYPES. EACH TYPE OPERATES IN A UNIQUE WAY.
WE'RE PUZZLE PIECES THAT ARE PART OF A WHOLE.

MANIFESTOR

YOU'RE THE SPARK THAT INITIATES ENERGY.
YOU'RE AN INNOVATOR AND TRAILBLAZER.
HERE TO START THINGS - AND NOT NECESSARILY FINISH.

GENERATOR

YOU SPREAD AND AMPLIFY ENERGY.
YOU'RE HERE TO BE LIT UP BY WHAT YOU DO
AND IN TURN YOUR ENERGY LIGHTS UP THOSE AROUND YOU.

MANIFESTING GENERATOR

YOU MAGNIFY THE ENERGY AROUND YOU.
YOU'RE HERE TO INITIATE LIKE A MANIFESTOR AND BE LIT UP LIKE A GENERATOR.
YOU HAVE THE ENERGY TO DO THINGS THAT EXCITE YOU.

PROJECTOR

YOU GUIDE AND ALCHEMIZE ENERGY.
YOU'RE A NATURAL GUIDE.
HERE TO SEE OTHERS DEEPLY AND SHOW A BETTER WAY.

REFLECTOR

YOU REVEAL AND ECHO ENERGY.
YOU ARE OPEN AND RECEPTIVE. HERE TO REFLECT BACK TO US.
YOU ARE A REFLECTION OF YOUR ENVIRONMENT.

WWW.LIVINGYOURHD.COM

Each of these types carries with it a specific energy and theme. A perfect example of conditioning is what we have been led to believe and subscribe to in the US—that life is about the hustle and grind. The truth is, most of us are not designed to behave, let alone work that way. This is why burnout and fatigue are so prevalent in our society today.

When we look at Generators and Manifesting Generators (MGs for short)—this is the only group designed to work long hours for extended periods of time. I compare this group to the Energizer Bunny, they are directly plugged into an internal energy source that lights up and turns on when they are excited and more importantly, aligned. Generators and MGs are designed to find the thing they are passionate about and do that thing for as long as it's exciting and turns them on.

Generators and MGs are the reason the world exists, and why we have technology, buildings, medicine, and advancements. Because of your passion and commitment to getting shit done, the world goes on! Generators get their energy by saying "Hell Yes," to the things that get them excited. They do need to be cautious of saying "Yes," when they really mean "No." Saying "Yes," to everything will quickly put a Generator into a tailspin. It's really easy to spot a misaligned Generator/MG—they are frustrated, confused, and angry. They believe life feels like a hamster wheel, and they are out of control.

Projectors, Manifestors, and Reflectors are on the opposite end of the spectrum, we get our energy in cycles or spurts. We need lots of downtime and rest to rejuvenate and restore our systems. This group is not necessarily cut out for the nine to five day-in, day-out routine, but gets to design a work life more suitable to their needs.

Self-care and boundaries are important for every type, but even more so in this group. Their energy comes from being aligned, when they are out of alignment and operating out of conditioning they are bitter, angry, and disappointed. When they are acting out of Type, they are more prone to burnout, depression, and illness. This happens when they are trying to behave like Generators (go, go, go) and failing. They cannot keep promises, so they feel out of integrity. They try to initiate and force recognition and get rejected. More commonly, they are hasty or impulsive and make quick decisions out of fear or scarcity, versus taking their time and trusting their intuition.

Projectors are our guides or coaches, here to evaluate and audit what currently is and give feedback on where improvements can be made. This is a special gift Projectors have, but also one that needs to be invited in. We all know that friend who gives great advice (even though we don't want to admit it) but when it's invited, it lands versus feeling like a judgment or critique.

Manifestors are our initiators, they're here to get the party started. To inspire and make us question, "Why?" They are the early adaptors, the innovators, the visionaries. Hard to nail down and sometimes even harder to understand, but their presence is strong and is felt the minute they walk into the room.

Our last group is the Reflectors—a small, but mighty group. Reflectors literally reflect back to us the environment. They amplify everyone and everything around them. We look to them to know if we (personally) are on track or (globally) are heading in the wrong direction. Reflectors absorb and reflect everything around them and are the most chameleon type. They are our mirrors.

So imagine, you've been sold this idea that if you're not moving at 100 miles an hour, hustling, constantly creating, inventing, reinventing, and "being on," you won't be successful—what happens when you finally crash? This is not sustainable. Or the idea that whatever you start, you must finish; this is not true for a lot of us. Nearly half the population is here to be the spark, to get the party started, not the flame to keep it going. This alone could be the game-changing information you need to start living more in alignment.

This is conditioning!

Just knowing this bit and diving into your Human Design Type can give you so much insight into a better way to work, operate, be in relationship, and help you begin to align more with the future and lifestyle you want—without the guilt.

Now! I'm not saying walk into your boss' office tomorrow and demand a new work schedule, proclaiming, "It's because I'm a reflector, and I work in spurts." That may not go too well, but you can begin to figure out what you do need. Where is all your energy going? Where are the energy holes, and vampires in your life?

Anna ~

A good friend of mine, Anna, was an overloaded, exhausted accountant for a big firm. The kind of firm where your bosses know you by work reviews and numbers, rather than anything personal. She wasn't enjoying her work anymore and was definitely hitting burnout; on top of that she'd recently gotten married, suffered a miscarriage in the past year, and was struggling with her mental health. Stuck in a loop of needing to live to work, meet goals, and keep everyone in her family happy, Anna was close to hitting a wall.

When we finally had a chance to sit down and go over Human Design, the a-ha's and revelations were palpable. Her energy literally could be felt shifting throughout the call. It turns out she is a Projector (acting like a Generator) and the 50-hour-plus work weeks were draining her dry. Her body was sending her messages that rest was needed, but her mind and ego were telling her, "If you stop, you'll fall behind." "You don't need rest, don't be lazy." "People won't respect you if you don't finish."

We learned in her Human Design that she thrives within her network—that her true abundance will come from tight-knit relationships and referrals versus cold calling. That her desire to research and learn wasn't just a hobby, but a form of security that she needed. As a Projector, she's here to guide us and show us easier, simpler ways of 'being,' but that starts with herself.

Part of her purpose is to learn these lessons, heal her body, mind, and spirit, and teach others what is possible. In other ways, her Human Design showed her that she wasn't living in the right environment conducive for her to thrive and that her nutrition and exercise routines could also be changed. HIIT classes and Bootcamps were adding to her stress and high cortisol levels; compounded with the pressure she was feeling at work and home. It was creating an emotional overload in her body. So switching to calmer, quieter environments (Pilates, Yoga, Meditation, and Breathwork) would better regulate her system. Allowing her time to process information, and emotions and make sound decisions that she could feel good about.

This reading gave Anna a lot of clarity and pause—she was able to see where in her life and career changes could be made. It wasn't about quitting her job but reevaluating what she said "Yes," to and honoring the time and energy commitment being asked. She found someone she trusted at work to confide in, which gave her the confidence to inquire about what other opportunities there were that would offer more flexibility. Lastly, she reached out to her close circle (her network) to let them know she was open to a change and inquired if anyone had any recommendations.

She learned to stop beating herself up for 'Needing to know more information,' and realized that was the best way for her to make sound decisions; and when she didn't, mistakes were made. Human Design helped Anna to remember how powerful she actually is and when she listens to her body and trusts her intuition, she'll make decisions correct for her. Her daughter at the time was five years old, she knew she wanted to be a role model for her and show her that respecting your body, honoring your needs, and resting is just as important as doing it for others.

Inner Wisdom ~

One of the things I love about Human Design, and this book you hold in your hands is that, instinctively, there is nothing in here that you don't already know. Your soul was drawn to this book because of the answers your mind is seeking. But as you'll start to realize or rather (re)awaken to is that inner wisdom. In Human Design, we call this your Authority. Everyone is born with innate wisdom and an internal compass that directs you to what is resourceful or not for you. For some of us, it's our heart (Ego Authority), our gut (Sacral Authority), our spleen (Splenic Authority), or even the granddaddy of all, our emotions (Solar Plexus Authority).

DECONSTRUCTING YOUR HUMAN DESIGN CHART

3. AUTHORITY

YOUR AUTHORITY IS YOUR INNER GUIDANCE, YOUR INTUITION PER SE. IT'S ABOUT MOVING AWAY FROM THE MIND TO MAKE DECISIONS AND INSTEAD CONNECT TO YOUR COMPASS AND PROCESS.

INNER AUTHORITY

SOLAR PLEXUS EMOTIONAL
- WHAT ARE YOUR FEELINGS TELLING YOU?

SACRAL
- WHAT IS YOUR GUT SAYING?

SPLENIC
- WHAT ARE YOUR INSTINCTS SAYING?

EGO
- WHAT ARE YOUR CORE DESIRES?

SELF-PROJECTED
- WHAT ARE YOU HERE TO SAY AND EXPRESS?

OUTER AUTHORITY

SOUNDING BOARD
- TALKING OUT LOUD OR TO SOMEONE TO PROCESS THOUGHTS

LUNAR CYCLE
- TIME HELPS YOU PROCESS AND GIVES YOU CLARITY

WWW.LIVINGYOURHD.COM

That is why when you hear the <u>truth</u>, it resonates with you to your core. Your mind wants certainty and is always seeking clarity, but this can only be found in your soul. Ra would always say when tasked with a decision—check your authority, it's always black or white (yes or no). When you begin to question or waiver, know that that is the mind coming in.

I know you're thinking, "OK, do I need to check in with my Authority for everything?" The answer—yes and no. We say, "Why not?" Especially for the *"big three"*—What you will do, Where you will live, and Who you will love, in short—career, life, and love. Of course, there might be other important situations that fall in between, but for everyday matters—what to have for dinner, washing the car or not, cleaning the house today or tomorrow, maybe not so much.

So I ask you to imagine there's a book that tells you exactly what to do in order to experience more peace, calm, abundance, and RICHNESS in your life with more ease, clarity, and trust. That book is the **Book of YOU**. It's your Human Design.

In order for this book to not just be another personal development book on your bookshelf, take the time to sit and reflect. Our greatest gifts lie in trusting in our Authority and understanding our definition. This is how we tap into our highest wisdom.

Our Centers ~

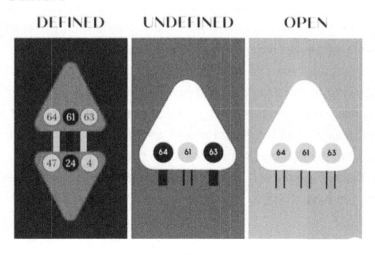

DEFINED   UNDEFINED   OPEN

When you look at your Bodygraph, you'll notice there are shapes similar to the Chakra System—these are called Centers in Human Design. Some will be colored in (this means they are defined) and others will be white (this means you are open). The shapes that have color represent "energy" that you have consistent access to, for example:

If your Head is defined, you are constantly coming up with questions and questioning everything—this is how you learn and enlighten others. If your Head is white, then you are constantly filtering out (sometimes random) questions, questions of others and may be known to have 'shiny ball syndrome.' This is because you are open and taking in the energy of everything and everyone around you.

So let's look at the gift and wisdom here—the gift of definition means you will always dive deeper, never take anything at face value, and you'll always push others to question versus just believing.

The wisdom of openness is that you will try new things and be open to new ideas, that you will be led astray (sometimes), but that is where you'll learn and be able to put that bit of knowledge into your pocket to serve at a later date.

You see, understanding your design will give you insight into why you do and act the way you do, and not how to hide or stop, but to turn these things into your superpowers to help you get everything that you want.

For years, I judged others by comparing their ability to work hard, to how hard I was willing to work. Many people didn't pass my test, and some surpassed me. I admired them. I drove myself sick and into serious fatigue three different times, trying to keep up with this idea that working 'myself to death and being busy' was a badge of honor.

My design showed me that my defined heart a.k.a. Will Center means that no matter what I will find a way, and I will carry on even to the detriment of myself. I am willing to sacrifice. My defined root means that I always feel pressure and drive to keep going and that others around me who do not have a defined root will feel that too. It will either motivate

78

them or turn them off. These two defined centers made relationships challenging for me. Until I learned how to use this superpower.

I had to become conscious that it was MYSELF plus conditioning that made me think, that working endlessly without proper rest and boundaries in relationships was acceptable. Just because I felt I could didn't mean I should say "Yes," to take on more. I had to learn that the pressure I felt to keep up was internal, and not because of an actual threat or fear. The gifts I bring are when I'm in, I'm all in—you can count on it. I have the drive, and the will to see things through. My wisdom comes in knowing that I get to stop and inform when I need rest. That I can allow myself to not see rest or self-care as a weakness, but as an integral part of my routine and how I love and honor myself. My superpower is that I now get to teach this to others. I have lived it, I am living it and I can spot it a mile away.

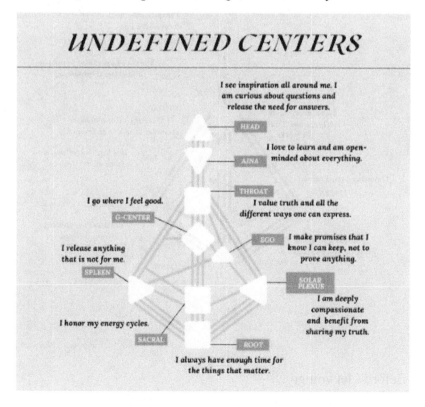

UNDEFINED CENTERS

I see inspiration all around me. I am curious about questions and release the need for answers.

HEAD

I love to learn and am open-minded about everything.

AJNA

THROAT

I value truth and all the different ways one can express.

I go where I feel good.

G-CENTER

EGO

I make promises that I know I can keep, not to prove anything.

I release anything that is not for me.

SPLEEN

SOLAR PLEXUS

I am deeply compassionate and benefit from sharing my truth.

I honor my energy cycles.

SACRAL

ROOT

I always have enough time for the things that matter.

There are probably things crossing your mind right now that you do (or don't do) and you're wondering, "Is that part of my design or did I pick that up somewhere?" We used to say that knowledge is power, but I believe knowledge applied is power. Knowing something and then doing something with it is truly where the power lies. Using your Human Design Bodygraph, refer to this graphic below to see what your open and defined centers say about you! Paying close attention to the 'Not Self Themes and Beliefs.' These will show you areas to be aware of and bring intention to where you have experienced living in the shadow energies.

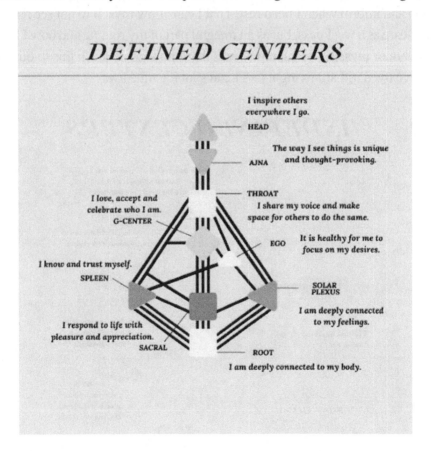

DEFINED CENTERS

I inspire others everywhere I go.
HEAD

AJNA — The way I see things is unique and thought-provoking.

THROAT

G-CENTER — I love, accept and celebrate who I am.

I share my voice and make space for others to do the same.

EGO — It is healthy for me to focus on my desires.

SPLEEN — I know and trust myself.

SOLAR PLEXUS

I am deeply connected to my feelings.

SACRAL — I respond to life with pleasure and appreciation.

ROOT — I am deeply connected to my body.

Before I let you go …

They say, every good book starts with the Hero's journey, well my friend, this is yours. Chances are you came to this book because you're ready for something to change. You're no longer satisfied with what is, and you know you are destined for more. Life has thrown you a few curveballs, and you're on the hill asking, "Is this all there is?"

This is the moment your guide presents you with a choice, and this is the <u>book</u> that can forever change your trajectory. The question now is, are you truly ready? Ready to embrace the abundance that is within You and become the hero of your life's story?

Brandi Daniels

Brandi Daniels, a trailblazer in human design and business expertise, is fervently dedicated to the empowerment of entrepreneurs and business owners. Her passion lies in guiding them toward building businesses or careers that not only nourish their minds, bodies, and spirits but also cater to their aspirational lifestyles. As an amplifier, she magnifies potential; as a community connector, she bridges gaps; and as a creative, she brings innovative solutions to the table. Her mission transcends the ordinary—it's about simplifying life, finding a peaceful existence, discovering one's flow, and ultimately, leading a "rich life." Brandi's commitment to this cause is unwavering, making her an invaluable resource in the realm of business development and personal growth.

Connect with Brandi at www.LivingYourHD.com.

CHAPTER 8

Step 2—Identify

Your beliefs become your thoughts, Your thoughts become your words, Your words become your actions, Your actions become your habits, Your habits become your values, Your values become your destiny.

~Mahatma Gandhi

In the labyrinth of life, there are often invisible shackles that keep us from realizing our full potential and living in abundance. These shackles manifest in various forms: disempowering stories, limiting beliefs, negative language, destructive habits, and even toxic relationships. In this chapter, we'll dive deep into step two of the Anatomy Of Abundance™ Framework, the process of identifying and reframing these elements that are holding you back.

Unearthing the Disempowering Stories

Our lives are often shaped by the stories we tell ourselves. These narratives, formed over years of experiences and conditioning, can either propel us forward or keep us stuck. Identifying these disempowering stories is the first step to rewriting your life's script.

Unmasking Limiting Beliefs

Beliefs are the bedrock upon which our thoughts, words, and actions are built. Limiting beliefs function as barriers, preventing us from reaching our true potential. We'll explore how to uncover these beliefs and, more importantly, how to replace them with empowering ones.

Transcending Negative Language

The language we use can be a powerful indicator of our internal dialogue. Negative self-talk and the words we choose can reinforce disempowering stories and beliefs. We'll delve into techniques to transform this language into a source of empowerment.

Breaking Destructive Habits

Habits, whether conscious or unconscious, shape our daily lives. Identifying destructive habits that keep you stuck is essential for personal growth. We'll discuss strategies for breaking free from these patterns and creating new, positive habits.

Navigating Toxic Relationships

Sometimes, the people we surround ourselves with can either uplift us or drag us down. Toxic relationships can drain your energy and hinder your progress. Consider how to identify these relationships and establish boundaries that promote your well-being.

Healing Underlying Trauma

Many disempowering stories, beliefs, and habits have their roots in unresolved trauma. To truly move forward, it's crucial to acknowledge and heal these wounds. We'll discuss approaches for addressing and healing underlying trauma.

Charting Your Healthy Path Forward

Once you've identified and reframed these disempowering elements, you'll be ready to chart a healthier path forward. This path is unique to you, aligned with your authentic self, and free from the constraints of past narratives.

A Journey Toward Abundance

The process of identifying and reframing is not just about shedding the old; it's about making space for the new. It's about stepping into the light of your true potential and embracing a life of pure abundance.

By doing the inner work, you pave the way for a brighter, more abundant future, one where you are the author of your own story, unburdened by the limitations of the past.

Explore These Questions:

1. What are the most persistent challenges I'm currently facing in life, love, and my career?
2. What aspects of my personality am I hiding from the outside world? For example, am I suppressing my creativity, assertiveness, sensuality, or vulnerability?
3. What have been the consequences or outcomes I've faced due to suppressing these aspects of my personality? For instance, has quelling my creativity led to feelings of frustration or stagnation in my work?
4. How would embracing and expressing my authentic self enrich my life, relationships, and career? For example, would embracing my creativity lead to more innovative problem-solving in my job?
5. What am I afraid of losing if I were to fully embrace and express my authentic self? For instance, do I fear losing approval

from others, professional status, or a sense of security in my relationships?

How to Turn Your Brain from Success Saboteur to Abundance Amplifier

by Sylvia Becker-Hill

Dedicated to my beloved mother who, despite trauma, PTSD, and lifelong struggles with anxiety, was able to keep her ability to love alive and who inspired me to become the liberated, strong woman I am today, showing others how to be uncaged, unashamed, and unstoppable.

*Being your word is the foundation for success in life.
Not being your word undermines your trustworthiness
and turns your self-doubt whispers into a roaring
self-loathing monster.*
~Sylvia Becker-Hill

It is 2007, online marketing is gaining momentum. YouTube evolves, and anyone aiming to ride this wave must use social media for short videos. Armed with video marketing training and professional equipment, I aim to showcase Emotional Freedom Technique to corporate leaders. Timing is crucial: I want to be a trailblazer!

Despite my efforts, I stumbled over the tripod. The microphone baffles me. An urge for a restroom visit arises. A VIP client's email demands attention. A quick text to a friend needs dispatching. My script is left behind, requiring a return trip to my office. Seeing myself in a mirror, I notice my appearance—lipstick, unruly hair—needs fixing.

With these diversions, two hours vanished. I remember an impending client call, forcing a reschedule ...

Have you ever set intentions, like consistent content creation, negotiating a higher salary, or eating healthier, only to leave them unfulfilled? Feeling deeply frustrated wondering, "What's wrong with me? Why can't I follow through?"

My intention in this chapter is for you to realize:

There is nothing wrong with you!

You will gain the knowledge and a simple process that will allow you to say "goodbye" to self-doubt and become unstoppable in being your word!

Information doesn't provide transformation.
Your engagement does.
~Sylvia Becker-Hill

How many self-help books have you had the opportunity to peruse over the past decade—10, 50, perhaps a staggering 500 or more? Personally, I find myself immersed in three books each week. One, purely for pleasure and escape; another, to better serve my cherished clients; and the third, to nurture my personal growth. This equates to over 500 self-help books devoured during the span of a decade. Drawing from this experience and the insights gleaned from thousands of clients over the past 27 years, I can distill three fundamental principles about delving into self-help literature, much like the one you hold in your hands.

1. A single idea with the power to reshape your consciousness is worth the journey through an entire book.
2. Depending on your unique stage of self-development, the same book will offer varying insights to you, distinct from its impact on others.
3. Even the most profound and transformative book will remain inconsequential in your life unless you engage with it in a practical, actionable way that transcends passive reading.

Now, let's explore some practical techniques to deepen your interaction with this book:

- Employ a highlighter to mark and emphasize the quotes that resonate with you.
- Use a pen to jot down your thoughts in the margins, engaging in a personal dialogue with the author's wisdom.
- Utilize the blank pages at the end of the book as a canvas for extended reflections and references to key passages, allowing for easy future access.
- Share your discovery with your circle of friends and consider forming a book club to discuss your insights collectively.
- Keep a journal ready to respond to the questions posed within my chapter, as there's an intimate connection between handwriting

and the depths of one's emotions. This bridge between your conscious and subconscious mind can strengthen the whispers of your intuition!

And, if you are active on social media, why not share your newfound insights with the world? Your learning holds significance, and you might unknowingly inspire others in their journeys.

Sometimes trash becomes art by being put into a museum.
Simple ideas gain power through context.
~Sylvia Becker-Hill

To foster genuine learning and the potential for true transformation as you engage with my chapter, we must first establish a common understanding of certain terms. This groundwork will enable you to immerse yourself deeply in the context in which the ideas I present may resonate within your mind AND body, potentially bringing about profound change through my written voice.

Before delving into the questions below, I encourage you to take a moment to center yourself, to ground your thoughts in your physical body. Breathe deeply, allowing your analytical mind to momentarily step aside, and instead, let these questions evoke feelings and physical sensations that guide your responses:

1. What does the term "SUCCESS" mean to you at this present moment?
2. Has your definition of success remained constant over time, or has it evolved?

3. From where does your current definition of success originate?
4. To what extent is it influenced by external factors, such as your parents, spouse, friends, societal norms, health, religion, and so on?
5. What proportion of your definition of success is authentically your own?
6. Consider the motivations behind your perception of success—how much is driven by fear, and how much by love?

Within the confines of this book, we place our focus on the notion of "abundance" as a framework for living a fulfilling and successful life. "ABUNDANCE" is a term that has gained prominence in recent years. For some, abundance may feel like an overwhelming tsunami of obligations, opportunities, and distractions, inducing a sense of impending drowning—a sentiment often referred to as "overwhelm." Others view it as an "insatiable beast of capitalism," relentless in its pursuit of more possessions, and the exploitation of Earth's resources, other people, and even oneself to achieve greater productivity and to reach higher levels of status.

Here, within the pages of the *Anatomy of Abundance*™ book, we employ the term in a positive context. However, it is crucial to recognize that every author and, indeed, every reader will have their distinct way of experiencing it. As you embark on this exploration, I offer you a few examples drawn from my own experiences and those of my clients.

As women, our hearts yearn for:

- Greater inner serenity.
- Freedom from the shackles of our past.
- A deeper sense of purpose in our work.
- More moments of unbridled laughter.
- Enhanced connections and love, both within and beyond.
- Financial security and peace of mind.

- Heightened energy and vitality.
- Time aplenty for friends, cultural discoveries, and cherished hobbies.
- An infusion of levity, play, adventure, and the uninhibited expression of our creativity.
- A more profound impact on the lives of others and the wider world.
- Liberation from self-sabotage and the ceaseless critique of our inner voice.
- And so much more ...

You see, abundance assumes diverse forms, and what it means to you is a matter of personal sentiment. Take a moment to journal your reflections.

Regardless of your interpretation, the key, my dear reader, resides within you. More precisely, it lies within your IDENTITY—a tapestry woven from:

- Your beliefs about yourself.
- The narratives you weave from your past experiences.
- The emotional energies that dwell within your body.
- The aura and mood you project into the world.
- And your actions that sustain your constructed identity of what and who you are as a self-referential feedback loop.

My mission is to unveil to women their extraordinary capacity to shape their own identity—to uncage their minds, unshame their emotions, and make their actions unstoppable.

I will illuminate the path to harnessing neuroscience-based cognitive strategies, allowing you to embody the essence of an abundant woman. When you truly embrace BEING abundance, living it becomes second nature—effortless, natural, and joyous.

Understanding your brain's design gives you
the power to design yourself.
~Sylvia Becker-Hill

The society we inhabit today bears the scars of a profound disconnection between humanity and "mother" nature. This chasm widened further as we clashed over resources in the wake of dramatic climate shifts and the subsequent population explosion resulting from the advent of agriculture. The prevailing societal model called "patriarchy" is attributed to the "father," serving as the archetype for God (derived from the Latin "padre," meaning father). This model, rooted in male-centric principles and systems meticulously engineered to fortify male dominance, is a mere 7,000 years old. We currently find ourselves in the tumultuous throes of its disintegration, paving the way for an emerging post-patriarchal world that has yet to be officially named—one characterized by collaboration, diversity, and inclusivity.

Given this historical backdrop, women have been conditioned for the last 7000 years to perceive themselves as powerless victims. I intend to furnish you with scientific insights into your brain that will unlock the keys to liberate you from this sense of powerlessness and victimhood, allowing you to step into your innate power and creativity. The latter is the divine spark in you that allows you to express yourself and shape the world.

Please know:

You have always been powerful.
You have always mattered.

It's merely a case of your belief system being molded by your parents, culture, and society to suggest otherwise. Allow me to impart a few brain-related facts before sharing personal stories illustrating how you can transform your brain from a Success Saboteur into an Abundance Amplifier.

Brain Fact One:

I invite you to consider the age of your smartphone, reflecting on when you last upgraded your device. Despite these compact marvels having significantly greater computing power and longevity than the earliest rocket ships that transported astronauts to the moon in the late '60s, the majority of people in the USA acquired a new smartphone within the past three years. The reason is not merely clever marketing or the allure of trends; it's rooted in our diligence to update both: our software and hardware. By failing to do so, we risk losing compatibility with our technological environment. How does this relate to your brain, you ask? It's a pivotal connection.

Your brain doesn't operate on software that's merely one, ten, or twenty years old, nor is its hardware design a decade, half-century, or century behind. The biological evolution process proceeds at a significantly slower pace, and it's vital to realize that the model your brain harbors is approximately **25,000 years old**. Irrespective of your biological age, ponder the implications of walking through life NOW with a brain model designed 25 millennia ago! This knowledge is paramount. Just as my old Nokia phone from 2000 lost compatibility with the ever-evolving app-rich environment, certain aspects of the brain's design are ideal for the year 23,000 BCE when mere survival was a cause for celebration. However, these facets aren't as ideally

94

suited for modern women of our time, who wield technology that would appear as sorcery to their cave-dwelling ancestors.

Brain Fact Two:

The human brain, which evolved over millions of years, especially the frontal lobe or "neocortex," the seat of our conscious mind, is a highly intricate organ that consumes a substantial portion of our body's energy and resources. Its design prioritizes the conservation of precious energy, employing the ingenious construct of "brain biases." **Biases** represent hardwired proclivities to respond in specific ways, stemming from the brain's desire to minimize energy expenditure when faced with decisions. Imagine a fork in the road, with one path sloping gently downhill and the other featuring steep, imposing rocks. A ball rolling down this path will invariably select the one with the least resistance!

There are over 160 recognized biases, but fear not—I will introduce only a select few in this chapter, elucidating them through practical stories to enhance your understanding. These insights will equip you to identify and address the most common self-sabotage patterns prevalent among us women on our journey to success.

Brain Fact Three:

The brain serves among other functions as the carrier of your mind: generating thoughts, ascribing meaning to perceptions, forming and retaining memories, producing inner voices, images, and dreams, transmuting perceptions and emotions into feelings, shaping decisions, building automated patterns that lead to habit formation, housing your ego and inner child, and storing your stories to maintain your self-image and more!

To conserve energy and operate with agility, evolution bifurcated the mind into two components: the smaller, newer **conscious mind** behind our forehead and the predominantly **subconscious mind** that occupies the majority of cranial real estate in the back of your head above your neck.

One of the brain's biases stipulates that the subconscious mind is substantially more potent and resilient than the conscious mind. You likely encounter this daily—when you make a morning commitment to your health, planning to embark on a hike at five p.m. after work and abstain from eating after seven p.m. If your day unfolds smoothly, and you still possess energy reserves, you fulfill your commitment. However, a taxing day marked by unrelenting busyness and a lack of respite depletes your conscious willpower, which lets you cancel the hike at five p.m. By eight p.m., you succumb to the allure of whatever your pantry offers, guided by the false belief that junk food will replenish your energy or serve as a buffer to suppress feelings of irritation stemming from your day. This underscores the "Two Minds Bias": when pitted against each other, the subconscious mind invariably emerges as the victor!

Brain Fact Four:

Until around 1990, scientists adhered to the belief that the human brain undergoes its most significant growth until the age of roughly six years, with certain factions claiming that its full maturation occurred at the end of puberty, around the age of 24. Irrespective of the school of thought, both groups were in agreement that, post "maturity," the brain's trajectory skewed only toward decline. In this view, factors like alcohol, drugs, lifestyle choices, illnesses, accidents, and genetic predispositions could contribute to a diminishment of brain cells, with little hope for redemption.

Fortuitously, the '70s witnessed remarkable advancements in imaging technology, with commercialized MRIs in the '80s affording an unprecedented glimpse into the functioning of healthy, living brains. These modern imaging techniques provided conclusive evidence of neuroplasticity—an idea initially conceived in the early '60s. Here's the great news for you: Regardless of your brain's "antiquated model" (Brain Fact One), its pre-established biases (Brain Fact Two), and the dominance of the subconscious mind (Brain Fact Three), your brain is inherently plastic! **This implies that it can grow new nerve cells and form new connections among them until your last breath!!!** (The sole caveat pertains to severe imbalances in neurotransmitters and neurochemicals, as observed in Alzheimer's and dementia patients.)

Your brain worries only about your safety.
Your happiness is your job.
~Sylvia Becker-Hill

Our brain, with a model dating back 25,000 years, is inherently programmed with its primary directive: "**safety first**." This imperative stems from the brain's ceaseless vigilance in ensuring your survival. Your brain perpetually scans your environment for three key elements: danger, sustenance, and opportunities for procreation. Yes, sex! I've now piqued your interest, haven't I?

Remember my story at the start of this chapter, how I sabotaged my video shooting efforts and with that my marketing success in 2007 through procrastination and distraction patterns?

Let's pause for a moment to reflect on what was going on:

I had a clearly defined conscious objective.

I was consciously well-prepared.

I was consciously well-versed in the process.

I had consciously acquired the requisite equipment.

With the allotted time scheduled, I was both consciously competent and brimming with confidence.

However, it seemed like I was possessed by a demon committed to keeping me from what I had declared I was going to do!

What I'm demonstrating through that true story is the brain's "safety first" bias, intertwined with the second bias, "subconscious mind over conscious mind power." My subconsciousness had deemed my intended action—sharing video content publicly—as **dangerous, triggering a series of distractions aimed at safeguarding me from an unspecified threat.**

This procrastination pattern persisted for weeks, prompting my coach at the time to offer reassurance: "It's just a matter of mindset, Sylvia. We've discussed this. You're apprehensive about marketing, finding it too sales-y! However, you cherish your community and your content. Push through your resistance, stay focused on your love and your impact goal, and it'll become easy."

Have you ever encountered similar advice from coaches, mentors, or self-help authorities?

I, being a diligent student, adhered to his counsel: I focused on my love for my community while pushing through my resistance. Superficially, there was progress—I managed to record a few videos. However, here's the twist:

The videos were utterly disastrous—unusable.

In the first, I was in tears.

In the second, I trembled uncontrollably.

The third video captured me in a state of paralyzing anxiety, resembling a deer caught in headlights.

Do you still relate to this narrative? Something that should be straightforward, an endeavor you witness others undertake daily, yet you find yourself unable to accomplish it. Perhaps, for you, it's not video production but a different challenge. Nevertheless, **the common**

**thread is the perpetual inability to follow through despite conscious
objectives, competencies, and plans.**

Society offers an array of well-intentioned solutions: "Exercise more
discipline," "establish stronger boundaries," "summon willpower,"
"fully commit," and "seek accountability partners." However, the more
we fail to take action, the deeper our self-doubt spirals, exacerbating
feelings of shame and self-loathing which we women are already
primed to feel due to our history of being second-class citizens without
power and fewer freedoms than men.

The predicament? These solutions stem from the conscious mind,
neglecting the undeniable fact that the subconscious mind possesses
immeasurably greater influence. Additionally, they overlook a brain
bias known as the "**blind spot**," where we're unaware of what we
don't know—a cognitive phenomenon that bridges gaps in perception
with surrounding information, fostering the illusion of comprehensive
understanding.

Sadly, women often navigate self-doubt when ensnared in
procrastination loops, attributing their struggles to personal
shortcomings. They remain unaware of the latent factors residing in
their subconsciousness —an unresolved trauma, a deep-seated vow,
or early childhood loyalty issues—that drive self-sabotage, protecting
them from reencountering past turmoil.

The solution? Employing specialized tools or processes, either
individually with skill or with the guidance of a trained professional.
These might encompass deep self-inquiry, Intentional Creativity®,
Emotional Freedom Technique, somatic coaching, and guided self-
directed neuroplasticity … all aimed at excavating the subconscious
content and releasing the barriers borne of the past.

And so, the story of my procrastination in video production draws
to its resolution.

I had to confront my anxiety symptoms head-on, deploying attention management and emotional intelligence to trace the source of my triggered state.

Through the practice of the Emotional Freedom Technique, I unearthed a long-forgotten memory—a traumatic incident from my final year in middle school:

A morning in the fall of 1983: I enter the school building to find my peers chatting and giggling in small groups. As I approach, they cease their conversations, turning their backs or breaking into laughter. The strange sensation of something awry grips my stomach as I walk the hallway and climb the grand staircase. Everywhere I go, the same reactions! Finally, I reach the door to my homeroom and spot a massive poster beside it.

The poster features a collection of 20 to 30 photos from an overnight bus trip my entire class had embarked on, complete with a disco dance party. However, one image is prominently enlarged and centered: me, dancing in a white top with ruffled sleeves and an exceedingly short skirt, arms outstretched, head thrown back, my long hair cascading. The image, captured from a peculiar angle, renders me a distorted and ungainly figure, like an alien spiraling out of control on the dance floor. I appear ridiculous and grotesque ...

*The entire school was abuzz with laughter at my expense. If I had possessed greater confidence or self-assured beauty, I might have taken it in stride, perhaps even adding a humorous comment. Alternatively, if I felt the freedom to express anger, I might have torn the poster down and discarded it. But in my insecure, frequently bullied, bookish nerdy persona, the experience was **overwhelmingly humiliating**. In response to that mortification, **I made a solemn vow: "Never again shall embarrassing pictures of me be exhibited in public."***

Over 35 years later, my subconscious mind still clung to that incident and my vow. It doesn't matter that self-made videos for YouTube didn't exist in 1983! The subconscious mind isn't rational! For it, the visual exposure online equaled the danger of ugly printed photos!

Confronting my anxiety allowed me to unravel this ancient trauma, and to release it emotionally and energetically from my body.

Since then, shooting videos and sharing them online has become a seamless and joyous endeavor. It even led me to be featured in a reality business documentary online on Apple TV, witnessed by millions of viewers!

Do the opposite of what society and your brain
want you to do and you'll be fine!
~Sylvia Becker-Hill

In capitalist societies, numerous companies and a select few individuals profit immensely from exploiting your emotional distress and anxieties. They do this through various means: tempting you with 'retail therapy' in advertisements, bombarding your social media feeds with images of escapist lifestyles, promoting substances like alcohol, illegal drugs, and pharmaceuticals as quick fixes, and marketing self-help programs that promise miraculous solutions through bypass strategies and the doctrine that "life is supposed to feel good." This all results in billions of dollars reaped from your brain's natural inclination to seek pleasure and avoid discomfort.

Our brain's bias for seeking comfort, unfortunately, keeps us subconsciously trapped in the very issues we're striving to overcome

or heal. All those coping mechanisms and avoidance strategies provide momentary relief—a Netflix binge paired with copious amounts of pizza and vanilla ice cream makes me forget everything!—but they ultimately keep us entrenched in what we're trying to escape.

The way out is deceptively simple but not easy. It involves doing the exact opposite of what your brain is wired for (protecting you from pain) and what capitalist societies encourage (exploiting your needs by selling products you wouldn't believe you need in the first place if you weren't running from your pain to stay comfortable).

After 37 years of research and 28 years of professional coaching and neuroplasticity work, my definitive answer to all your struggles and pains is this:

FACE IT!

Before delving into the 'face it' process, let me address some pervasive misconceptions about 'pain' in our culture. **Pain** is often labeled as 'bad' and 'dangerous.' Additionally, women have been conditioned to believe they are the 'weaker sex,' 'fragile,' and 'too sensitive to endure pain.' It's amusing to me, and I can't help but chuckle while typing this sentence, because **the opposite is true**. Women's nervous systems are wired to endure significantly higher levels of pain than men could ever fathom. Any woman who has experienced excruciating menstrual cramps or has given birth knows exactly what I mean.

Regardless of the false narratives surrounding our 'feminine softness,' pain itself has been unfairly stigmatized. Pain is neither inherently good nor bad; it's simply information. It's a vital part of our bodies, our subconscious minds, and our soul's language! Pain communicates when something is "off" and when there's a misalignment with our values, expectations, and intentions. It can range from a gentle whisper to a deafening scream, saying: "Wake up! Pay attention! Look and feel! Something isn't right," and you are called to change. In essence, **pain is an invitation to seek new alignment.**

Attempting to escape, suppress it with medication, or distract from it will only result in a harsher reckoning down the road. Please do not misinterpret me. I'm not saying, "No pain no gain!" We can create huge gains without pain! I am just busting the myth that "pain is always bad," that "feeling uncomfortable is bad" like too many Law of Attraction teachers preach.

The height of your success is defined by your
willingness to feel uncomfortable.
~Sylvia Becker-Hill

My core process in **7 steps to turn your brain from a success saboteur to an abundance amplifier** follows the acronym "Face it!" Use it every time you are experiencing yourself doing the "wrong thing," "sabotaging your own intentions," or "feeling off."

F—Focus inward.

A—Acknowledge what you're doing and thinking.

C—Call out the lies and conditioned beliefs.

E—Emotions need to be felt without resistance knowing you're safe to feel them.

I—Identify an alternative aligned action that expresses your truth.

T—Tell an accountability buddy (diary or friend or coach) your new choice.

!—Celebrate your resilience, your commitment, and your courage to change.

Go to the link at the bottom of my biography. There you can access a free training guiding you through the 7 steps including an EFT tap-along "procrastination-buster" and my new lyrics to the song "I like to move it" from the movie Madagascar designed to rewire your brain to never forget to "Face it!" what is sabotaging you.

Sylvia Becker-Hill

Sylvia Becker-Hill is a true Renaissance woman, a multiple-published author, and a seasoned edutainer who has empowered thousands of executives and business leaders since 1997. In 2002, she became the first German coach to earn the coveted title of Professional Certified Coach from the ICF, establishing herself as a pioneer in the coaching world. Her impressive educational background boasts two university degrees, while her portfolio showcases over 30 certifications in various change modalities, including her most recent accreditation as one of the world's few Certified Master Neuroplasticians.

Located in the picturesque landscape of North County San Diego, Sylvia shares her life with her New Zealand husband and two teenage sons. Beyond her global client service from her home office, Sylvia can be found in her art studio, nestled within a charming children's playhouse beneath a majestic Peppertree in her backyard. Here, she masterfully crafts vivid, brain-rewiring paintings that reflect her passion for vibrant expression.

Sylvia's core belief centers on the profound impact of understanding one's own brain function—a key to unlocking the full spectrum of human potential. In her engaging presentations, she seamlessly merges education and entertainment, imparting design principles, unraveling cognitive biases, and sharing happiness-boosting brain hacks. Sylvia's mission is clear: to guide individuals in transforming their brains from mere success saboteurs into abundant amplifiers, fostering prosperity in every area of life.

Connect with Sylvia at www.becker-hill.com/faceitgift.

IDENTIFY —
FOUNDATIONAL LAW

Your Soul's Path to Discovery

by Dr. Michelle Wolford, ND

I was asked to write on the foundational law of identity, the structural component. How one discovers, embodies, and evolves their identity without allowing the victim or hero to rule their story, but to live as your ever-expanding self in your unlimited potential. Your state of true abundance. And, how to identify what is holding you back from your greatest version of self.

Without structure, we lack form and purpose.
Foundation is everything.
It will predict your level of impact.

Before we move into the heart of our journey together, I want to share some foundational concepts to offer you a comprehensive understanding of what shapes your identity, including how the brain (psyche and nervous system) plus the body (cellular growth and communication), life experiences and energetics impact your sense of self, the *"I"*—the co-author of your life.

Let us begin. *The Identity.* The identity is a set of characteristics, beliefs, and experiences that define who you are. It encompasses your overall sense of self, including personal, social, and cultural aspects, and how you view yourself in relation to the world. On the other hand, your personality is the unique set of traits, patterns of thinking, feelings, and behavior that make up who you are. It is how the world interprets and responds to you, and you to it. Your personality influences your personal reality.

The identity is the structure of the home.
Your personality is how you choose to decorate it.

Our identity first forms on a cellular level and develops over time through body maturation, and personal experiences that impact your psyche. Evolution occurs when we meet challenges or glory. Conflict brings awareness for change. Expansion for greater abundance arises when we acknowledge and evaluate the conflict, and then shift into exploration, decision, and alignment.

Take a look at the diagram below to see the different aspects that form your identity and pave the way for your soul's path to discovery.

Foundational Concepts of the Identity:

Souls Path

The Identity

Psychological Development

Organ System & Cellular Maturation

Trauma vs Glory

Clinical Phases of Brain Development

Identity Identifiers

7 Tiered Chakra System

Identity Expanders

6 Aspects of Human Expression

- Genetic
- Biochemical
- Physical
- Mental
- Emotional
- Spiritual

This journey of understanding The Identity begins on the cellular level. Every cell in your body is programmed to mature during a specific time of your life, solidifying its cellular identity (i.e., its job). Until the time of peak maturation for each organ system, those cells are learning who they are, the job they're meant to perform, and how to communicate with other cells. This systematic maturation process creates cellular identity and forms coherence (togetherness) in the human body.

Disruptions in this maturation process negatively impact your cellular identity, impacting your sense of self and how your body functions. You are the culmination of all your cells. And when they don't perform their job well or send false messages, they create internal disharmony and lack coherence. This manifests physically as symptoms, or energetically through experiences we attract. The most common culprit is trauma- mental, emotional, spiritual, physical, or biochemical insults. Examples of a biochemical trauma include drug use, vaccine injury, and environmental toxins. Examples of the other categories may be more obvious for you to imagine.

Trauma comes at any time, in any form. Ideally, with acknowledgment, time, and healing, we can always find our center, regain coherence, and continue to thrive. When any part of our cells isn't thriving, they are in a state of disharmony (surviving or suffering), which is the antithesis of abundance.

When trauma occurs during one of the stages of organ system maturation, it interrupts your cellular growth and development leaving that organ system at an increased risk for showing imbalance or weakness when the human body is under stress. Study the chart below and highlight the years of *impact experiences* to see which organ system(s) may have stunted cellular maturation or poor cellular communication disrupting your identity.

Dr. Gerard Gueniot Map of Organ System & Cellular Maturation:

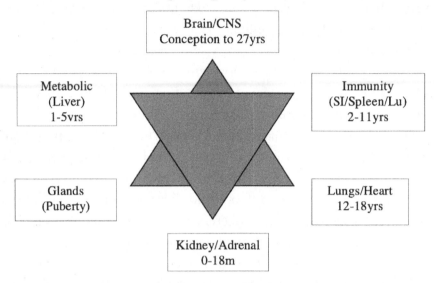

Kidney/Adrenal- Electrolytic System (Birth- 18months): Survival. Beginning of cellular communication. Physical: Easily stressed, living in high cortisol state. Energetic: Fear/Anxiety vs Grounded. Chakra chart: Root.

Liver/Digestive/GALT Immune/Thyroid- Metabolic System (18months – 5yrs): Self vs. non-self, nutrient absorption, cellular waste. Physical: Skin and digestive issues. Energetic: Boundaries (healthy vs unhealthy), self-confidence or lack of. Chakra chart: Sacral, Solar Plexus.

Lung/MALT Immune- Immune System (5 - 11yrs): Continuation of differentiating self vs. non-self and immune system maturation. Communicating with the external world about self. Physical: Skin issues and chronic lung afflictions. Energetic: Grief, poor communicator. Chakra chart: Heart.

Pituitary Gland- Hormonal System (11- 14yrs): The hormonal system controls the behavior of all cells. A system that is living in coherence (unity), communicates a clear message to other cells, allowing the cellular identity and identity of an individual to blossom as one. A toxic oasis creates cellular confusion and conflict, which leads to cellular degradation and dis-ease which can manifest physical, biochemically, or psychologically (mentally, emotionally, spiritually). Physical: Hormonal imbalances (Thyroid/Sex Hormones), Issus with growth and metabolism. Energetic: Sexual confusion, lacking intuition. Chakra chart: Throat, 3rd Eye, Crow.

Heart- Circulatory System (12- 18yrs): Including lymphatic system (drainage pipes of the body), venous, arterial and acupuncture meridians (lines of energy). It ensures communication and exchange with the self (heart) and with the external world (lungs). This is how we come to understand and express our identity. We are also programmed to explore the opposite of our foundation (home life), as a survival mechanism to find the best way to thrive. We often come back to our foundation with nuancal improvements (if we had a safe, healthy home), or massive improvements (if we had a traumatic home). Without proper guidance or unresolved trauma, we can easily be led astray to a false identity. This is a very impressionable period of time and one filled with many emotions. Physical: Heart or Circulatory issues. Energetic: poor relationships, communication and connection with others. Chakra chart: Heart, 3rd Eye.

Brain- Central Nervous System (Conception – 27yrs): Our nervous system balances and governs impulses, emotions, intellect, thought, action and behavior. When properly attuned, it also governs our intuition. It is believed in TCM that the soul fully incarnates around the age of 12 (the merging of our spiritual self and physical body, united as one). Chakra chart: Crown.

* Through my own study, I have altered this information slightly, however, it is based of the work and study of Dr. Gerard Gueniot, MD

I want to emphasize that micro-cosmically your cells are forming an identity, while macro-cosmically, your psyche is forming an identity, constantly asking, "Who I am?" Therefore, mind-body coherence is key to achieving health, wealth, purpose, and abundance.

Similar to cellular maturation, your *psychological development* also happens in distinct stages and gives insight into how the brain matures and interprets the external world, which impacts your sense of self. How you identify yourself is partly how you identify the world around you.

Highlight the age(s) of significant trauma or memories, and let your mind shift into curiosity, reflection, and contemplation. Questioning and acknowledgment open a window to self-discovery, which offers insight into what is holding you back in different aspects of your life, creating room for expansion (i.e. achieving and attaining what you desire).

Erik Ericksons Phases of Psychological Development

Trust vs. Mistrust (Infancy, 0-1yr): Infants learn to trust their caregivers when their basic needs (food, comfort, love) are consistently met. A sense of trust is established when caregivers are reliable and responsive.

Autonomy vs. Shame and Doubt (Early Childhood, 1-3yrs): Toddlers begin to explore their independence and develop a sense of self-control. Encouragement and support for autonomy lead to a healthy sense of self, while excessive criticism can lead to shame and doubt.

Initiative vs. Guilt (Preschool, 3-6yrs): Children explore their world, develop a sense of purpose, and begin to make decisions and take initiative. They may feel guilty if they perceive their actions as wrong or disruptive.

Industry vs. Inferiority (Elementary School, 6-11yrs): During this stage, children engage in tasks that require effort and diligence, such as schoolwork and extracurricular activities. Success in these tasks builds a sense of competence, while failure may lead to feelings of inferiority.

Identity vs. Role Confusion (Adolescence, 12-18yrs): Adolescents explore their identities and develop a sense of self. They may experiment with different roles and values to establish their identity, which can result in confusion or a clear sense of self.

Intimacy vs. Isolation (Young Adulthood, 19-40yrs: Young adults seek intimate relationships and develop the capacity for love and commitment. Failure to establish these connections can result in feelings of isolation.

Generativity vs. Stagnation (Middle Adulthood, 40-65yrs): Adults focus on contributing to society and future generations, often through work, parenthood, and community involvement. Those who do not find ways to contribute may experience stagnation.

Ego Integrity vs. Despair (Late Adulthood, 65+): In retirement, individuals reflect on their lives. If they feel a sense of fulfillment and accomplishment, they develop ego integrity. If they harbor regrets and unresolved issues, they may experience despair.

The two diagrams above are the behind-the-scenes imbalances and programs that are ruling your sense of self due to impact during your prime years of maturation.

Some literature would claim that *conception to 7 years of age* are the most impactful maturation years, while other literature would suggest the time between *preconception to 27 years of age* has the greatest significance in determining one's sense of self from both a cellular and psychological perspective. You could also argue that since we are ever-changing and evolving beings, any stage of development has an impact. However, I would say preconception to 27 years of age is when we create the initial neuro-pathways that construct our foundation of self. This foundation can be harder to deconstruct and reconstruct the older we get.

I like to compare the highlighted areas from Dr. Guenoit's Map of Organ System & Cellular Maturation and Erickson's stages of Psychological Development with the Chakra guide to see more clearly where physical, psychological, and energetic imbalances are manifesting.

Chakras are energy centers in the body that correspond with organ systems, sounds, smells, colors, vibrational patterns of energy, and emotions. Look below to see where you are prone to imbalance and how those imbalance(s) are expressing for healing. It's the body's language of communication requesting attention for healing.

CHAKRA GUIDE - Foundation

Dr. Michelle Wolford, ND

	ROOT	SACRAL	SOLAR PLEXUS
Color	Red	Orange	Yellow
Location	Base of Spine	Pelvic	Naval
Body Organ	Kidneys, Adrenals	Reproductive Organs	Digestive System
	Legs, Feet	Pelvis	Skin
Element	Earth	Water	Fire
Life Area	Survival	Sexuality	Will Power
Balanced	Grounded, Secure	Flow, Flexiblity	Power, Will, Determination
	Safe, Stable, Trusting	Express Healthy Emotions	Sense of Self, Boundaries
Unbalanced	Low self-esteem, Indecision	Closed/Guarded, Bordem	Limiting Beliefs, Judgment
	Confusion, Addiction	Uninspired, Lack Intimacy	Lack Motivation/Drive
Gemstones	Ruby, Red Agate	Orange Calcite	Citrine, Tigeres Eye
	Blood Stone, Obsidian	Carnelian, Moonstone	Yellow Agate
Essential Oils	Sandalwod, Cederwood	Orange, Neroli	Bergamont
	Vetiver, Patchuloi	Gardinea	Lemon, Clove
Herb	Nettle, Ashwaghanda	Don Quai, Maca, Vitex	Ginger, Milk Thistle
	Ginseng, Red Clover	Mugwort, Saw Palmetto	Dandelion, Chamomile
Food	Root Veggies, Protein	Seed cycling, Spices	Grains, Dairy
	Beans, Nuts, Seeds	Root Veggies, Citrus	Citrus, Herbs
	Red Foods	Orange Foods	Yellow Foods
Affirmations	I AM	I FEEL	I DO
Qualities	Survivial, Grounding	Sexuality, Desire	Personal Power, Strength
	Stablity, Satisfaction	Pleasure, Sensuality	Authority, Self-Control
	Vitality, Courage	Relationships, Creativity	Social ID, Inner Harmony
	Aceeptance of Life	Union with Nature	Self Acceptance

CHAKRA GUIDE - Expansion
Dr. Michelle Wolford, ND

	HEART	THROAT	THIRD EYE	CROWN
Color	Green	Blue	Violete	Indigo
Location	Heart	Throat	Brow/Forhead	Top of Head
Body Organ	Heart, Lung, Thymus Circulation, Lymph	Thyroid Ears, Nose, Throat	Pituitary, Pineal Gland Brain, Eyes, CNS	CNS Head, Cervical Spine
Element	Air	Ether	Light	Consciousness
Life Area	Love, Relationships	Communication	Intitution	Consiousness
Balanced	Compassion Ability to Give & Receive	Ability to Manifest Self Expression	Connected to your Intuition Clarity of Thought	Sense of Oneness Living with Purpose
Unbalanced	Feeling Rejected, Self-sab Lacking Connection	Difficulty Expressing Familial Patterns	Indecision, Lack of Empathy Unable to Relate to Others	Disconnected, Isolated Lacking Puurpose
Gemstones	Jade, Rose Quarts Aventurine, Tourmaline	Torquoise, Aqua Marine, Blue Lace Agate	Lapiz Luzuli Azurite, Celestilite	Clear Quartz, Amathist Selinite
Essential Oils	Geranium Ylang, Ylang	Eucalyptus Peppermint, Sage	Clary Sage, Lavendar Sandalwood	Frankincense Jasmine, Rose
Herb	Hawthorne, Rosemary Thyme, Basil	Licorise, Marshmellow Rhiola, Melissa,	Passiflora, Holy Basil Guta Kola, Juniper	Guta Kola, Myrrh Lotus Blossom
Food	Leafy Greens Veggies of all Variety Green Foods	Berries, Watermelon Cucumber, Watery Foods Blue Foods	Foods High in Flavinoids Soups, Water Purple Foods	Water Fasting Cleansing
Affirmations	I LOVE	I SPEAK	I SEE	I UNDERSTAND
Qualities	Unconditional Love Harmony, Healing Compassion, Devotion Transformation	Freedom, Independence Self Expression Shared Thought Inspiration, Truth	Intuition, Independence Clairvoyance, Imagination Manifestation Peace of Mind	Bliss, Enlightenment Understanding Universal Consiousness Divine Wisdom

Facing change can be intimidating because we grow very attached to our identities, however, to continue expanding into what you want to do, be, have, achieve, represent, and experience requires some adjustments from your old identity into a greater version of self. It's an accepted death for a chosen rebirth.

That's why it's important to address someone's healing experience through the *6 Aspects of Human Expression* - the genetic, biochemical, physical, mental, emotional, and spiritual self.

Genetic: We often talk about our genetics from a physical perspective. My mom has blonde hair; I have blonde hair. My father is tall; I am tall. My grandmother had breast cancer; I may be at risk of breast cancer. My family lineage is Italian; I am Italian. There are many aspects to genetics – physical traits, biochemically the way your body is programmed to function, and adaptations for survival.

There is also our Bio-Energetic DNA (bio = body, energetic = the stories of our ancestors that live in our cellular memory) and Epi-Genetics, which is how our external environment (chemical exposures) and internal environment (lifestyle choices, emotions, mental thoughts) can turn on or off genes, for better or worse.

In medicine, we see interesting links between the mind and body. Example: Ashkenazi Jews are more prone to digestive disorders such as ulcerative colitis and Crohn's disease. It's speculative, but due to their confinement and treatment during Auschwitz, it could be surmised that the physical and emotional trauma left an imprint on their cellular memory that was passed down through generations. The body is still expressing that trauma for healing, which can manifest physically as digestive issues impacting one's daily life, or once healed, catapult one forward to greater abundance. The key: discover the imbalance -> heal -> thrive -> purposeful living.

If you think about it, it makes sense. Our digestive tract's job is to digest the outside world by taking in nutrients and removing waste from food. We also emotionally/energetically digest the outside world through experiences—what is safe vs. unsafe—and all varying experiences in between. If any system is out of balance, you are out of balance. In this example, physically you may feel impacted by what you can eat and the toilet's proximity. Biochemically your body is stuck in an inflammatory state, while energetically you don't know what to trust or not trust, which manifests into a confused immune system (auto-immune), or unsuccessful relationships.

In other examples, you could argue nature vs. nurture, i.e. what is passed down genetically vs. what is passed down through familial patterning (observation and reenactment). That said, the concept of Bio-Energetic DNA is a magnificent source of insight and power that can lead to incredible healing and change.

Furthermore, an interesting concept to reflect on is this: in the acute (early stages) of trauma, or when our genes adapt for survival, these expressions generally serve us initially. However, if we get stuck in a state of modification that leads to imbalance, or if the external world has evolved where our genetic imprint no longer serves us, we must adapt (change). This is where identifying your body and energetic patterns gives you the power to heal and live your most abundant life.

Physical: Traits, function, expressions of disease, and external exposures.

Biochemical: Our genetics programmed our biochemistry to have an innate (instinctual/natural) response to our external and internal environment. However, we can also make choices that positively or negatively impact our biochemistry. Examples: the food we eat, meditation/prayer, and herbal medicine can offer healing, while exposures to damaging chemicals in herbicides, pesticides, cleaning, and cosmetic products can disrupt our biochemistry.

Our external environment (people, places, toxins), and our internal environment (mental, emotional, and spiritual experiences), impact our biochemistry. It's dominos. One impacts the other. It's a massive network of constant communication that impacts the cells' sense of self, which impacts your sense of self.

Mental: Our genes and biochemistry influence brain function. Our personal experiences, emotional intelligence, and spiritual path add layers, and all three either work well together or are in conflict, impacting our sense of self and how we interact with the world around us.

Emotional: Our genes, biochemistry, mental health, age, experiences, and spiritual path all have a voice that impacts our level of awareness and emotional intelligence, i.e. knowing what is worth responding to and how we choose to respond. Some responses are conscious (known), and others are unconscious (unknown until discovered, which is often a Bio-Energetic program or learned behavior).

Spiritual: Our genes and the stories our genetics want to tell for greater spiritual healing will beg to be heard. Your spiritual or religious beliefs, culture, how you view the world, and how your mental-emotional framework is shaped will also impact your spiritual perspective. No matter your religious beliefs, I think we can agree we have a soul, and that soul has a mystical presence and a pull on us. We must learn to listen and distinguish between the power of fear, pain, and ego vs. intuition (our souls path).

Lastly, there is value in looking at the basic *Identity Identifiers* that impact your construction of self, others, and the world. Some of these identifiers are primary (govern the majority of your identity and how you make decisions), and some are secondary (have impact, but can be overruled by primary identifiers). The tertiary identifiers are typically the chameleon-like characteristics we flux in and out of in different situations or groups. The brain is expansive, but its primary objective is survival, so if it feels threatened, your primary identifiers will rule your response.

Understanding your primary, secondary, and tertiary identifiers can shine a light on what is holding you back. Example: If one of your primary identifiers is "I'm a successful businesswoman," and then you want to shift into parenthood and work part-time, or maybe be a stay-at-home mom, that can create some internal conflict if not resolved, and be an unconscious obstacle to whom or what you attract, the decisions you make, your view of self, and how you feel.

Identity Identifiers:

Common Words: words we use or would love others to use to describe us.

Biological Identity: genetic makeup, biological sex.

Cultural Identity: where we came from or where our ancestors came from, plus the elements of that culture such as food, music, colors, smells, dance, ancient wisdom and healing practices.

Gender Identity: your internal sense of your own gender, which may or may not align with your biological gender.

Sexual Orientation: emotional, romantic, and sexual attractions.

Spiritual or Religious Identity: beliefs and practices that relate to your spiritual beliefs.

Social Identity: how you see yourself in relation to various social groups including aspects like ethnicity, race, nationality, socio-economic status, and/or the roles you occupy in society such as your profession or how you give back/contribute to society.

Personal Values and Beliefs: your personal values, ethics, and moral beliefs.

Interests and Hobbies: interests, passions, sports, hobbies, art, dance, music, crafts, things you enjoy doing.

Experiences and Life Events: significant life experiences, such as education, accomplishments, work, travel, relationships, triumphs and trauma.

Self-Concept: your perceived self, including your strengths, weaknesses, and self-esteem.

External Validation: how others perceive you and validate your identity.

Mystical Sciences: astrology, enneagram, gene keys, human design.

You can see that forming and establishing an identity is complex. Any individual 0-27 years of age is in a constant ninja-warrior matrix seeking their ever defining and refining *"I."* After 27, we are living an extension of our traumas or greatness, while simultaneously deconstructing and reconstructing the past for a greater future.

The key is your foundation. With a strong foundation, you create longevity, stability, power, and impact; even when you are going through upgrades. If you lack a strong sense of self, you are lost. Morals, values, ethics, principles, self-love, compassion, and faith in a higher power is the necessary framework to be grounded in yourself for greater expansion and expression. It is the anatomy of your abundance and the central pump (heart) to every other organ system that is working for a dynamic and optimal you. Everything else is decoration. Without a solid center, you can't build anything sustainable to weather the storms of life.

This foundation forms from preconception to 27 years old. I say pre-conception because ideally parents consciously conceive their little spirit being(s), and have done the interpersonal work prior to conception to create an optimal foundation for growth and development in the womb and thereafter. Conception is the first introduction to the formation of self, with an emphasis on 0-7 for psychological development, and 0-27 for physiological development.

And the soul? When does it have influence over your identity? It is believed in many ancient cultures that the soul doesn't fully incarnate into its earthly being until age 12. This concept was taught in my Traditional Chinese Medicine classes and shared with me when I was working with the Samburu tribe in Kenya, and a shaman in Peru. Similarly, when studying in an ashram in India, we were taught to avoid spiritual healing work on children under 12yrs. because it could disrupt their Karmic and Dharmic path, and you as the healer could assume part of the child's Karma (the sum of a person's actions in this and previous states of existence, viewed as their fate in future existences).

*   *   *

The human experience is meant to be a journey of self-discovery, but one could argue that if we lived in greater rhythm with ourselves and nature, we could avoid the *dis-ease* we predominantly see in Western culture; a culture where everything is at our fingertips, imbedded in instant gratification, disassociated from nature with the illusion of ultimate freedom, and lacking roots in a well-developed sense of self (morals, values, ethics, purpose). I love Western culture for many reasons, but excess of anything creates an imbalance. And a lack of foundation creates internal chaos. Internal chaos creates an unstable identity, which causes us to lose our truest sense of self and purpose; how we give to others.

We begin to have internal conflict. When our view of self conflicts (+/-) with what we show the world or how the world interprets us, we have what feels like misunderstandings, an identity crisis, or a little trauma-drama.

Take a moment to list the top 5-10 words that come to mind in each category below. Be honest! Learn where you are unconsciously living out of alignment. List the words that come to mind in each category, highlight the ones that are congruent in all three categories, and circle the ones you want to embody. The rest are left for you to evolve out of—to let go of that action, emotion, behavior, identifier, or personality trait. You can now see more clearly where you are congruent or out of alignment with yourself, others, and the world.

See Self As	Project to the World	Others Experience Me
_____	_____	_____
_____	_____	_____
_____	_____	_____
_____	_____	_____
_____	_____	_____

Once you have established a clearer idea of who you are, what you want to evolve out of, and what you want to embody, take a moment to explore the *Identity Expansion* questions to create greater abundance in your life.

Identity Expansion:

Self-Awareness: The first step is to gain a deep understanding of yourself. This includes recognizing your strengths, weaknesses, values, beliefs, and emotions. Can you list yours?

Self-Acceptance: The next phase involves accepting yourself as you are, without judgment or self-criticism. Embrace your authentic self. Are you proud of your skills/gifts? How you show up in the world?

Goal Setting: Now you can set clear and meaningful goals for yourself that align with your future self. Set 1-3 goals for each aspect of your life: career, family, personal, health, community/friends, partnership, financial.

Continuous Learning: Adopt the mindset that because life is every changing, you too must continually support your growth and development for positive change. There will be times, one part of your life takes president over the other, but it is like a wheel that is constantly turning. What do you want to focus on next?

Resilience: Life naturally presents ups and downs, therefore, continued attention to self is important to maintaining resilience and evolution. It also strengths your sense of self and confidence. What needs the greatest support, attention, or healing in your life?

Healthy Relationships: Building and maintaining healthy relationships is key to an ever-expanding identity. The company you keep is a reflection of you and impacts your greatness. Who needs go? And what are the attributes of a new friend, boss, co-worker or romantic partner you want to attract?

Contribution and Giving Back (Purpose): The greatest gift in life is how we can give back to others. Resolved trauma prevents egoic pursuits. The deeper our sense of self is, the greater our ability to impactfully contribute to others through acts of kindness, volunteering, mentorship, or purposeful creation! How do you want to give back?

For greater perspective and clarity, I also like to ask thought-provoking questions that are scenario-based—"What would you do if you won a billion dollars? What would you do if you were given 1 year, 5 years, 20 years to live? If you could do, have, or be anything, what would you create for yourself and others? Is there anything heavy on your heart or mind that you would like to share with someone in your life? When you die, how do you want to be remembered?"

Questions like these offer insight into what has the greatest value to you, what is fun and frivolous, what attachments need breaking, or where your fear governs your decisions, your ego wants control, and your pain is misleading you.

Perspective keeps us in alignment with what has the greatest value to our heart and soul, while also highlighting what would behoove us to let go of, and where we can have more faith and courage! Faith is believing in yourself, but more importantly a higher wisdom. Courage is loving yourself unconditionally through all the iterations of you.

Our identities are ever-evolving. Understanding where trauma and praise have shaped your identity and how that created room for healing offers powerful lessons, empowerment, and growth. When you couple acknowledged areas for healing with where you are misaligned, it is a powerful combination for reshaping who you want to evolve into.

Contrast creates clarity

Ironically, what typically holds us back from our most abundant self is ourself. But there is power in that because you hold the power for change. The next step is to be willing to do something different; commit to whom you want to be next, then change your thoughts and behavior. And, ideally, your commitment will be for the greater good of you and those around you.

Questions:

    1) How do you want to give back?

2) How do you want to be remembered?
3) Name three life experiences that would make you feel more complete.
4) What are the top three most important things to you?
5) Where are you living out of rhyme with your divine self?

Are your answers authentic to you? Are they what you spend your time and thoughts aligning with? Or, do you get distracted by what your family, society, fears, ego, or pain think are better answers? We often make decisions based on how we think others will interpret us. Can you differentiate true-self from projected-self, or even from the need-self? Need-self is the part of you stuck in survival mode that didn't fully heal and needs to be seen. When this character is running the show, we are often influenced greatly by others' projections.

One of the biggest mistakes we can make in life, although I don't believe in mistakes, just delays, is to allow someone else's projections and perceptions to temporarily dictate our path. The best thing you can do is take the time to LEARN your most authentic self and follow your inner guidance. And create a foundation.

One of my governing principles in life is to live in AIRE: *Authenticity, Integrity, and Responsibility for the Enrichment of your life and mine.* If what I'm doing, saying, or thinking is out of AIRE (i.e.: out of alignment with my best self), a warning sound goes off in my head, and sometimes a battle between me and my ego ensues. Then I get to take a deep dive back into the self.

Every time these moments happen, I am humbled by my humanness, and I get to learn more about my fears, traumas, ego, and praise; the moments in our life that shape a false identity. An identity that offers pain instead of abundance.

The purpose of this chapter is:

1) Understand the foundation of *The Identity.*

2) Learn ways to enhance, attune, align, support, heal, or expand *yourself.*

3) Surrender into the concept that life is not a destination with an ending, but a journey with many expressions and an eventual end that ideally is reflected upon as loved and complete.

I've given you a lot to think about and multiple ways you can identify and expand your identity. The closer you get to your inner truth, the more confident and ready you will be to let go of that which no longer serves you (past identifiers), and step into that which will serve you better today (your more abundant self).

Many of us want to achieve our purpose, but our purpose is usually not some big, grand plan. Our purpose is often quieter, more internal, with equal impact. Our purpose is not something we find, it's something we are and something we do (how we give back to others). Our purpose lives within us, not outside of us. When on purpose, we positively impact others with our light and love.

Of course, sometimes we have to take an external journey, whether that's through planned or unplanned experiences (birth, death, sickness), travel, learning, mediation, prayer, healing experiences such as acupuncture, somato-emotional release, naturopathic medicine, reiki, or studying the pseudo-sciences like astrology, gene-keys, human design or psychological testing such as Myers-Briggs or Enneagram. But most of these external things offer a perspective, something we can look at that reflects a version of ourselves back at us for clarity. It's not truth, it's potential. It's one option amongst many in the field of possibility. You and a higher intelligence are co-creating your identity and life path, but first, you have to heal before you unconsciously create, or you will keep creating from the old self, and nothing will change.

The way I create this sustainability for my patients is through my iDreamWellness® program. It's my 7 pillars of daily living to embody the most abundant life possible!

iDreamWellness® Program by Dr. Michelle Wolford, ND

I = Intention Setting: Get up every morning and set your intention for the day

D = Diet: Eat clean, organic, earth grown foods; appropriate portions and only when hungry

R = Remedies: Take appropriate doctor recommended remedies (raw materials for detox and healing); herbal medicine, homeopathy, flower essences, nutraceuticals, etc.

E = Exercise: Daily body movement to strengthen bone, muscle and mind. Plus, increase agility and flexibility, and support detox pathways

A = Affirmations: Take a moment daily to affirm your greatness and where there is room for improvement by using supportive language to grow into an upgraded version of self

M = Mediation: Mediate daily to quiet your mind, lower your stress response, align with God's voice and wisdom

Wellness = Do things you love that brings you joy, adventure, creativity and self-expansion. The goal is to expand your identity, not shrink or stabilize it

In closing, I'd like to speak further about the healing power of nature's medicine. My specialty as a Naturopathic Doctor is Biotherapeutic Drainage Therapy. This therapy is a combination of botanical medicine and homeopathy designed to restore the natural function of the human body through draining it of its toxic load and restoring cellular coherence and communication to create an environment for healing. Toxic load confuses a cell, creating a lack of coherence and poor cellular communication, and you are expressing it! Once a cell is properly drained of its toxic load, it then has a greater ability to heal, which in turn restores its natural function, restoring health.

The mind affects the body.
The body being out of balance affects the mind.
The goal is to heal the mind and body together
as they are a cohesive team.

Therefore, we must look at metrics (labs) in addition to choosing remedies that are in the greatest alignment with your genetics, personality (temperament), and immune system. Further, we must know the mode of action of each remedy for healing. Plants have their own natural chemical composition that communicates to cells what they are to do. Energetic remedies such as homeopathy and flower essences have a vibration that re-attunes a cell to its natural state. These remedies speak to the physical body as well as the unconscious mind and the entire cellular network.

The brain and body are ever-evolving. It's important to remember, the body is always seeking a homeo-dynamic balance and the brain remains adaptable (neuroplastic, meaning changeable) if we take care of it!

People are bound to the familiar, but often daydream of change.
To truly shift course is a practice, a dedication to the dream.

Hopefully, I've offered you a new way of viewing your brain and body and the layers within to help you understand how your identity was formed (spiritual path + family, culture, and social influences) and what aspects you want to deconstruct to build an upgraded version of you. Some deconstructions may include things that no longer fit or old stories that hold you back. Either way, honor the experiences of the past with gratitude, for they played a role in who and where you are today. Next, clearly decide your new destination and stay focused on the path ahead. This is where the fun begins because once you have let go of your old self, you are available to rebuild and claim your new identity. It's time to decide what you are committed to doing differently. Take a thorough look into what your body is expressing, and heed the call. Your body and mind are a microphone to the soul, and the soul doesn't lie. You can only heal that which you acknowledge needs healing. You can only change that which you are dedicated to changing. Until then, the old self is your conductor.

Dr. Michelle Wolford, ND

Dr. Michelle Wolford, ND, is a licensed and board-certified Naturopathic Doctor running a successful worldwide telemed and clinical practice treating kids and adults for a variety of acute and chronic conditions.

She's traveled the world working with top doctors, herbalists, Shamans, and Gurus to expand her knowledge of both Eastern and Western medicine for your optimal healing experience. She is a thought leader, who combines advancements in modern science with her medical training and extensive knowledge of plant medicine, energy medicine, nutrition, body movement, nature's rhymes, meditation, breath-work, ancient healing traditions and spirituality. She is The Sage and Scientist.

She has been a keynote speaker for the Natural Living Speakers tour, interviewed by Forbes, voted Best Naturopathic Doctor in Encinitas, CA, and a guest writer for the Journal of Alternative Medicine. She continues to guest speak on podcasts and in public forums.

Connect with Dr. Wolford at www.DrMichelleWolford.com.

CHAPTER 9

Step 3—Sacred Selfcare

"Balance is not letting anyone else love you
less than you love yourself."
~Patrina Wisdom

In the hustle and bustle of modern life, it's all too easy to neglect the most essential relationship—the one you have with yourself. Step 3 of the Anatomy Of Abundance™ Framework is Sacred Self-Care. Sacred Self-Care is a profound practice that extends beyond bubble baths and spa days. It is the art of caring for your mind, body, and spirit with the reverence and devotion you'd offer to the divine. It's about recognizing your intrinsic worth and prioritizing your well-being. In this chapter, we'll explore how to cultivate this practice and create daily routines that support your flourishing.

The Divine Within

At the core of Sacred Self-Care is the recognition that you are a divine being. Your essence, your soul, is a sacred spark of the universe. Treating yourself as such is not a form of arrogance but a celebration of your inherent worth. There has been a prevailing narrative, and societal programming, meant to associate selfishness with negativity. I invite you to shift this belief and consider the concept of self-fullness instead.

Mind, Body, Spirit

Sacred Self-Care is holistic, encompassing your entire being. It involves nourishing your mind through practices like meditation, mindfulness, and positive affirmations. It includes tending to your body through regular exercise, a balanced diet, and adequate rest. And it addresses your spirit by exploring your deeper purpose and engaging in practices that foster spiritual growth.

Daily Routines and Rituals

Creating daily routines and rituals is the cornerstone of Sacred Self-Care. These routines function as anchors in your day, grounding you and providing a sense of structure. They can include morning and evening rituals, exercise routines, meditation practices, and moments of reflection. The key is consistency and intentionality.

Relationship with Money

Abundance is bestowed on those who cultivate a healthy relationship with it and practice good stewardship of it. Your relationship with money is an integral part of Sacred Self-Care. It involves cultivating financial mindfulness, understanding your financial values, and making choices that align with your long-term goals, and financial well-being. When you treat your financial health with reverence, you create a solid foundation for abundance to flourish.

Nurturing Relationships

Sacred Self-Care extends to your relationships. Just as you dedicate time and energy to your own well-being, it's crucial to nurture your connections with loved ones. Date nights, heartfelt conversations, presence, and quality time spent with those you cherish are all forms of self-care that strengthen your bonds.

Boundaries as Acts of Love

Perhaps one of the most powerful aspects of Sacred Self-Care is the establishment of strong boundaries. Boundaries are not barriers to keep others out; they are acts of love to protect and honor yourself. They allow you to define what is acceptable and what is not, ensuring that your well-being remains a top priority.

The Art of Saying, "No"

Learning to say "no" is a significant aspect of self-care. It's about recognizing your limitations and respecting them. Saying "no" as a full sentence, without explanation, is necessary, not selfish; it's an act of self-preservation.

A Life of Abundance and Fulfillment

Sacred Self-Care is not a luxury; it's a necessity for a life of abundance and fulfillment. It's a commitment to yourself, a promise to honor and care for the divine spark that resides within you. By embracing this practice, you not only enrich your own life but you also radiate abundance and love into the world around you.

Explore These Questions:

1. What are my three key strengths when it comes to self-care? For example, do these strengths involve maintaining a consistent exercise routine, practicing daily mindfulness, or effectively managing stress?
2. What are my three primary weaknesses or areas requiring growth in terms of self-care? For instance, are these related to

neglecting exercise, insufficient sleep, or not setting boundaries in personal relationships?

3. Am I prioritizing my own needs, desires, and aspirations? For instance, am I dedicating enough time to pursue my hobbies, work toward my career goals, or nurture my relationships?

4. Am I at ease with intimacy and my sexuality? Do I embrace my sexual empowerment? For example, am I confident in expressing my desires and boundaries in intimate relationships?

5. Am I in tune with and effectively channeling the energies of the divine feminine and divine masculine within myself? For instance, am I balancing qualities like nurturing and assertiveness in my personal and professional life?

Anatomy of Pure Abundance

by Stacey McKay

---

*To Mom & Dad: "Though you are no longer here with me
in the physical sense, your presence remains alive in my
memories and the values you instilled in me."
To Michael: "You're amazing just as you are,
and that's why I love you."
To my son Nick, whose love has enriched my
life beyond measure.*

The Moment

My relationship with my mom has always been pretty good. Of course, there were times we would disagree, as being a young person I "knew everything." That changed as I, too, became a mom and began to understand why my mom would do the things that she did. I was fortunate enough to have a loving mom, caring, spoke her mind, and was overall a genuine woman.

On September 16th, 2013, I spoke to my mom. Little did I know that would be the last time I would hear her voice. On September 17th, I received a phone call from a medical center in Bend, Oregon informing me that my mom had collapsed. She was unconscious but, thankfully, still alive on a ventilator. Many thoughts ran through my mind. I thought, "Oh my God, really? This isn't happening."

A few days later, I was forced to make the hardest decision of my life, the decision to pull the plug and release my mom forever. At that moment there was a shift within me, an awakening of sorts. It was at that moment that I realized that life is short and I needed to live ... I needed to thrive; something I wasn't doing up to that point.

I was not living my best life, I was always putting others before myself, over-giving, and neglecting my own self-care. I didn't even know, at the time, what self-care meant. Before my mom's passing, I was a people-pleaser. I didn't know how to say "no" and said "yes" to too many things such as invites to events, taking friends somewhere, or assisting them even though I didn't really have the time, or the desire to engage. Physically, I was in decent health, not overweight, yet not in the best shape either. I didn't maintain a healthy diet. At that time, I was consuming more processed and highly saturated foods, in part because I ate out most of the time.

When I called my brother and told him that our mom passed, there was a defining silence on the other end of the phone. His response was, "Okay sis, I'll be there on Wednesday." My brother was a truck driver and worked long hours. During this time of mourning our mom's death, not once did we disagree. Not once did we say anything to each other that would hurt the other. Being 13 years apart as siblings, we came together and said, "Let's take care of this."

For those of us who grew up in a generation where we didn't touch our parents' things without permission, the thought of us going through our parents' things when they passed was very odd. I cannot begin to tell you what it was like for my brother and I to have to go through her things because it felt like a violation, but together we got through it.

They say grieving is a process, and I totally agree. When you are dealing with a loss or transition, it's important to have a support system, or as some call it—your "inner circle," to support you. The truth is that death is inevitable. There's no way around it. So why not live your life with happiness and fulfillment now, so that when the time comes for you to pass on, you feel good knowing you have succeeded in doing the things you've always desired to do with no regrets?

As we were gathering and splitting up Mom's things between my brother and I, it dawned on me again that I had a life to live. There was more in store for me. At that moment, I knew it was time for me to start tapping into abundance, something I hadn't ever thought of, let alone knew how to do. I realized that I was merely existing day by day, getting up, going to work, dropping my son off at school, picking him up and doing it all over again the next day. I was married at the time and although he was there physically, he was not there for me emotionally. You see, at that time, I was married to an alcoholic. I was a people pleaser and an enabler. An enabler is a person who either protects someone or chooses to stay in a toxic relationship for fear of being alone. It's a form of co-dependency.

I had wanted to be a real estate agent for quite some time but hadn't started studying for my real estate license. My excuse was, "I don't have time," and I had a deep belief that I wouldn't be successful, but this was just a form of procrastination stemming from low self-esteem. Certain experiences can make you think that you are not worthy of accomplishing a goal. But you can shift that narrative and say to yourself, "Oh no, I am worthy, I am loved, I am adored."

Death can make you re-evaluate your life. Think about it, if you have ever been to a cemetery, you get an eye-opening dose of reality, as you imagine how many buried there have regrets; all the should of's, would of's, could of's. We all come into this world with a birth certificate and leave with a death certificate. It's how we spend the time in between that matters.

After my mother's death, I started soul-searching and questioning the quality of my life and my faith. I decided to work on myself and get to know who Stacey really was. Up to this point, I had been in denial. In denial about my mom's passing, in denial about my failing marriage, and in denial about the things I was doing to myself and not accepting responsibility for. I stopped procrastinating, finally got my real estate license, and committed to start taking better care of myself.

I also met with a friend who had been sober for over 20 years in Alcoholics Anonymous (AA), and they introduced me to Al-Anon. Both programs work as a 12-step program. You don't have to be of any sect or religion, it is about you getting better and improving your life by implementing the steps. One of the steps that I found most valuable while in Al-Anon was the fourth step which is to do an inventory of yourself. When you do an inventory of your soul, you will uncover your demons and the skeletons in your closet. I learned that it's your childhood, and how your parents raised you that affects your life choices, you begin to look at why you do the things that you do. Certain patterns, behaviors, and habits are revealed. As I began to do an inventory on myself, it was scary and challenging, but it woke me up to say, "You know what? I'm not a victim." … "I know I can get past this," "I'm 100% responsible for my life." This was when I really started making good decisions in my life, like starting to meditate and doing breathwork. One of the things that happened to me after my mother's passing was that I contracted bronchitis, something I did not have before. It was scary, and I had to take time off from work. This was another experience that reminded me that I needed to make better decisions for myself. I started seeing a holistic doctor to have my blood and general health evaluated. Of course, the diagnosis was that I needed more self-care.

My doctor recommended that I see someone who taught yoga, meditation, and breathing exercises. This is when I met a lady named Anne who, to this day, is a very dear friend of mine. When I met her, we clicked immediately, and I started seeing her on a regular basis. This was my official introduction to self-care. Another life-changing decision that I made during this time was to divorce my husband of eleven years. This was not easy, as in my family, the majority of the women, my mom included, had divorced. I felt like a failure and didn't want to admit that I had failed in my marriage. During the first five years, my marriage was blissful and the last six were toxic. I knew I needed to leave, but how? He had taken care of my son since he was three years of age and was a good stepfather to him. I endured verbal and emotional abuse in the relationship but with no support from my mother. I felt trapped in a relationship where my sanity was questioned daily. I was mentally and physically exhausted from doing everything around the home and managing the finances, in addition to dealing with his drinking habits and emotional and verbal abuse. Of course, I was also to blame, as it takes two to be at fault. Divorcing him wouldn't be easy. In 2015, I made the decision and filed for divorce.

I started to see a therapist and a psychiatrist. We call them mental health advisors. Once I started seeing them both. I began peeling back the layers of my life, like an onion and started to look at why I chose the type of men that came into my life.

During this time, a good friend of mine introduced me to a spiritual path known as Nichiren Buddhism. To this day, I practice a mantra, chanting, Nam-Myoho Renge Kyo. One of the reasons I started this practice was that I needed to do soul-searching for myself. I needed to process my mom's death and what I was going through. This practice allowed me to take responsibility for my life and own the things I was doing right, such as self-care and owning my shortcomings along with the things I was doing wrong, so I could take responsibility for my actions. One of the major commitments I made to myself was that I would take a two-year hiatus to focus on self-care, and healing myself, and to become a better person. I was in a season of searching and discovering, there were no men in my life, and I was fine with that. I had luggage and I wanted to leave that luggage behind so as not to carry it into my next relationship.

In April of 2017, I was laid off from the aerospace company I was with for 25 years. Mind you, this was not the first time I had been laid off. It came at a time when I really wasn't ready. Then again, are we ever ready for when life hits you with a two-by-four moment? The answer, honestly, is no. But I had my real estate license, so why not actually do real estate? I signed up with a local broker during my layoff and I've continued to grow my real estate business since.

I continued with my mental health counselors until 2018, after that, I felt that I no longer needed them. I did the work, got the tools, and it was time to take off my training wheels.

Fast forward. March 2018, only a few months later. My brother started to have medical difficulties stemming from heart bypass surgery done in 2013. He was in the first stages of dementia, so I became his Power of Attorney and found a care home that allowed persons with dementia to live there. He was physically fine, however, his mental faculties were failing him. It was only five years after losing Mom, I was working in the real estate industry, and I was responsible for my brother's health and well-being. Taking care of him and his finances began taking a toll on me and I fell back into old habits; not meditating or keeping up with my Buddhist practices. My inner people pleaser reared its ugly little head again, but this time, I had the tools learned from my previous mental health advisors and the Al-Anon program that had so successfully assisted me.

I surrounded myself with a positive sphere of friends and got back on track with my journey back to me, by re-committing to my self-care.

Let's take a look at the Wikipedia definition of Self-care—Defined as the process of establishing behavior to ensure holistic well-being of oneself to promote health, and actively, manage illness when it occurs.

Self-care does indeed involve prioritizing your own well-being and needs, but it's not necessarily about putting yourself above others in a selfish or harmful way. Instead, it's about recognizing that you cannot effectively care for others or meet your responsibilities if you neglect your own physical, emotional, and mental health. It's about finding a balance where you take care of yourself so that you can better care for others and fulfill your obligations.

Here are some key aspects of self-care that involve putting yourself first in a healthy and responsible way:

Physical Health: This includes things like eating nutritious meals, getting regular exercise, getting enough sleep, and seeking medical care when needed. Prioritizing your physical health ensures you have the energy and strength to fulfill your responsibilities and support those around you.

Some things I do are fitness training, walking, eating healthier, and regular doctor checkups. These are vital to women's self-care.

Emotional Well-being: Acknowledging and processing your emotions is a form of self-care. It's okay to take time for self-reflection and emotional healing when necessary. This can involve practices like journaling, therapy, or simply allowing yourself to feel and express your emotions in a healthy manner

Reading books and journaling are important. This lets you stop the "negative chatter." Sometimes you have to stop the toxicity of relationships for your emotional well-being. This means disconnecting from those you know who do not have your best interests at heart and might mean even disconnecting from family members for the sake of sanity.

Mental Health: Taking care of your mental health is crucial. This can include practicing mindfulness, managing stress, setting boundaries, and seeking professional help when dealing with mental health challenges. A healthy mind is essential for making sound decisions and maintaining relationships.

Putting your mental health first is not selfish, but a necessity.

Setting Boundaries: Sometimes, self-care involves saying no to certain commitments or requests to protect your own well-being. Setting healthy boundaries ensures that you're not overextending yourself and becoming emotionally or physically drained. The best advice I can give to this is learning to say, "No."

Saying "No" is not selfish, it is required.

Pursuing Personal Interests: Engaging in hobbies, interests, or activities that bring you joy and fulfillment is another form of self-care. It allows you to nurture your individuality and recharge your spirit.

I am currently involved in Toastmasters and do speeches regularly. I also have a healthier eating lifestyle now, no beef, and focus on plant-based meals. Currently, part of my future planning is for my retirement. I want to live a life without regrets and I have a bucket list of items to complete.

Seeking Support: Don't hesitate to seek help or support from friends, family, or professionals when needed. You don't have to face challenges alone, and asking for assistance is a sign of strength, not weakness. Have a positive sphere of friends that don't gossip or create chaos. Seek a mental health professional if you feel that every day you wake up and dread even going outside. Have a positive sphere of friends, and seek therapy when needed from a professional.

In essence, self-care is about maintaining a balance between your own needs and the needs of others. It's recognizing that you are worthy of care and attention, just as much as anyone else, and that by taking care of yourself, you become better equipped to support and care for those around you. Self-care isn't selfish; it's a vital aspect of overall well-being and resilience.

Now you might be thinking, "I don't have time for me," with children in school, baseball games, soccer, etc. Let me explain, I too, have a son who is now an adult. I realized that if I didn't have "ME" time I would get burnt out with work during the day, assisting him with homework and sports activities at night. When he was young, I had my mom, significant other, or a friend take him for a day, so I could do ANYTHING I wanted. Even if it was sitting at home all day watching a movie or just doing something for myself. I would use my time to write, reflect, and say to myself, "How can I be a better person?" "What can I contribute to this world?" not only to my son but to the world.

Schedule time for self-care. Take that time to read a book, go hiking, take a day at the spa, something that allows you to reset. After four deaths within a decade, I realized that it is vitally important to practice self-care. Go for walks on the beach, journal every day, even if it is a few words of how you're feeling, and breathe.

"No one is without problems. As long as you're alive, you'll have problems of one kind or another. Problems are an important source of growth and a driving force for victory" (Daisaku Ikeda World Tribune September. 1st, 2023, pg. 3)

Life is either happening to you or for you; the key is not to be a victim. My wish for you is to prioritize your mental health and well-being.

Stacey McKay

Stacey McKay is currently an author, Project Manager, and realtor based out of Southern California.

Her professional experience includes writing a best-selling book and she works in the field of aerospace and real estate as a project manager and realtor. Her skills in public relations, communication, project management, and real estate have had her working for notable companies such as Boeing, Northrop Grumman, and Virgin Orbit.

Her achievements include:

- Realtor- Probate and Trust Specialist
- Project Management Professional (PMP)
- Vice President of Education for Toastmaster's International Organization

When she's not immersed in her professional life, we can find her strength training, reading a good conspiracy novel, and hanging out with friends, you can also find her at the shooting range or attending classic car shows. These activities not only provide a great source of relaxation but also inspire her creativity and drive.

Her clients have praised her for her character, integrity, and trust and she takes 100% responsibility for her own life. Some of her self-care regimes include meditation, journaling, and breathwork. These values have been instrumental in shaping her approach to life.

Currently, she is deeply involved in authoring a book called Anatomy of Abundance, Conscious Guide to Creating Prosperity in All Aspects of Life, and is excited about the potential impact it will have on feminine leaders.

Connect with Stacey at https://www.instagram.com/staceymmckay/.

Own Your Beautifully Bent Journey: Every Curve Tells a Story!

by Daisy Jones-Brown

---

*To my beloved family with a special dedication to my
son, Quinten, who fills every page of my life with joy
and purpose, and my devoted husband, Lovorn, whose
unwavering support has been my anchor throughout this
journey. I dedicate this chapter to the unwavering love and
blessings they've bestowed upon me. Above all, I thank God,
the author of our lives, for weaving our stories together in
His grand tapestry. This is for you, my cherished trio.*

The Introduction:

I had never heard the words 'abundance' or 'sacred self-care;' that's the real start of my story, and I believe some of you might have shared a similar beginning. I had been constantly told, "God will make room for your gifts." But what if you felt you had none? Then there was the mantra, "The more you have, the more you give." For me, it meant, "Work endlessly, then give away whatever you've earned to those who have even less." It painted a picture of a life without the possibility of true abundance, one defined by tireless labor only to part with the fruits of that labor.

It was much later that I recognized the profound truth: abundance is mine to claim. The pivotal shift came with understanding the power of "I AM." That is more than just words; it's a potent declaration of self-worth. It isn't just a mantra; it's a testament to our divine heritage. Oh, how things might have been different had I grasped this earlier! But I hold no regrets for my journey; every step has been invaluable.

Over time I learned abundance isn't exclusive, reserved for those of a certain appearance or privileged background. And it's broader than mere financial wealth; it encompasses every facet of life. The true magic happens when you realize that abundance isn't something you chase; it's an energy you EXPAND into.

So, what's the bedrock of this, I AM- embracing "Sacred self-care." It's the wellspring from which abundance flows, the path to the phenomenal life we all deserve. It's all about wholeheartedly embracing oneself. Life, with its twists and turns, never handed me a blueprint. I've had my moments when days blurred into nights, times when lingering traumas weighed heavily. But even in the darkest storms, the resilience of "I AM" emerged, ever persistent and hopeful, reminiscent of a rose thriving amidst thorns.

We enter this world amidst the trauma of leaving the protective environment of our mother's womb. Yet, when we first open our eyes to the world, the beauty and wonder of life capture our attention. We announce our presence with our first cry. It's a peculiar coexistence— trauma and magnificence coexisting in a single moment. I think life hands us this peculiar coexistence over and over.

For a time, bliss dominated our days until life or someone else's trauma disturbed the honeymoon. It is then we start seeing the darker facets of existence and feeling that serenity moves farther out of our reach, at least that is what happened to me. However, something deep within me always insisted, "You belong here." That elusive something guided me, although I couldn't put a name to it for years to come.

The Beginning:

My family home was filled with joy and laughter, even though we lived in extreme poverty. I was seven years old before we had a house with a bathroom and running water. Financial prosperity seemed so out of reach that I couldn't even fathom it. However, the love within our home made me feel wealthy. Outside our home, I struggled to understand why we seemed to have so little, besides love. I would look at the grand houses in town with wonder, not fully realizing that many of them were built on the sacrifices of my ancestors. My parents toiled as sharecroppers, and we resided in a shack in the midst of a peach orchard until I turned seven. Our move that year was triggered by the heart-wrenching loss of my 17-year-old brother. The grief was too much for us, especially my mother, to bear in that place where he tragically drowned. This relocation led to a better job opportunity for my father, and we eventually bought a house before his retirement.

At ten years old, my first job involved picking peaches under the scorching summer sun. I, along with 20 others, would be driven on the back of a pickup truck to vast peach orchards. With a sack, a punch card, and instructions in hand, we would work tirelessly. Despite the sweltering heat, we wore long-sleeved shirts and pants. The fertilizers sprayed on the trees would irritate exposed skin so severely that one felt the urge to scratch it raw. After such grueling days, I'd think, "There must be something better than this." But I needed clothes for school, and in our household, everyone contributed.

I didn't know much, but I knew I didn't want to live the rest of my life trading my hands for work, I was determined to elevate my mind. I aspired to expand my horizons mentally. I dreamt of attaining the "milk and honey" spoken of at church. To me, these dreams were a glimpse of what abundance could be and a reflection of our deeper, divine selves. I wanted to pursue these dreams, but my formal education dampened my spirits. At school, I was continuously reminded of my humble beginnings, often feeling discouraged to aim higher. The education I received seemed misaligned with my personal aspirations. It felt as though someone had superimposed their limited dreams upon me, and I had mistakenly believed them. There was this unrelenting pressure to conform, to accept being ordinary, and to settle for working in a factory, serving someone else's dream.

It was a summer night and I had played all day, as most children did, at least when I was growing up. I grew up when you went outside when the sun came up, played all day, made your adventures to blackberry bushes, and plum bushes, made dirt pies, and ran back to the jug of water my dad put on the step to quench my thirst.

I grew up in the country, so everything smelled fresh, and playing all day out in the warm hot sun was refreshing. I had no cares in the world as I laid my 10-year-old head down to sleep that Friday night, who was I to care who was visiting for the weekend?

I shared a bed with my sister, she was older, but I insisted on getting my way, I called the outside of the bed. The way my house was built you had to pass through our room to get to the bathroom, weird huh, but the bathroom was an addition and they didn't bother to finish the space in between. My family went all the time at night, and we were never awakened. But later that night I was awakened by this intense pain between my legs, it awakened me on the spot, and I will never forget what I saw next ... a big image of where the pain was coming from ... the pain made me freeze as his hand penetrated my vagina. I tried to pretend I was not awake, and I managed to make out the person and realized that it was the friend who stayed over. I just lay there until he finished, crying in silence. I asked myself what just happened, can I name it, who do I tell and how could I explain it? I felt helpless. I remembered knowing it was wrong and not being able to go back to sleep. He visited me again the next night. It was the longest weekend ever … and a few more nights as the summer passed. When I tried to reclaim my body and remove his hand he just went right back until he pleasured himself. I never woke my sister and I never told, for the rest of my childhood. But I changed, my innocence was gone, and I could feel that I was enraged, but I turned it inward and was sad, my honeymoon was over.

Life can often seem like a perplexing maze, seemingly designed to test us, intensify our traumas, and push us to our limits. However, even during times when I felt overwhelmed, an inexplicable force prevented me from breaking down. This force felt tangible, yet I couldn't pinpoint its origin. It wasn't rooted in my religious practices, as those often clouded my judgment. This notion of God felt distant, like an unreachable deity that demanded perfection, making me feel unworthy. Consequently, I began searching elsewhere for answers, leaving me in a state of confusion.

The Search:

My momma was my soft spot to land. I was a momma baby; I know a lot of girls are daddy babies but for me, it was my momma. I loved my daddy, but momma was my go-to. Ever since I could remember I wanted to be around my momma. When I was tiny, I used to smell the intoxicating aroma of Maxwell House that would permeate our house every morning, and I would beg her for some of this forbidden fruit. I kept asking, "Could I have a taste?" One day, my persistence paid off. My mom conceded, poured a tiny bit into her saucer from her fancy mug, and passed it to me. And that's how our morning coffee ritual began, a tradition that would last for 12 years until I joined the Air Force at 18 years old.

The military was my escape from the factory that I didn't want to work in and college was never an option anyway. I was going along discovering this new world when one day I received a heart-wrenching call. My mother was critically ill. Stomach cancer had taken over her body. From our almost daily phone calls, I knew something was wrong, but this floored me. I got to see her once after that dreaded call, and I promised to come back, but she passed away before I could get home.

No more morning coffee, no more wisdom-filled chats. I went from the comforting ritual of morning coffee to feeling like my life had plunged into an abyss of darkness. The aroma of coffee would calm and overwhelm me, bringing back wonderful and painful memories, and reminding me of my mom's absence. I started wandering through life, wondering how to fill my empty cup. My go-to answer was to pretend everything was okay. I started collecting cups as I traveled all over the world in the military. And I didn't know why. How do we refill our own cups, so that they overflow? How do we find the strength within to let our abundance spill over into our own saucers? I understood these more and more as life went on. I understood coffee with mom wasn't just about sipping coffee. It was our shared time, a platform where my mom imparted her wisdom, where I found an oasis of calm before starting my day. Soon after losing my mom, came more personal trials: heartbreak, financial woes, bankruptcy, a quick marriage, and divorce by 22. My life felt like it was spiraling, I was surviving, but not thriving. At that time, I thought GOD was punishing me and I had no idea how to get to good. I am convinced this is where GOD's GRACE and MERCY showed up and carried me. I walked dead into complex trauma.

For me, it showed up as the Strong Black Woman who was beating the odds. It looked like I was thriving against the odds and thriving despite it all. I was collecting the letters behind my last name; I was proving my worth to myself and to the world. But inside, I was slowly dying, chipping away at my core.

Seeking clarity and understanding, I delved into psychology. Eager to alleviate my suffering, I became a Licensed Professional Counselor and embarked on personal therapy sessions. These sessions were instrumental in my journey of self-discovery and healing, guiding me toward a sense of mental tranquility. I immersed myself in self-care, journaling, and embraced gratitude wholeheartedly. For the first time, I grasped the concept of holistic care and began to find the inner peace I so desperately sought. However, the intersection of religion and spirituality in my life continued to perplex me. I adopted an abundant mindset, recognizing and valuing the myriad possibilities life presented. My studies in psychology and personal therapy experiences taught me to transition from a mindset rooted in fear to one overflowing with hope, optimism, and resilience. As a counselor, I firmly believe that one's traumas shouldn't confine them; instead, they can act as a refining fire, forging a resilient spirit. Converting pain into power isn't just feasible; it's crucial for finding true peace. Yet, despite these realizations, I felt an unaddressed void. Though I thrived professionally, on a personal level, I felt fragmented. I had the knowledge and expertise, but aligning my emotions and actions proved to be an ongoing challenge.

Becoming a mother transformed me, leading to significant personal growth. Despite earning a decent income, I found myself financially strapped. My money management skills were non-existent, and my self-esteem had been eroded by tumultuous relationships and the stigma of bankruptcy. I was barely scraping by, living from one paycheck to the next, and even had my car repossessed. I frequently relied on floating checks, but one day, this risky habit backfired. At the grocery checkout, I got flagged. It was my three-year-old son's words that truly shattered me: "Mommy, why are we leaving our food? I want my cereal." Overwhelmed, I realized I'd hit my lowest point. That rock bottom pushed me to educate myself about finances. There are moments when the motivation to change doesn't come from within, but from the need to be better for someone else—for me, that motivation was my son. On that day, I vowed to him that I'd never find myself in such a dire financial situation again. Overcoming those deep-seated beliefs from my past was challenging; their grip was tighter than I'd imagined. While I became resolute in improving my financial mindset and stability, I neglected to address other lingering issues in my life.

Picture selling the dream, while living a nightmare inside. Over time, I felt trapped in this duality, torn between my current self and the person I yearned to become. On the surface, everything looked perfect–a devoted family, a beautiful home, and a commendable salary. Yet, lurking beneath was a torrent of unresolved pain: experiences of sexual abuse, heartbreak, grief, microaggressions, overwhelming stress, and the pressures of corporate America. My world was shaken when I lost my sister. She, too, had been projecting an ideal life while struggling inside. Her passing served as a poignant reminder: living the dream was far more crucial than just selling it. I needed to BE the dream.

The Integration and Path to Sacred Self-Care:

Thus began my most profound transformation. I chose to aim higher, to truly become more. I became fully committed to a path of self-empowerment. Rather than merely seeking abundance, I aimed to embody it. I decided to grow, to evolve, to EXPAND. While the idea of an abundance mindset is valuable, I realized it's not just about mental perception. I delved deeper, understanding that real abundance is anchored in our spiritual essence, our intimate bond with the divine, and, most specifically, in the "I AM" presence of God. This belief suggests that we're all naturally entitled to abundance, and our journey to embrace it starts with spiritual enlightenment that subsequently illuminates the mind. Once this became clear to me, my epiphany arrived. That persistent inner voice whispering, "You belong here," had been echoing a simple, profound truth: "I AM."

The phrase "I AM" holds significant weight in religious and spiritual dialogues, often signifying God's self-acknowledgment. It's more than just a declaration of existence; it delves into the core of our very being and our profound connection with the divine. The "I AM" underscores God's omnipresence within us, highlighting that we are vessels of divine abundance, endowed with gifts and abilities. It signifies that, like the Creator, we are meant to create, and through that creation, our prosperity emerges. I recognized my innate gifts and talents, and I believed that God would ensure they found their place. By distinguishing religion from spirituality, I had an epiphany: abundance was my innate right, and I was ready to fully embrace it.

By resonating with the divine principle of "I AM," we confirm that our lives aren't bound by earthly constraints or feelings of insufficiency. We are, by nature, abundant, thriving, and brimming with potential, being directly linked to a boundless reservoir of prosperity — the divine. This spiritual bond, once nurtured, guides our mindsets. It was this foundational understanding of how the spirit, soul, and body harmoniously work together that was enlightening for me. While the concept might seem straightforward, it's both intricate and immensely potent. This profound alignment ushered in a mental tranquility for me, enabling me to deeply engage in sacred self-care and connect with my true essence. Recognizing our spiritual richness allows our minds to truly grasp and maintain a perspective of abundance, enriching the therapeutic experience. We come to see that the universe is abundant, and as facets of the divine, we partake in this bounty. This spiritual enlightenment liberates us from fear and scarcity, refocusing our minds on the numerous blessings and possibilities in our lives. Hence, by aligning with our spiritual essence, we prepare our minds to discern and cherish the omnipresent and internal abundance. Our journey to self-awareness isn't a straight path but rather a labyrinth, each route directing us back to our divine core.

My first trip to Africa provided profound clarity. It wasn't mere coincidence that this journey took place at the end of 2019 during the Year of Return, right before the global emergence of COVID-19. This intersection of events served as an awakening, allowing me to deeply connect with my "I AM." Visiting Africa felt like a homecoming. Passing through the 'Door of No Return' and subsequently the 'Door of Return' and being given an African name was not just an honor for me but for my entire lineage. This journey also brought a realization, a bittersweet understanding of how my own homeland systems of oppression had ingrained in me a sense of insignificance, a second-class citizenship narrative that had blinded me to my true heritage of abundance.

In Ghana, I connected with my roots and discovered my ties to an ancient culture filled with dynamic rhythms and profound spirituality. In this birthplace of civilization, my true essence came alive: I am Love, Beauty, Greatness, a Queen, and the embodiment of all that is good. My spirit is intrinsically linked to the Divine. The story of the transatlantic slave trade took on new dimensions in Ghana. I saw the full narrative, beyond the snippets in my history books. My travels and immersion into various cultures now made sense. I realized I had been steered away from my inherent greatness. All my life, I'd been pushing against the tide of my identity, with both personal and societal traumas complicating my journey to embrace abundance and self-care. I understood the need to connect with God, not through rote religious practices, but from a deeper, more genuine place: my spirit. I learned that in many African communities, dance isn't just entertainment; it's a heartfelt conversation with our ancestors, spirit guides, and our very selves. By drawing strength from my core and the generations before me, genuine healing began. It wasn't just about overcoming pain—it was about reclaiming my story. I sought places where my voice resonated, where my narrative wasn't merely acknowledged but deeply felt. I delved into sacred self-care, not just for relaxation but as a bold stance. Every ritual, every introspective moment, became a potent declaration to the world—and crucially, to myself—that I am valuable and that prioritizing my well-being is essential.

I believe the sacred space you seek lies neither in external religious rituals nor strictly within the clinical realms of psychology. It resides inside you, in that tranquil space that emerges when you peel away layers of trauma, societal pressures, and self-doubt, choosing instead to EXPAND. It's a celebration of your entirety and a space to honor your journey, recognizing your bond with the divine. It's about heeding the inner guide that has accompanied you since your very first moments in this intricate, wondrous world.

Life's traumas tried to label me; societal norms attempted to mold me. The whispered judgments, the pointed glances, the lurking insecurities—all tried to suppress my core. Yet, with every challenge to my spirit, an inner chant arose more potent: "I AM more than my history. I AM more than this hurt. I AM resilient. I AM deserving." It took time, countless moments of anguish and reflection, to truly grasp the power of those words. "I AM" became the spark that revived the inner flame, linking me to a lineage of formidable, indomitable Black women who stood tall, proclaiming, I AM A QUEEN!

To every woman reading this, understand that your core, your "I AM," is a potent force. Embrace it, cherish it, and let it lead you from the maze of sorrow to the expansive meadows of abundance. Your mind will align, and your body will naturally yearn for sacred self-care. Our narratives aren't mere survival tales; they are powerful songs of triumphant resurgence. Sacred self-care emerges when you walk in your true essence, constantly BECOMING and EXPANDING.

Today, I stand tall not because I've forgotten, but because I remember—and I AM evolving. Every scar, every tear, every memory has molded me into the woman I am today and the woman I am becoming on this journey. I've not only held onto my family, home, and dreams, but I've also reclaimed my joy, peace, and well-being.

Here's the crucial point: Change cannot be faked. You must embody the change. Whether in your business or personal life, you must present yourself as the person you wish to attract. Your life will not exceed your own growth. Remember, your story is significant and is not solely yours to keep; it serves as a guiding light for others on their healing journey. It's time to activate your ancestral strength, break the cycle, and claim the life you deserve.

One of my favorite quotes is:

Self-care is healing work for your entire being, from your mind to your body and to your soul. When you heal yourself, you create an earth-shattering legacy. The lineage of women who come after you will be healed. Your inner circle of Black women around you, healed!
By actively choosing yourself, you are breaking the generational curses or traumas that have cycled through your family.
You activate your ancestral strength.
~Oludara Adeeyo

Brown Suga Wellness: Where every woman of color should be "well and wealthy" is dedicated to showcasing the power of honoring one's journey and retaking one's story to cultivate a life of abundance.

We aim to awaken you to your inherent greatness, helping you flow seamlessly with life's currents and elevate your side hustle to six figures or more. Go to the link at the end of the biography to download our Flourishing in Full Color: A Woman of Color's Guide to Prosperity and Peace.

Daisy Jones-Brown

Daisy Jones-Brown, holding an MA in psychology from The University of West Florida, stands out as a seasoned Licensed Professional Counselor. Her illustrious journey spans significant contributions to social services, especially in areas of military resiliency, peak performance, and guidance counseling.

At the Department of Justice, Daisy manages federal grants that address paramount concerns such as sexual assault and domestic violence. Her service with the Air Force was marked by her leadership in pivotal installation programs encompassing Violence Prevention, Suicide Prevention, and the Sexual Assault Program. Notably, as an Air Force Reserves retiree, her deep-rooted understanding and expertise within the military community are unparalleled.

But Daisy doesn't stop at corporate achievements. Her entrepreneurial flair is evident in her ventures, Born Beautiful, LLC, a premium natural wellness product brand, and Brown Suga Wellness.

Here, she's dedicated to guiding women of color to not only prioritize their well-being but also to scale their side hustles, ensuring they align with their dream lives. Firm in her belief that everyone deserves to thrive both in wellness and wealth, Daisy also shines as a Life Strategist and stands tall as a Hello7 Business Certification Cadet for Business Coaching.

Presently enlightening minds as an adjunct professor in the Psychology department at Mississippi State University, Daisy balances her professional feats with personal joy, cherishing moments with her husband, Lovorn Brown, their son Quinten, and her treasured stepchildren, Natasja, Whitney, and Jaden.

Connect with Daisy at www.brownsugawellness.com.

CHAPTER 10

Step 4—Declare

To be yourself in a world that is constantly trying to make
you something else is the greatest accomplishment.
~Ralph Waldo Emerson

The fourth step in the Anatomy Of Abundance™ Framework is a powerful one—Declare. It's about stepping boldly into your truth and declaring to the world, "This is who I am." This declaration is not a proclamation of who you've been or who others expect you to be. It's a resounding announcement of your authentic self.

The Masks We Wear

For so long, many of us have worn masks—masks of conformity, masks of people-pleasing, masks to fit in and be accepted. We've operated from a place of scarcity, fearing that if we revealed our true selves, we might lose love, acceptance, or opportunities. In this process, we've not only deceived others but, more importantly, we've deceived ourselves.

Reintroducing Yourself

The Declare step is about reintroducing yourself to the people around you. It's a reset, a redefining of your boundaries, values, and beliefs. It's the unveiling of your true identity, unapologetically and authentically. This process can be both liberating and challenging.

Training Others How to Treat You

By declaring your true self, you're also training those around you how to treat you. Boundaries, which are a crucial aspect of Sacred Self-Care, come into play here. Boundaries are not walls; they're bridges that establish how others can interact with you. They set the tone for the type of relationships you want to cultivate.

The Courage to Be Honest

Operating from a place of scarcity may have led you to be less than honest about your values, desires, and boundaries. Now, it's time to muster the courage to be honest. It's time to have those conversations with loved ones, colleagues, children, and friends where you express your true self. It may be uncomfortable, but it's essential for your growth and well-being.

The Power of Authenticity

When you declare your authenticity, you step into your power. You no longer need to conform to societal expectations or wear masks to gain approval. You attract people and opportunities that align with your true self. Authenticity is magnetic, drawing into your life those who resonate with your values and mission.

Embracing Change

Declaring your truth also means embracing change. It's acknowledging that as you evolve, your relationships and circumstances may evolve as well. Some may celebrate your declaration and join you on your journey, while others may resist. Be willing to let go of the things and people who are no longer in alignment with where you are going. Either way, it's a testament to the power of authenticity.

A Life Aligned with Abundance

The Declare step is about aligning your life with abundance. It's about living in harmony with your values and boundaries. It's a declaration of self-love and self-respect, and declaring that you are worthy of a life of authenticity, abundance, and fulfillment. I've discovered that clarity and vision possess the remarkable ability to propel you forward and generate momentum as you distance yourself from old patterns.

Explore These Questions:

1. What's your personal mission statement and purpose in life?
2. I am worthy of abundance in love, finance, and spirituality because?
3. What are three abundant experiences or emotions that I am currently manifesting in my life? For instance, am I drawing in feelings of joy, financial security, or deep connection with loved ones?
4. What are three individuals, emotions, or experiences that I aim to eliminate from my life? For example, am I working to release negative influences, feelings of self-doubt, or stressful situations?
5. What is the detailed, long-term abundant vision I am nurturing for my life?

Declare It! BIG Vision Energy

by Nikki Lewis, PhD

Until you make the unconscious conscious,
it will direct your life and you will call it fate.
~Carl Jung

Did you ever want something really deeply then, for various reasons, it fell off your radar? Maybe you didn't know all the steps upfront to complete it and that uncertainty led to procrastination for weeks, months, or years. Maybe the dream was so amazing and out of the ordinary that you were afraid to even let yourself admit that you wanted it. The dream was so monumental that it didn't seem plausible to be in your realm of what is achievable for you. Or perhaps, because of multiple demands on your time and other resources, you felt as though you had to choose between pursuing this magnificent dream and handling your seemingly "required" day-to-day tasks and projects? Well, chances are that we all have had those experiences where we put a dream on the back-burner or write it off as unfeasible; whether we desired to start or finish that graduate degree, take a much-needed and deserved lengthy island vacation, pursue a dream career in a different field that won't seem like work, or even take a self-imposed sabbatical to rejuvenate our body and mind.

Well, the good news is that we can reclaim and begin to materialize our dreams anytime, including now. If I said that you can elevate every area of your life and it could start by writing your vision and making it plain, how would you respond? Would you say sign me up now? Would you be skeptical? If I said that you can attract more of what you desire in your life with ease and flow, not hustle, would you be curious? As stated in the opening quote to this chapter it is important to make the unconscious conscious, meaning the unconscious has a significant role in determining the reality of our life. The things we think about and do unconsciously produce results in our conscious reality. Thus, we can co-create our lives by being more intentional about our unconscious thoughts, desires, and behaviors.

The purpose of this chapter is to provide you with guidance on how to begin to materialize your dreams using the power of vision and declaration. Vision and declaration are effective tools to transform the programming in your unconscious and conscious doing, being, and having. This chapter provides some fun and easy exercises that will walk you through a process of determining and stating the experiences, feelings, and traits that you desire in your life. By the time you reach the end of the chapter, you will have been guided through the creation of three declarations related to your highest vision for your life. When I refer to "your life," I mean all parts of you that contribute to your life: self-identity, spirituality, relationships (familial, romantic, and friends), career, leisure, finances, and personal development. So, let's begin with a reflection on why it is important to declare.

The Benefits of Declaring Intentions

The word declare is familiar to most people. We hear phrases such as, "The couple declared their love for one another" or a more formal use such as the "Declaration of Independence." The dictionary definition of declare is to make clear or to state firmly one's intentions. In this chapter, we will declare what we intend to do, be, and have in our lives and how we desire to feel. First, it is important to declare because it forces us to state our desires. What do you value? What do you want to accomplish? Who do you want to be? How do you want to feel? Secondly, the declaration helps us to keep our goals front and center. In the absence of a declaration or written reference to what we desire, we take a chance that it will be overshadowed by less significant, seemingly more urgent, or even easier pursuits. However, by declaring (preferably mentally and then in writing) we further imprint our goals into our consciousness. We create neural connections that bring the ideas back to us when we see or hear similar ideas. Lately, coaches and mentors are talking more about the Reticular Activating System (RAS), which is a biological explanation for the phenomenon that occurs when you think of or have a conversation about a certain object, then you seem to see more of the object in the next week than you recall seeing in the previous month. This is because the RAS, which is located in your brain stem, serves as a filter and spends time looking for things that match your thoughts and that are aligned with your beliefs. Consequently, the more you declare a "thing" the more you attract it and similar things to your life. Thirdly, it is helpful to have and to refer to declarations because they can provide momentum to keep moving in the intended direction and they can promote resilience in times of difficulty or uncertainty. If you only have a passing thought about something without any grounding it is likely to remain a passing thought.

However, if you can establish connections (e.g. feelings, beliefs, experiences) to the idea of having it you have a greater chance of it or something better taking form and becoming a reality.

Tips for Preparing to Declare

As mentioned earlier, this chapter intends to help you jumpstart the materialization of your dream(s) via visioning and declaring. You will be asked to reflect on and describe your dream life, the feelings that you would like to prevail or be dominant in your heart and mind, and the qualities that you believe an individual (you) must embody to have the type of life that you described. For you to get the most out of the declaration process in this chapter and any intentions you set in the future, you must be mindful of three important things. First, you must think BIG, which in this context stands for built-in greatness. When you are asked to describe your dream life do not be concerned about the details of how it will happen, instead focus on what you would desire when anything is possible. In creating your declarations, consider prompts such as, What does Source/God/Creator [use the term of your choice] want for my life? What are my gifts and talents? How are my gifts and talents best used to serve others? Think along the lines of being given the charge, "Don't stop until you are proud," then brainstorm and brain dump.

Secondly, you must use positive words. For example, do not write, "I will not be tired." Instead write it in a way that is aligned with what you desire, in this case, "I am well rested and energetic." Another example of what you would not write is, "I do not hate my job" but instead, "I have a career that I love." Using positive words and avoiding "not" keeps the focus on what you desire and creates a higher vibration.

Thirdly and finally, speak about your intentions in ways that reflect your level of resolve or commitment. If something is not a major priority we may see it as a "maybe one day" idea. However, if we are serious about it and intend to commit to it we speak of it in that way. When expressing desires in levels of intensity, on the weaker or less committed end of the continuum we have wishes and hopes. On the other end, we have more resolute desires such as intentions and declarations. This can be illustrated by the following example of three sentences expressing the same idea with different intensity levels. Read each sentence and pause after each: 1. I *want* to write a book this year. 2. I *hope* to write a book this year. 3. I *intend* to write a book this year. Do you notice the different feelings and impressions that result from the change of just one word in the sentence? The first sentence seems casual, there is desire but I do not have plans yet. The second sentence also expresses desire but has an added element of optimism with hope. The third sentence gives the impression that a plan is in place or forthcoming.

Declare. Declare. Declare. Now the real fun begins with 4 Steps!

If you are anything like me, at this point you might be thinking that you will glance at the instructions for the exercises and then do them another time. However, let me encourage you to stay the course. All the exercises can be completed in about 30 minutes total. If you get in a flow and lose yourself with Step 2, it might take an extra 10 minutes or so. You do have 30 minutes to jump-start setting the foundation for your new life, right? Ok, let's do Step 1 immediately after you read the instructions; it is simple and can be completed in just a few minutes. Before beginning the exercises, decide where you will write or type your responses. Will you type your responses on a note or document on your phone, tablet, or computer? Or will you write them on a physical note pad, journal, or other paper that you will keep?

Step 1. Complete your gratitude list. Create a list of at least 21 things for which you are grateful. You can go back as far in your life as you wish, you can focus on this month or any period of your choice. You can pull from as many aspects of your life as you wish or focus on a few; you can include people, experiences, things, or whatever strikes your fancy. This is a quick exercise with significant benefits. Expressing gratitude is associated with feelings of fullness, joy, inspiration, hope, and even courage. This should take less than five minutes. Ready, set, go!

I am grateful for the following:

You did write down at least 21 things, right? Completing this brief exercise will put you in the right frame of mind to successfully complete the rest of the steps and bring you closer to your dream life.

Now, on to Step 2.

Step 2. Declare Your Dream Life. Think of and describe the most desirable and divine life you can imagine for yourself. Write in present and/or past tense as if the experience is true in physical reality or it has already taken place. Allow at least 12 minutes to complete this exercise.

For example: I am elated about my life and everyone and everything in it. I am healthy. I grow my own food in my garden and create delicious meals for my friends and family. My children and spouse are happy and healthy. Our home is beautiful, wonderfully decorated, and full of love and joy. I have an abundance of free time. I travel the world for fun vacations. I donated money to fund 20 full scholarships to Hampton University, and I donated $4 million U.S.D. toward research on Black maternal health. I just won third place in a golf tournament last week and first place in a tennis tournament the previous month.

When doing this exercise recall things that you have fantasized about and that you would love to do, be, and have. Here are some questions you might answer. Feel free to add to the list as you wish.

Where are you? How do you feel? How do you use your gifts and talents? What do you do to nurture your spirituality? Where do you travel for fun and how often? What is your family like? What kind of friendships do you have? What kind of residence(s) do you have? What kind of staff do you have, personal and professional? What do you do for fun? What do you eat? What kind of clothes and shoes do you wear? How is your physical health? What do you do to move and take care of your body? How do you earn money? How do you use your money to help others?

Okay, your turn. Set a timer and write in your journal for at least 12 minutes. If you need more time, that is fine.

Step 3. Declare Your Desired Feelings. In this exercise, you will identify five or more feelings that you desire an abundance of in your life. This exercise is to help you identify how you intend to feel or "be." Complete the statement "I embrace..." or "I embrace being ..."

For example: I embrace joy. I embrace being loving. I embrace freedom. I embrace being sexy. I embrace being playful. I embrace being relaxed.

Examples of feelings that you might use include the following: acceptance/accepted, balance, blissful, cheerful, energetic, excited, forgiving, freedom, fulfilled, joyful, kind, loving, peaceful, playful, relaxed, respected, secure, thankful, validated, valued, and whole.

If you need ideas for additional feeling words, the internet has many feeling charts and wheels that you can consult. Remember, feelings are the soil in which we plant our intentions and goals. If your dominant feelings are along the lines of stress, pessimism, etc., these will be reflected in your energy, your mindset, and your life.

In your journal complete five or more embrace statements with the feelings that you want an abundance of in your life. "I embrace ..." or "I embrace being ..."

Step 4. Declare Yourself Capable and Equipped. In this exercise, you will create a list of qualities in your journal that you feel are needed to accomplish the dream life that you wrote about earlier or for any version of your dream life. The prompt is "I am ..." What are five traits or qualities that someone with the life you described would need to or likely embody? In other words, what traits would support someone in achieving and sustaining the type of life that you imagined and described? Complete the phrase with one or two words.

Examples from one word added to two words added: I am creative. I am decisive. I am patient. I am persistent. I am solution-oriented. I am action-oriented. I am a risk-taker. I am a good listener.

Other words that you might consider include: adaptable, analytical, authentic, capable, caring, courageous, creative, dependable, determined, disciplined, effective, enterprising, empathetic, flexible, focused, generous, good leader, honest, imaginative, intelligent, intuitive, observant, optimistic, organized, positive, prepared, productive, purposeful, resilient, responsible, skilled, talented, trustworthy, victorious, visionary, wonderfully made.

Great work! You are finished with the exercises.

Congratulations! If you are reading this, hopefully, that means that you completed all four steps.

How do you feel? You can go back and make changes anytime, you can update the feelings and traits if you later find something more inspiring and authentic, and of course, you can revise any part of, "Your Dream Life" if your vision changes and as you accomplish things from the current version.

Next Steps. Now that you have created your Dream Life Vision, we want it to continue to resonate with you. If you intend to continue to benefit from the exercises, set a goal to read your embrace statements, Dream Life Vision, and I am statements at least three times a week. As you read them repeatedly, over time they will feel more and more realistic and aligned with your reality. Additionally, repeated reading of them will cause you to feel more confident and courageous, even if those words are not on your list. You declared it, now believe, and make choices and changes that will move you closer to doing, being, and having all that you envisioned and declared. Some people will choose to start with small changes and gradually work their way up to more transformational changes. Others will be all-in and start making major changes immediately. Whichever approach you take, stay in your Built in Greatness (BIG) energy that you visualized, and sooner than you think you will materialize more and more of your dream self and dream life. I declare that for you.

Nikki Lewis, PhD

Nikki Lewis, PhD is a university professor and evolving health and lifestyle mentor. Several years ago she was in a motor vehicle accident outside of the U.S. which she miraculously survived. However, she sustained numerous physical injuries, including a brain injury. While recovering she used many of the personal and spiritual development practices that she had read about years earlier and until then had used intermittently. During this time she engaged whole-heartedly in self-healing, self-love, spiritual development, and meta-physical exercises to handle the barrage of issues that ensued. As a result, even today she continues to prioritize well-being in her life and encourages others to do the same.

She holds a PhD in Educational Psychology, Measurement, and Evaluation from the University of North Carolina at Chapel Hill (UNC-CH), earned in 2007, a MEd in Education Administration from Virginia

Commonwealth University, and a BA in Psychology from UNC-CH. Her academic career spans more than 12 years as a full-time professor and includes mentoring PhD students; teaching courses in psychology, program evaluation, statistics, and research methods; and conducting research on diversity in the Science, Technology, Engineering, and Mathematics (STEM) professoriate and professor well-being. She has presented her research at institutions such as the National Science Foundation, Harvard University, North Carolina A&T University, and in academic settings worldwide.

When not conducting academic work Dr. Nikki's calendar typically comprises time for family and friends, playing tennis, meditating, and traveling the world to healing destinations including Costa Rica, Ghana, and Japan.

Connect with Dr. Nikki at dr.nikki@professornikki.com.

Love, Money, and Happiness: Cultivating Abundance Through Interdependent Thinking

by Dr. Karen Kramer

T*o my clients and my children who have been my teachers about life.*

---

*"It is not until we break the patterns of our lives that we
are able to see the chains that keep us there."*
~Dr. Karen Kramer

Ponder this scenario: sharing your deepest desires and dreams with others, only to receive bewildered or unsupportive responses. Additionally, your own internal voice, shaped by life experiences and beliefs, may create obstacles to your aspirations. These internal and external voices have played a pivotal role in defining who you are and shaping your beliefs, values, and perceptions of what is attainable or beyond reach.

Within the pages of this chapter, you will find the key to unlocking a transformative mindset—one where love, money, and happiness cease to be distant dreams and become achievable realities. We embark on a journey through the intricate labyrinth of thoughts, desires, and beliefs, aiming to harmonize our inner yearnings with the external world.

Welcome to the path of turning dreams into tangible realities.

Cultivating an Interdependent Abundance Mindset

In the quest to cultivate an interdependently abundant mindset, we embark on a journey of transformation and self-discovery. This section includes two case studies that delve deeply into the nuances of embracing loss, understanding a scarcity mindset, and shifting from scarcity to abundance.

Embracing Loss

Our society offers abundant education and encouragement for success, acquisition, and the pursuit of love, money, and happiness. Our educational systems, books, seminars, podcasts, and YouTube channels are overflowing with "How-to" guides for dating, career development, and personal finance.

Yet, there's a noticeable void when it comes to preparing and guiding individuals through the inevitable experiences of loss, letting go, and the grieving process. There's a lack of resources addressing how to cope with the challenges of grieving a breakup or divorce, releasing long-standing friendships, managing job loss or financial setbacks, facing foreclosure or bankruptcy, handling the necessity to downsize or relocate, or engaging in a healthy grieving process after the loss of a parent, child, or sibling.

Grief provides us with an opportunity to explore the inner psychology that shapes our being. It enables us to identify unhealed wounds, triggers, and significant emotional events from our past, fostering personal growth and resilience. Additionally, it equips us with coping skills to navigate change and uncertainty, facilitating quicker recovery during challenging times.

Before exploring abundance, it's crucial to recognize that each of us will encounter various forms of grief or loss in our lifetime. My intention is to help you develop better coping skills when faced with life's adversities and losses, focusing on those most common throughout your life.

In my book *Healthy Grief: Normalizing and Navigating Loss in a Culture of Toxic Positivity*, I provide a five-stage Healthy GRIEF Framework to help process major to minor losses in life—experiencing a deep sorrow when what once was is no longer.

At its core, here are the Healthy GRIEF Framework questions to assess your progress, identify necessary shifts, and support your unique path through times of loss:

1. **Gather:** What's missing? What's essential for your next decision? What do you need to know today?
2. **Relate:** What emotions are you feeling? Where do you feel them in your body? What beliefs do you have about the loss, yourself, and others? Are they accurate? List three things you're grateful for today.
3. **Involve:** What's your goal for today? What are your three main targets or activities? What actionable steps can you take for each one, and how will at least one of these activities support your journey of healthy grief?
4. **Ease:** What type of support do you need, and who can provide it? How will this support benefit you and others?
5. **Focus:** What outcomes are you aiming for? What's your vision of the "new normal"? What's one step you can take today to get there?

Understanding Scarcity Mindset

In our quest to harness the power of interdependent thinking for abundance, we must first confront the formidable adversary that stands in its way—the scarcity mindset. *The scarcity mindset* is a pervasive way of thinking that revolves around the belief that there's not enough to go around. It's a perspective rooted in fear, competition, and a constant struggle for limited resources.

Before we can effectively embrace interdependence, we need to recognize and challenge the limited beliefs that have held us back.

Recognizing Limited Beliefs

As a Neuro-Linguistic Programming (NLP) Master Practitioner and Hypnotherapist, I can easily identify the layers of beliefs frequently preventing a client from reaching their desired goals. At their core, the most common underlying belief is "I'm not enough." It comes in many forms such as "I'm not good enough," "I'm not young/old enough," "I don't have enough," "I'm not smart enough," and many more. This is the foundation of a scarcity mindset.

These fallacies limit your ability to fully embrace your life and create abundance. Unfortunately, these beliefs lay in the deep crevices of your unconscious mind, and are not always obvious to your own conscious awareness.

Conscious and Unconscious Minds

In NLP, the concepts of the conscious mind and the unconscious mind are used to describe different aspects of mental processing. These concepts are not necessarily aligned with traditional psychological definitions but are used within NLP to understand human behavior, communication, and change. Here's how NLP typically distinguishes between the conscious and unconscious mind:

The *conscious mind* is associated with your immediate awareness and thoughts in the present moment. It is responsible for logical thinking, analysis, and decision-making; it processes a limited amount of information at a time and is primarily concerned with the here and now. It deals with rational thoughts, language, and objective thinking.

The *unconscious mind* is the repository of all your memories, experiences, emotions, beliefs, and behaviors. It is responsible for managing automatic processes, emotions, and your response to stimuli; it is vast and can process a tremendous amount of information simultaneously and plays a significant role in forming and storing beliefs, habits, and patterns of behavior.

Limiting beliefs are housed in the unconscious mind, driving our behaviors. For example, if I believe I'm not deserving enough for a happy and healthy relationship, I will attract and manifest unhappy and unhealthy relationships.

Where do the beliefs come from?

Critical Faculty

To explore this question, we must delve into the concept of the *critical faculty*. In NLP, the critical faculty acts as a mental filter that shapes how the mind processes and accepts information, serving as a crucial bridge between the conscious and unconscious realms.

It acts as a gatekeeper, regulating the flow of information between the two realms. This filter rigorously evaluates incoming information to determine whether it aligns with the existing beliefs and safety mechanisms stored in the unconscious.

The conscious mind, closely tied to the critical faculty, assesses new thoughts, beliefs, or suggestions for consistency with the individual's current belief system.

The critical faculty's purpose is to ensure that any new information harmonizes with existing beliefs in the unconscious mind. Information passing this scrutiny is more likely to influence behaviors, emotions, and beliefs. Information that doesn't meet the critical faculty's criteria is typically rejected or met with resistance by the unconscious.

So, how can a belief such as "I'm not enough" circumvent the discerning scrutiny of the critical faculty?

Imprint Period

In NLP, the *imprint period* identifies a phase in one's life when their unconscious mind is highly receptive to absorbing information and experiences that significantly influence their beliefs and behaviors. This phase typically occurs in early childhood, varying from person to person but generally spanning from birth to around seven years old (or up to 10 in some theories). During this period, children are remarkably sensitive to their surroundings and the people in it.

The imprint period involves a process of "imprinting" where children observe, absorb, and mimic the behaviors, beliefs, and values of their caregivers, family, and society. They learn and internalize language, cultural norms, social rules, and emotional patterns. It's crucial to shield them from disturbing or inappropriate concepts, as these can lead to misguided beliefs that persist into adulthood.

What's absorbed during the imprint period is primarily stored in the unconscious mind, forming the basis for an individual's lifelong beliefs and behaviors. These early experiences and beliefs profoundly impact an individual's adult life, influencing their decisions, self-image, and relationships. Whether these beliefs are limiting or empowering determines if they contribute to a scarcity mindset.

It's worth noting that not all limiting beliefs are necessarily negative; the key question is whether a belief supports or hinders one's ability to achieve his or her goals. If a belief impedes progress, it becomes a part of a scarcity mindset.

Case Study: Client Danya

To illustrate the real-world implications of a scarcity mindset, let's examine a compelling case study of a client who grappled with a limiting belief and the profound impact it had on her life.

"I HATE MEN!" You should have seen the look on my client's face when she blurted that out. She was so surprised! Yet, I wasn't.

Dayna* (not her real name) was in her late 40s, a nurse with long flowing blonde hair and crystal-clear blue eyes. She had spent tens of thousands of dollars on dating coaches, dating programs, and online dating profiles over the three years prior to working with me, and had still not found, attracted, or married Mr. Forever. How could she with this underlying belief?!

She was easily attracting men, yet had challenges keeping them past a few dates. As we peeled back the layers of her unconscious programming and limiting belief, we identified the root cause—an interaction she had with her dad at a young age, a time when she formed the attitude of "I hate men." Her unconscious mind was secretly sabotaging her laid-out conscious plans.

How, then, do we identify the root cause of our limiting beliefs?

As we journey deeper into this chapter, remember that recognizing the limiting beliefs of a scarcity mindset is the first step in freeing ourselves from its constraints. By understanding its grip on our lives and learning from the experiences of others, we open the door to a profound shift in our thinking. Let's explore the steps to break free from these constraints and embrace the interconnected abundance that interdependent thinking offers.

Shifting from Scarcity to Abundance

Now, it's time to roll up our sleeves and step into the transformative journey of shifting from scarcity to abundance. Abundance is not just about having more; it's a mindset, a way of perceiving the world and one's place within it. By understanding the psychology behind abundance, we can begin to reshape our thinking. To shift to a mindset more focused on abundance, you must unearth the scarcity mindset or limiting beliefs that may be holding you back from getting what you want.

Challenging Limiting Beliefs—Cartesian Logic

Transitioning from scarcity to abundance is often a complex journey. It necessitates the crucial step of challenging and confronting limiting beliefs that have held us back, opening the door to abundance thinking.

Cartesian Logic provides a valuable tool for unraveling thought processes and identifying potential limiting beliefs. This method enables us to break down mental barriers that hinder our thinking and decision-making. Cartesian questions serve as problem-solving questions that help us address issues that drain our energy, focus, and time.

These four simple and effective questions are essential for exploring the outcomes, consequences, and overall relationship between an action or decision and its impact on oneself and the environment (especially in interdependent thinking):

1. What happens if you DO X?
2. What happens if you DON'T do X?
3. What doesn't happen if you DO X?
4. What doesn't happen if you DON'T do X?

	Will	Wont
Do	What WILL happen if you DO 'X'	What WONT happen if you DO 'X'
Dont	What WILL happen if you DONT 'X'	What WONT happen if you DONT 'X'

To help explore and identify what some of those beliefs are that may be keeping you stuck requires a trained practitioner well versed in uncovering hidden subconscious programming such as a Master NLP Practitioner or Hypnotherapist.

"You cannot solve a problem with the same
mind that created it."
~Albert Einstein

However, by employing Cartesian Logic, we can unravel and challenge limiting beliefs, facilitating the shift from scarcity to abundance thinking.

Case Study: Erica Davis

There are a number of inspiring case studies of individuals who have discovered deep joy and fulfillment by embracing interdependent living. One of those stories is Erica Davis.

Erica's journey into athleticism began at a young age when her mom ran a 10k race in the Bay Area, and three-year-old Erica crossed the finish line beside her. This marked the beginning of her passion for sports. She excelled in various sports and pursued a degree in Exercise Science and teaching credentials. In her senior year, she joined the cross-country team and faced the challenges of a 5K race.

After completing her education, Erica aimed to participate in the Hawaii Ironman. However, a medical condition altered her life. At the age of 24, she was diagnosed with Transverse Myelitis, inflammation of the spinal cord, which left her paralyzed from the chest down.

Erica faced numerous hospitalizations and physical challenges but maintained her spirit. She returned home and began the journey of relearning to stand and regaining movement in her toes. Supported by her family and friends, she discovered the world of adaptive sports, particularly hand-cycling.

Erica ventured into triathlons, marathons, and hand-cycling races, winning over 30 of them. She trained with Paralympic teams, advocating for equal monetary rewards for Paralympians. She embraced various activities, including kayaking, and competed at World Championships.

In 2009, Erica received the opportunity to climb Mt. Kilimanjaro, becoming the first female paraplegic to summit it. She overcame physical, mental, and emotional challenges, reaching the summit with her team.

Erica's story serves as an inspiration for resilience, determination, and embracing new opportunities despite life-altering setbacks. She remains committed to conquering challenges and embracing new chapters with optimism.

Applying an Interdependent Abundance Mindset

This section delves into the cultivation of abundant love, wealth, and happiness, underpinned by real client case studies.

Building Abundant Love

In our journey to develop an abundance of love through interdependent thinking, we come to the heart of our connections with others. This section explores how interdependence can enhance relationships followed by a client case study.

Love thrives within the web of interdependence. We'll begin by examining how recognizing the interconnected nature of our relationships can deepen the love we share. By understanding that our well-being is closely tied to the well-being of our loved ones, we can nurture more profound and lasting connections.

Case Study: Client Joyce

Here is the story of my client Joyce* (not her real name), who transformed her relationship with her daughter through interdependent thinking. This real-life story highlights how interdependence not only deepened their love but also created a positive ripple effect that extends to others.

In 2022, the unexpected news of becoming a first-time grandma filled my client, Joyce, with joy. However, her unvaccinated status raised concerns, especially in the context of the ongoing COVID-19 pandemic. The dilemma of choosing between personal health choices and the desire to be present for their grandchild's birth became a profound struggle.

Joyce threw a baby shower, while battling mixed emotions, aware that she might not hold her grandchild due to their vaccination decision. Despite the sadness and grief over the loss of this expected moment, anger was never directed toward their daughter's wish for her child's safety.

Joyce eventually found a way to express their stance and respect for their daughter's boundaries in a heartfelt message. The news of the grandson's birth was eventually learned through another relative, stirring complex emotions of hurt, sadness, and jealousy.

An unexpected surprise visit on Joyce's birthday led to the first cradling of their grandson just before his three-month birthday. Despite differing stances on vaccinations and COVID-19, this family's journey concluded with an enriched bond based on respect and love, with Joyce cherishing their autonomy and the understanding that allowed her to reunite with their grandchild.

Luckily, her interactions with her grandson increased. COVID-19 and vaccines remained unspoken. Not all stories conclude as Joyce's did. Her steadfast decision, her daughter's understanding, and the eventual reunion enriched their bond. She cherished her autonomy and counted herself fortunate that they were able to navigate this chapter with respect and love.

Creating Abundant Wealth

Throughout this book, you will find numerous chapters on specific tactics and strategies for financial abundance. This is not one of those. Instead, this section delves into practical techniques that can help individuals manifest abundant wealth.

Positive affirmations and visualization are powerful tools to program your mind for success. Repeating positive statements about financial goals helps rewire your unconscious mind and build confidence. Visualization involves mentally rehearsing the achievement of financial goals. This vivid mental imagery creates a sense of reality and motivates you to work towards those goals.

Case Study: Dr. Karen

In this real-life case study, my own, I witnessed a transformation towards financial abundance.

The journey begins with a legacy of thriftiness, instilled in my parents who were born in the 1920s and raised during the Great Depression Era. This created a belief that "money is to be saved, not spent." A diligent upbringing in financial management and investing became a valuable foundation for my future.

In my late 40s, my story took an unexpected turn when personal circumstances changed, and financial dependency vanished due to a divorce. Amidst challenges, I committed to manifesting a dream—to transform my backyard into an oasis, despite skepticism from peers and the looming negativity of limiting beliefs. Through the deployment of visualization techniques and daily affirmations, I began to witness the transformation of my backyard, though moments of financial anxiety persisted, fueled by an internal dialogue of self-doubt.

However, my narrative significantly shifted when I encountered NLP and used its principles to dismantle the limiting beliefs that had eroded my confidence. This newfound liberation allowed me to navigate a demanding divorce mediation with composure and self-assuredness, eventually severing the ties of temporary spousal support on my own terms.

Within four years, my journey unfolded with the establishment of the VillaVision Wellness and Retreat Center followed by negotiations for a seven-figure deal to expand my business—a testament to the transformative power of affirmations, visualization, and overcoming limiting beliefs in wealth manifestation.

Nurturing Abundant Happiness

True happiness is not an isolated pursuit, but a state of being that flourishes through interconnected relationships, purposeful living, self-care, and mindfulness. Happiness is intricately woven into our connections with others and the world around us. Understanding this interdependence can help you foster enduring joy and satisfaction.

Pursuing Passions and Purpose - *Ikigai*

Passion and purpose are the heart of true happiness. Discover how embracing interdependent thinking can empower you to chase your passions and synchronize your life with a profound sense of purpose.

Enter *ikigai*, a renowned Japanese concept often hailed as the key to longevity and fulfillment. This multifaceted term embodies the quest for purpose, joy, and meaning in life. Visualize *ikigai* as the convergence of four essential elements: what you love, your strengths, the world's needs, and what you can be paid for. When these elements unite, they shape your *ikigai*, your daily reason for rising.

The link between *ikigai* and a longer, healthier life is profound. Studies reveal that individuals who unearth their *ikigai* often enjoy extended lives filled with contentment. This deep sense of purpose not only reduces stress but also fosters an optimistic outlook on life. Remember, longevity isn't just about adding years to your life; it's about infusing life into your years. *Ikigai* paves the way to a richer, more fulfilling existence.

Finding your *ikigai* is a personal journey that requires introspection and self-discovery. It involves a series of steps:

1. **Identify Your Passions:** Begin by listing the activities and aspects of life that genuinely ignite your enthusiasm. What makes your heart race, your eyes light up, and your spirit soar? These are often clues to your passions.

2. **Recognize Your Talents:** Consider the skills and talents you possess. What are you naturally good at? It could be a particular talent, skill, or expertise. Recognizing your strengths is crucial in defining your *ikigai*.

3. **Understand What the World Needs:** Reflect on the ways your passions and talents can be of service to others and society. How can you make a meaningful contribution to the world? This step aligns your *ikigai* with the greater good.

4. **Determine What You Can Be Paid For:** While financial aspects are not the sole focus, they are important. Identify how your passions, talents, and contributions can be financially sustainable. This will ensure that your *ikigai* supports your livelihood.

5. **Seek the Intersection:** The heart of your *ikigai* lies at the intersection of these four areas. It's where your love, skills, societal needs, and financial viability converge. Your *ikigai* is your North Star, guiding you toward a life filled with meaning and vitality.

Exploring your *ikigai* is an ongoing process that may evolve over time. It's about aligning your actions, profession, and daily life with the essence of who you are and what you're meant to do. Your *ikigai* will provide the compass for your life journey, leading to a longer, more purposeful, and fulfilling existence.

Case Study: Client Jan

Jan, a successful technology company manager, faced a challenging shift when she retired. Her career was filled with accomplishments, yet retirement left her isolated and adrift. This case study illustrates how Jan embraced the principles of *ikigai* to reignite her passions, purpose, and abundant happiness in her post-retirement life.

Jan's retirement felt abrupt and lonely. Her career had provided structure and purpose, and now she felt disconnected and unrecognized. She missed the camaraderie and challenges her job had offered.

Navigating retirement, Jan discovered the concept of *ikigai*. She realized her passions, talents, and contributions needed alignment for happiness and purpose. Her journey had four phases:

1. Jan discovered her love for art and the desire to learn and grow. This became central to her *ikigai* pursuit.

2. Strengthening bonds, especially with her daughter and grandkids, brought immense joy and fulfillment.

3. Jan engaged in volunteer work, took art workshops, and embarked on solo adventures like exploring Scotland, fueling her growth and learning.

4. Jan formed an art group, received commissions, and found recognition in several states, contributing to society and aligning with her *ikigai*.

Jan's journey redefined her post-retirement life, viewing it as a new chapter filled with opportunities. Her focus on new experiences, creative pursuits, and contributions revitalized her sense of purpose, bringing abundance to her life.

Jan's case demonstrates the transformative power of *ikigai*. By aligning her passions, talents, societal contributions, and financial stability, she reignited happiness and purpose in retirement. Her story highlights the significance of staying connected, seeking new experiences, and embracing creativity, enriching her post-retirement life.

Conclusion

The path to abundance through interdependent thinking is a lifelong journey. It's a journey that acknowledges that our lives are interconnected, that our well-being is tied to the well-being of others, and that the pursuit of love, money, and happiness is enhanced through collaboration and shared purpose.

As you move forward, remember that interdependence isn't about forsaking your individuality but enhancing it by recognizing the strength that comes from our connections with others. It's about fostering a world where love, money, and happiness are not limited resources but boundless possibilities.

So, take this wisdom and apply it to your life. Embrace interdependent thinking as a guiding principle. Recognize the abundance that comes from deep, meaningful relationships, financial security, and a profound sense of happiness. As you walk this path, know that you're not alone; you're part of an interconnected world where the well-being of one can uplift many.

Scan me

To support your journey to a more abundant life, go to bit.ly/AbundanceLMHR or click on the QR code to access your FREE resources.

May your journey toward love, money, and happiness through interdependent thinking be rich, fulfilling, and abundant beyond measure.

Dr. Karen Kramer

Dr. Karen Kramer is a guiding light who has transformed the lives of countless individuals around the globe since the early 1990s.

With a profound understanding of the human mind and a grief recovery expert, Dr. Karen's true passion as a coach, speaker, and author lies in helping navigate heart-wrenching experiences such as divorce, loss of loved ones, and traumatic events.

Corporations and nonprofits (including United Way, American Express, Nike, Boeing, and Google) have sought Dr. Karen's invaluable counsel. Her expertise also embraces entrepreneurs, actresses, and retirees.

As a faculty member, program manager, and executive coach at the Center for Creative Leadership, Dr. Karen guided leaders from new managers to C-suite executives. She also served as a co-facilitator and program director for Teen Wisdom Inc., certifying teenage girl life coaches. As the Head Coach for Recalibrate360, Dr. Karen played a pivotal role in certifying individuals in Neuro-Linguistics Programming (NLP), Time Line Therapy®, and Hypnotherapy.

In 2022, Dr. Karen unveiled the awe-inspiring VillaVision Wellness & Retreat Center—a sanctuary of tranquility, nestled in sun-drenched Southern California. Here, women overcome grief while rediscovering happiness, health, and inner wholeness through one-on-one Breakthrough Immersion coaching, women's retreats, and day events.

As a woman-preneur and a mother who successfully raised five children in a blended family, she intimately understands the art of juggling life's priorities while maintaining a semblance of sanity.

Connect with Dr. Karen at www.DrKarenKramer.com.

CHAPTER 11

Step 5—Organize

Success is not a destination. It's a bi-product of a life built
on who you are and how you want to live your life.
~Patrina Wisdom

The Organize step of the Anatomy Of Abundance™ Framework is where the foundational laws, strategies, and implementation truly come into play. It's the stage where you transform your aspirations into concrete plans, paving the way for the manifestation of your long-term goals. Whether these goals relate to health, relationships, spirituality, finances, or any other facet of life, this chapter will guide you on the journey of transformation.

Creating Your Blueprint

At the heart of the Organize step is the creation of a blueprint for your life. It's about crafting a vision for your future, breaking it down into achievable milestones, and outlining the steps to reach those milestones. This blueprint becomes your roadmap, guiding you toward your desired destination.

Productive Scheduling

At Pure Abundance Inc., we know that anything that's prioritized and scheduled gets done. A spacious yet productive schedule is key to success. It allows you to allocate time to your priorities while ensuring you have moments for rest and rejuvenation. It's about finding the balance between ambition and self-care. We'll explore time management techniques that support your goals without burning you out.

Investing in Your Transformation

One of the hallmarks of successful individuals is their willingness to invest in themselves. This includes seeking guidance and mentorship from experts in various fields. Fitness trainers, life and business coaches, psychologists, and healers—these individuals can shed light on your blind spots and provide invaluable support on your journey.

The Power of Coaching

It's no coincidence that many of the world's most successful individuals enlist the services of coaches. Coaches provide invaluable insights, unwavering accountability, and effective strategies that can significantly expedite your progress. If you aspire to reach the pinnacles of those you admire, contemplate adopting the same approach and investing in coaching. Pure Abundance Inc. is a platform thoughtfully designed to harness the power of collaboration and collective expertise, facilitating transformative growth for both individuals and organizations. We can assist you in pinpointing your current position on your journey and determining your optimal next step, including selecting the right expert to guide you.

Allocating Resources

To invest in yourself, it's crucial to allocate resources, both time and money, to support your growth. Just as you budget for your bills and daily expenses, allocating funds annually for personal and professional development is an investment in your future. It's a declaration of self-worth.

Your Worthiness

Remember, you are worthy of abundance, growth, and success. The Organize step is a testament to your commitment to creating a life aligned with your highest aspirations. It's an acknowledgment that you deserve the time, effort, and resources necessary to bring your vision to life.

The Courage to Continue

As Winston Churchill wisely noted, success is not final, and failure is not fatal. What truly counts is the courage to continue. The Organize step is not a one-time event but an ongoing process. It requires resilience, adaptability, and a steadfast commitment to your goals.

A Life of Abundance

As you embark on the Organize step of the Anatomy Of Abundance™ Framework, remember that you are not alone on this journey. You have the support of our experts, coaches, and, most importantly, your own inner strength. Your life is a canvas waiting for your masterpiece, and by organizing your path, you are painting a portrait of abundance, fulfillment, and purpose.

Explore These Questions:

1. What are the aspects of my life that I've overlooked and want to prioritize and schedule going forward? For instance, do I wish to prioritize my self-care, spending more time on personal growth, or nurturing my relationships?

2. What changes can I make to my daily schedule to accommodate the priorities I want to emphasize? For example, can I allocate more time for exercise, allocate specific time slots for work tasks, or schedule regular quality time with loved ones?

3. What beliefs, habits, and fears do I need to eliminate to make this a reality? For example, do I need to let go of the belief that I'm not good enough, break the habit of procrastination, or overcome the fear of failure?

4. What are the advantages or rewards of implementing these changes? For instance, could the benefits include increased productivity at work, improved physical health, or stronger relationships with loved ones?

5. What type of support should I seek at this stage to kickstart my journey towards a life of pure abundance? For instance, could this support involve hiring assistance like a babysitter or personal assistant, enlisting the services of a matchmaker, engaging a life or business coach or strategist, exploring therapy or mentorship, or becoming part of a community of like-minded individuals?

Financial Abundance for the Non–mathematician

by Lenka Holman

Why is it that the more information there is on a topic, the more confusing it is to find the "right answer?" Information overload complicated by hidden agendas is often the reason most people never move forward on the abundance scale. If there really was one solution, everyone would do it and everyone would be financially abundant. It may take some time to create your foundation for financial abundance, but it's like building a muscle. With practice, abundant choices will become much more intuitive.

Consider financial *abundance* as a sliding scale, rather than a simple on/off switch. Much internet chatter focuses on *scarcity versus abundance*. It's not that simple. We will focus on moving from *avoidance* and *conditional comfort* toward *abundance.* Cultivating abundance takes practice, and naturally, people slip back into old patterns, so we will share ways to keep focused on your vision. More importantly, we will discuss how the measure of success must be tied to personal values. Without that foundation, we can't know if we are living in abundance. All of this seemingly theoretical discussion will be supported by real-life examples of people I have mentored in the financial field over the last two decades.

The Abundance Sliding Scale

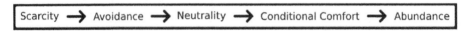

Scarcity: Living in fear.

Avoidance: Spending money on non-essentials with no idea of how to pay for them.

Neutrality: Feeling like your financial situation will never improve.

Conditional Comfort: We are comfortable if no one gets sick, gas prices don't go up, I don't lose my job, etc.

Financial Abundance: More resources are coming in than are required for my chosen lifestyle.

Imagine finally understanding why someone you love is always stressed about money and having solutions that can shift them towards abundance. Learning from my experiences will help you do just that.

This will most likely be the most controversial chapter in this book. Some may feel challenged due to strongly held beliefs promoted by society, religion, and even family tradition. Like any idea, values can be interpreted and shaped to fit an agenda. We will shift from viewing these values as right and wrong to using a process that allows:

1. Neutralizing the seduction of "financial entertainers."
2. Implementing plans with a timeless process.
3. The elimination of shame to allow true financial abundance.

Tube Tops and Tunics: One size does not fit all

Life gets complicated, so naturally people look for the easy one-size-fits-all answer. But just like with clothing, there isn't *really* such a thing as one-size-fits-all in a flattering way. Imagine if everyone's closet had sweatpants, tube tops, and tunics. Individuality would be completely lost.

I call the one-size-fits-all professional a "Financial Entertainer" because they often have a soundbite that easily goes viral, but doesn't treat people like individuals. That approach means a professional knows what you need before they have even met you.

People can feel abundant by making progress toward their *personal* goals. Focusing on your core values instead of a balance sheet creates more financial abundance, and financial wealth is simply a natural byproduct of that mindset. Financial abundance is about more flowing in than going out. No one has ever budgeted their way to abundance, which means budgeting alone can only move you toward **conditional comfort**. **Abundance** by definition is about expanding your goals; not reducing them.

To know where you are going, you must acknowledge where you came from.

A tale of three sisters ... and their parents

There is one family that has fascinated me for decades. The Smith sisters grew up like many in America. They all had the same goal of having a one-parent income that could support children in every way. But while all three of them had this end goal in mind, their differing values and levels of abundance led them to pursue it in very different ways.

This family started in Kansas and later moved to San Diego because, as a military contractor, Dad had more financial opportunities on the West Coast. This was a white-collar job that allowed them to buy a middle-class tract home in Carlsbad for the amazing price of $37,000. Even so, the girls grew up watching their parents constantly fight about money.

For both parents, the 1960s Midwest "standard of success" was for the husband to climb the corporate ladder, while the wife stayed at home with the kids. Eventually, the husband would retire with a nice pension. With these expectations in mind, the dad was constantly saying "We can't afford that" or "Do you think I'm made of money?" His *poverty* mindset came from being raised where both parents had to work multiple jobs, leaving him to effectively be raised by his older sister. *Security* was his greatest value, and having a pile of money in the bank was his idea of how to get it. Mom was a bit spoiled as an only child, and this followed her into adult life. Buying things was how she made herself feel better since her husband was watching every penny. *Spontaneity* was her greatest value, to the point that any planning was repulsive. *Avoidance* was where she lived on the sliding scale. This constant money conflict was one of the major issues that culminated in a divorce when the girls were in high school.

As promised, we won't spend much time on the *poverty* mindset, but this context is important to see how three sisters could be raised in the same financially toxic environment and have completely different money mindsets.

The oldest sister was constantly trying to prove that she wasn't like her parents and went to college for a degree in computer sciences. That led to a lucrative career in Silicon Valley which allowed her husband to stay home with the kids. Their kids were raised in a *conditional comfort* lifestyle with definite limits on extras. The husband was diligent in managing household finances and as a couple, they retired with a sizable 401k without any worry about running out of money. They were the textbook success as defined by traditional financial services. Their values were *security* and *connectedness*, but their focus on budgeting meant that sometimes they went without things they really needed. Every penny possible was diverted into the 401k and the fear of having "enough" was always present. One simple tweak to their outlook would be to segment goal progress. That would have likely moved them from *conditional comfort* to *abundance*. (More on that later.)

The middle daughter married a teacher at a major university which paid six figures but the family lifestyle led to a debt cycle that led to a paycheck-to-paycheck cycle. The husband often worked at multiple colleges to catch up, which meant that even summer school led to fewer vacations. The middle daughter was the "soccer mom" who engaged in every aspect of the kid's schooling. Multiple pensions translated into a six-figure retirement income, and they eventually moved back to Kansas because they "couldn't afford" California. This couple valued "not sweating the small stuff" and often scoffed at the older sister. Their children would never go without the latest toy, even if that meant something went on credit. Anything "expensive" for them was out of the question, but somehow the little things always added up to a constant cycle of debt. *Avoidance* was more their money pattern than *conditional comfort*. If they had examined and agreed that the "stuff" was detracting from their value of *time* with family, it could have removed the temptation to get into debt.

The youngest of the family was a rebel. She went to school and got a decent job, but it wasn't six figures like the older sisters had. What's more, she married a blue-collar worker who, while brilliant, never made a six-figure salary at his job. She and her husband valued *creativity* and *independence* more than anything else. When the kids were young this was a two-income household but this sister didn't want her children in daycare. When the kids were of school age, they decided that the wife selling real estate would be the way to go; not the easiest path, because her income was really needed. They often asked, "How can we make it happen?" In addition to his day job in construction, her husband often helped flipping properties to make enough for some of the extras that they both wanted. When they found a huge positive cashflow property, they went all in and created an income stream that nearly paid for their own home mortgage. Interestingly, while this family often only made half the income of the older sisters, asking "How can we make this happen?" was what led them to an *abundance* mentality.

The only level of abundance not represented by our family of 3 sisters is *neutrality*. The most vivid example I've seen of *neutrality* mindset is a room full of 20-somethings at UC San Marcos. When asked to educate on basic financial concepts I saw a glazed look in every eye. I stopped everything and said "Let's face it, none of you believe that you will be able to afford a house. High prices, extreme college debt, and low wages make you say, "____ it. I'm going for a latte and some avocado toast. My parents worked hard and can't get ahead so why shouldn't I enjoy today?" That was the first time they felt understood and the rest of the hour they were completely engaged. Acknowledging the concerns of a neutral person and offering hope opens up the door to progress. Small steps and stories of success can help that person move forward toward abundance.

Shame and Societal Pressures

Culturally, we've come a long way; it's no longer acceptable to judge others based on things like body image, sexual orientation, or relationship status. However, it seems that money is one of the last aspects of our lives where it's okay to shame someone.

The judgment that comes with not living in the perfect house in the suburbs, driving fancy new cars, or posting Instagrammable life moments shows up in many ways. For a while, after 2008, it was ok to be going through financial hell because it could be blamed on the state of the economy. When one in five houses was upside down or going through foreclosure or short sale, it was no big deal. But that was a symptom, not the actual core of financial stress. Overextending your finances to get into a bigger, better house was simply keeping up with the Joneses.

While so many people want more in their financial world, there are few who will even start on the first baby steps toward long-term security. Why? We live in a microwave society that expects instant results. The simple reality is that success requires choices. Everyone wants to be financially successful without looking "bad." Any suggestion of stepping back is seen as a temporary failure and *shame*.

Now for reality. Many of the richest and most successful people in the world got there because they were smart with their money. It isn't sexy to think of driving an old pickup when you have the money to get a new luxury car on payments; that would be just crazy but that's exactly what Warren Buffet did. Sometimes it takes a little crazy to be a real success.

Imagine that you're building a twenty-story skyscraper. There isn't a person in the world who would be ashamed of digging a deep foundation if the end goal is to build a skyscraper. But that's dirty, nasty work, where you see absolutely nothing going up, and quite frankly, everyone sees you going in the *wrong direction*. Building a foundation of habits and beliefs about money is *exactly the same*.

The moral of the story is that each and every time you are being told by the world that you should be ashamed of building your foundation and getting dirty, you need to reframe your mindset to understand that the deeper you go, the taller the end result can be without crumbling.

So, go get dirty and dig a solid foundation!

The VEGAN Cycle
(Don't worry, you don't have to give up steak unless that is your core value)

V -Values

E - Education

G - Guidance

A - Action

N - Nurture

While this acronym might be new to you, the principles have been around for thousands of years. For context, my integration of biblical financial principles came as I studied to become Crown Ministries' first San Diego "Journey to Financial Freedom" seminar instructor. As a student of the Bible, I have found that regardless of your spiritual or religious beliefs, the principles of money really are **B**asic **I**nstructions **B**efore **L**eaving **E**arth. The referenced verses in this chapter reflect timeless wisdom and can help in your financial journey.

Values—*Everything* starts with this, so we need to have a common definition to work from for the basis of this entire chapter.

Many may ask "What do I *own* of financial value?" Things like houses, cars, artwork, or jewelry would probably be on the list. Others might ask "What do *I* value?" *This* question is more likely to be answered with family, memories, and friends—those things that money can't replace. We're getting closer to this definition, but it still does not quite help us directly when determining our financial needs. Those personal values could be exactly the same for 10 people, but even between those same 10 people, we'll likely find that they have completely different *core* values. That is where we need to start if we are to get past the superficial conversation of getting beyond scarcity in finance. I have a simple exercise available to help discover core values.

Core values are expressed as actions and attitudes rather than things. If you (like many people) have your family at the top of your personal value list, think of how your core values can *support* your family. For example, my family is supported by my value of being independent. My daughters will agree that I have often told them, "It's not my job to take care of you. It's my job to teach you how to take care of yourself." When they were 10, that meant letting them choose what to spend allowance on. That empowered them to make choices, make mistakes, own both, and move forward.

For our discussion, I'd like to say that financial value means that something is offering value to your life proportionally to the cost or creating financial abundance.

Making a habit of focusing on your core values instead of financial values helps you avoid the pitfalls of external pressures.

Educate—"A fool and his money are soon parted" (Proverbs 21:20).

When it comes to our society, shortcuts are encouraged, but often dangerous. We will go to a salesperson to tell us what the hottest thing is or click on the top "get rich quick" Google search. What if you educated yourself on foundational principles first, then looked for resources on what to acquire? Here is where I'm discussing the concepts of spending and investing money for the future. Products and strategies might change, but the core concepts don't. To further educate yourself on these specific ideas, the most approachable book series on this topic is "How Money Works, Stop Being a Sucker" by Tom Mathews and "How Money Works for Women" by Kim Scouller and Sharon Lechter. As far as definitions are concerned, I appreciate Investopedia, but suggest avoiding the first few articles because they are generally sales pitches.

Guidance— "... a wise man seeks counsel" (Proverbs 12:15).

Guidance is most effective when you already have your vision of what you want to accomplish and have educated yourself on principles. My husband and I knew that building a rental house on our property would not be cheap or easy, but the vision was to turn an empty dirt patch into an income stream. We educated ourselves on all aspects of building, established that it would pay for itself in just over two years, and more than two decades later it is one of our most reliable income streams. But we still needed professionals to do the foundation, plumbing, and electrical. These were simply not "do it yourself" items. If a profession requires a license, there are two very good reasons: First, bad advice can be catastrophic. Second, it means that there is some entity that weeds out people doing harmful things. Hiring an electrician kept us from burning down the house. Do you get guidance from a licensed professional who knows your values and believes in abundance instead of fear and limitation? Do you have a lawyer, tax professional, and financial advisor? Building relationships with advisors begins with the first dollars you earn.

Action—"And God is able to make all grace abound to you, so that having all sufficiency in all things at all times, you may abound in every good work." (Corinthians 9:8) (Please notice the words good work.)

Many people have the hardest time with analysis paralysis. But when it comes to finances, visualization is only one step. If you find a $100 bill and don't take the action to pick it up, you are no better off. A friend of mine had multiple life events that could have completely destroyed her financially. During a time of economic downturn, she lost her job and was out of work for ten months, which led to debt. Then to top it off she had major medical issues that required surgery and tens of thousands of dollars in hospital bills. Instead of using things outside of her control to justify avoidance or scarcity, she looked at options and chose to begin paying back her debt by dog-sitting for people on a regular basis. Not only does she have a plan on how to manage a financial setback, but she is doing something she absolutely loves to accomplish the goal.

Nurture—This is where your vision board is most valuable. You know what you want and are ready to take action. Constantly reminding yourself why you are taking action can have two great effects: it can keep you from getting discouraged when things get difficult, and it may very well help you come up with ideas on how to achieve your goals in a more efficient manner. Notice I didn't say easier; you'll always need to put the work in, but sometimes it makes sense to take a different path to your goals than you initially expected. The most famous example of nurturing your vision is Jack Canfield's story of how *Chicken Soup for the Soul* became a huge success. A quick YouTube search will show why Canfield is a fantastic inspiration.

Once that is all done … you are just getting started.

Periodically you will need to revisit and slightly adjust VEGAN

VEGAN becomes:

V - Vision

E - Evaluate

G - Guidance

A - Action

N - Nurture

Values generally stay the same, but your **Vision** will evolve over time. Compared to when I was younger … my core value of being independent now means expanding my life to empower more people than my immediate family.

Educate becomes **Evaluate** if you're on track moving towards your Vision. My once 10-year-olds are now adults, and I don't have a say over their paycheck, but I still nurture their independence in other ways.

Guidance shifts slowly, but it never goes away. At specific benchmarks, you might need to check in and use your trusted advisors as a sounding board. My dog-sitting friend reaches out periodically, and sometimes I simply say, "You are completely on track. Congratulations!"

Action will keep you moving toward goals while you keep course correcting.

Nurture will always be critical as your environment and associations will either guide or distract from values and vision.

Get rid of the one-bucket trap

The magic is in the margins. Create a margin instead of saving "what is left over." Society teaches us to think of income as one source that fills one bucket. This is incredibly dangerous. Expecting that you can depend on one income from one company is a severely limiting belief that is rarely fulfilled by the companies we depend on. We need to shift our mindsets and realize that there are endless ways to attract money with our natural skills.

There are only four ways to "spend" money.

1) Taxes
2) Giving
3) Lifestyle
4) Debt

Taxes are automatic for most W-2 workers, but commission-based individuals can get into trouble if they don't accept that there is no way to legally eliminate them.

Giving is something I believe in, and I have seen those who give from abundance prosper at amazing levels. That being said be sure your giving is aligned with core values and appropriate resources. (2 Corinthians 9:6-8)

Debt in this diagram is the minimum debt payments, including housing, cars, student loans, credit cards, etc.

Lifestyle is a chosen range, not the default of "What is our income after taxes?" Had the middle sister in the story above decided how much she was willing to spend on lifestyle, the debt cycle could have been broken.

The rest is **Margin,** that we create, and that is what we can use for investing for future goals. This is where the magic of aligning our values with our finances really blossoms. Margin opens the door for opportunity when it comes knocking. Have you ever heard someone say that they really wanted something, but they didn't make enough money? Margin is something I've seen created in even modest incomes.

The most common mistake is that people see their finances as one bucket. W-2 workers take out taxes, faith-focused individuals give a tithe, and then everything else is spent on lifestyle. Get a raise, buy a new car, or at least get a new HULU subscription. When you decide the size of your lifestyle first, you will naturally increase your Margin over time.

This mindset focuses on investing for Future Goals. Society has a long list of what we "should" do, but as you go through this, please remember to keep your choices in alignment with *your* core values. When you're ready to examine how your values are supported by different goals, I have a worksheet that will guide you through the process.

So many people don't save for the future because they feel doing so will sacrifice their quality of life. Let me be clear; I have seen people who have worked overtime and never taken vacations, all so they can have a great "retirement." Sadly, some of those people passed away far too young. That is not what I'm proposing. Imagine, however, spending every penny on every possible extra during your working years, then having to completely stop all fun activities as soon as you retire. Worse yet, never having a "work optional" lifestyle and never experiencing the freedom of not having to go to work 40 hours per week. I prefer to consider a full life, where, at some point, we have the resources to reinvent ourselves for the next chapter. This is not a specific age; it is a level of maturity where our vision leads us in a direction that fully utilizes our life experiences to support our core values. My reinvention is to coach agents to grow a business that supports the next generation of clients.

Had the oldest sister in our story looked at her income in current and future lifestyle goal buckets, it would have been easier to see progress and allow for *abundant* choices, and as a result, given her a fuller, more relaxed life.

Financial Abundance is about designing your life using the VEGAN process, not an end goal in itself. Vision within the context of benchmarks allows your values to flourish. Fostering an environment of guidance from trusted advisors will allow you to focus on values as you stay in an abundance cycle. Now you have the tools to begin that journey.

Lenka Holman

Lenka Holman is a financial services professional who embraces the philosophy that investing is about more than balance sheets. Earnings translate to experiences, memories, and ultimately a Life WORTH Living that's unique to each individual. Beginning in 2003, she chose to move from being an office manager to becoming a student of money and how it can enrich lives. Becoming an educator for Crown Ministries was how she engrained Biblical principles and ethics into guiding clients. She makes decisions by answering to a "higher power."

Lenka was recognized in Forbes Magazine and professional designations include becoming a Certified Financial Educator and a fiduciary. This means that regulating officials mandate that her advice must always be what is best for the client instead of the lower level of "suitable."

This dedication to respecting her clients came from her early experience with financial services professionals. As a single mom of two, she felt that no one wanted to help set up "starter accounts" because they would not make sizable commissions for the advisor. With that foundation, she has been able to speak truth that has resonated with all clients from the starters to her sizably affluent families.

Her life experiences as a wife, parent, church member, and Girl Scout leader, and over 20 years with Wealth Wave have led her to create the platform of Life WORTH Living as a community of resources and connections for personal growth and empowerment that combine values and mentoring.

Connect with Lenka at https://lenkaholman.com.

ORGANIZE —
FOUNDATIONAL LAW

Clutter Created This Mess; Organize to Maximize

by Kymberly J. Spears

Dedication
Jeremiah 29:11: For I know the plans I have for you," declares
the Lord, "plans to prosper you and not to harm you, plans
to give you hope and a future.

She sat at her cluttered kitchen table, laptop open, the smell of dinner dishes wafting into the air. She contemplated whether or not to do them or finish the client cases that had been interrupted earlier. She wondered if she was a bad mother and partner, having put so many things off. She used to look forward to conversations with her husband over coffee. His love and their blended family have brought such joy into her life. Yet, juggling every dynamic, between in-laws, co-parents, and a growing number of business relationships, she was constantly revolving roles, holding things together like a linchpin. At that moment, she decided ... the dishes would have to wait until the morning ... their coffee connection would be postponed as well, and she would stay glued to her seat until further notice. Realizing she was hunched over, she sat up straighter in the kitchen chair. She longed for a separate space, but her family needed her there. Her thoughts spiraled, "Did she have the time to commit to financial freedom?"

She sat up with her heart heavy, conflated with responsibility. Things had become so cluttered in her household, her finances, and her relationships. Things were in constant disarray. This wasn't the first time she had felt paralyzed in her thoughts. For example, whenever she sat down in an attempt to open her bills, this overwhelming grief would sneak in and consume her. She hadn't bought herself new clothes. They hadn't planned any recent family trips, yet the debt kept climbing, maxed out credit cards from impulsive spending, and no savings in sight. Feeling choked up, she scurried to the backyard, the most organized space in their home, with only two decorative chairs, a wind chime, and a small side table. Again, her thoughts rushed past her like random objects in no particular order. Her clutter had created such a mess. This same clutter would have to be cleared from her mind first, then organized to maximize her faith. She could have abundance...she would create a path to achieving it all.

What is clutter?

Clutter can be defined in multiple ways; a confused or disordered state of collection. When used as a verb—to spread over, in a disorderly manner, or to make disorderly or hard to use by spilling over with objects. In electronics, clutter is seen as unwanted echoes that confuse observations of signals on a radar screen. How about the transitive verb to fill or cover with, scattered, or disordered things, which impede movement or reduce effectiveness? While oftentimes, we think of clutter in terms of our physical environment, more often than not, that same clutter may have manifested from an emotionally or mentally cluttered space within our mind. It can create a clutter of thoughts about the various roles we play in life, the values that we wish to maintain, the relationships we desire to nurture, the wellness we want to give our bodies, the peace of financial security, and its disciplined efforts. In this chapter, we will look at how clutter, in three key areas of our lives, can subtly exist. The chaotic experience and high cost when left unchecked, to the beauty in embracing your mess and the opportunity to organize with clarity and vision. The practical tips in this section are meant to encourage every individual who desires prosperity and fulfillment in their everyday life. My desire for you is that you build a skill set of clearing clutter and getting organized to maximize life's inherent abundance.

The Impact on the Mind

Before we embark on a journey to conquer clutter, we must first understand its nature. Clutter, at its core, is an overwhelming presence of unnecessary and chaotic elements. It is a physical or mental weight that pulls us down, obstructing our paths to progress. Yes, clutter can manifest tangible chaos in our homes, our relationships, and our finances. It is the culmination of these things that interrupts our ability to move forward in sound decision-making, ultimately causing the overwhelm and fatigue of an overstimulated mind. Let's discuss further how clutter of the mind can be seen in our everyday lives.

Have you ever been at your desk looking at a pile of papers, thinking about the unopened emails regarding an upcoming deadline, while also visualizing the cost of dinner that night, already sensing you are too tired to cook? These intermingling thoughts and concerns can be described as clutter of the mind. Clutter of the mind can be displayed in various ways. Overthinking about past decisions or future interactions. Trying to juggle multiple tasks at one time reduces productivity and focus, and the ever-prevalent information overload, which is the constant exposure to new ideas, opinions, and critiques, both in person and online. The dangerous implications of this type of disorder can range from inability to concentrate, constantly jumping between projects, feeling worried and anxious, and fear that you can't manage it all. The tangled web of stress and pressure we create in our minds when we don't establish routines, clear boundaries, and responsible financial planning, can cause a chain of events. This stress represents a struggle to operate efficiently and most importantly, being at peace and with faith that there's an abundance of time and resources to enjoy it all. Rest assured, by examining the nature of clutter, we can better understand when it's time to refresh and restore healthy and balanced behaviors that match our core values.

Starting with our relationships. Have you ever met someone who was a very compassionate and empathetic individual? They always tended to be the go-to person for their friends and family. Someone whose caring nature often leads them to a complex network of relationships that feel overwhelming and chaotic. For example, the person at work, who becomes an unofficial mediator between colleagues, often gets caught in interpersonal conflicts and office politics. Their role as the peak peacemaker is mentally draining, and they often juggle the expectations and emotions of their coworkers which can become burdensome. In their personal life, they are equally entangled. They have a wide circle of friends each with their unique demands on that person's time and attention. Their phone may be constantly buzzing with messages, and it seems like they're always on call to listen to someone's problems or offer support. Taking it a step further, their romantic relationships may have their own set of complications. They may be dating someone whom they feel is wonderful, but have clearly identified that they have different expectations about the future, and while one may seem eager to continue, the other feels pressured due to family values and beliefs and stays committed longer than their gut is suggesting. This type of clutter in relationships stems from emotional baggage, unresolved conflicts, and unhealthy dynamics that hinder the growth and harmony of connections with others. Unresolved conflicts and lingering disagreements between partners or family members is a form of emotional clutter, that often leads to resentment. The solution is to have space to invite others to have comfortable conversations and clear lines of communication. Toxic relationships, which are defined as relationships that are one-sided or leave one of the parties unfulfilled, often clutter life with negativity and drain emotional energy. This sends out a vibration that it is okay to be in a relationship with people who do not serve you and treat you well. The tendency to create unrealistic expectations of others can also lead to disappointments and misunderstandings causing resentment and frustration. Again, this sends signals to the mind that your needs cannot be met, and will result in a lack in the areas of love.

The last point would be a lack of communication overall. Poor communication or emotional withholding can clutter relationships with discouragement and emotional distance. Clutter that we carry in our relationships often leads us to feel pulled in multiple directions and overwhelmed trying to meet the emotional needs of others including friends, family members, co-workers, or otherwise. The inability to set boundaries can have us feeling mentally exhausted and constantly worried about letting someone down while our own desires and dreams take a backseat. This constant need to be a source of support, for everyone can leave one with little time and energy for self-care or the pursuit of our own passions. For many of us, our identities are tied to the quality of our relationships. It is important to organize your interactions in ways that are healthy, ways that enroll people in mutually beneficial dynamics, and allow each person to cater to their own personal needs, while allowing room to cater and be considerate of others.

This brings us to the next area and most recognizable culprit for collecting clutter, our households; the space that becomes our sanctuary, houses all of our things, and acts as the setting for our most valued engagements, and most intimate conversations When in disarray, the clutter within our homes can sabotage the best of intentions and devalue the most prized possessions. Imagine a home that physically reflects a cluttered life. It would be reflective of the type of person who constantly saves items for sentimental reasons or thinks they'll need it one day and it might come in handy. Over the years, this collection of possessions may have grown to an overwhelming scale. Walking through the door of this house, you would immediately notice the disorder. The living room might be filled with stacks of old magazines or dusty collectibles and piles of paper. The dining table, meant for meals and family gatherings, might be a sea of unopened bills and unpaid debts. The kitchen is cluttered with gadgets that really don't get used. And the pantry is stocked with expired food items. The bedrooms aren't any better. The children's playrooms are always a constant chaos of toys, broken puzzles or forgotten art supplies. The master bedroom is cluttered with worn clothes and the closet is always a jumble of shoes and accessories. Even the bathroom might be filled with half-used toiletries and expired medications. The garage, intended for the family car, may be so full of unused sporting equipment, tools, and boxes of who-knows-what, that the car has been banished to the driveway. There's barely any room to move around, let alone find anything when it's needed. Who would feel comfortable sitting amongst this mess? The thought of having serious conversations, or connecting over coffee, is immediately impeded by a visual distraction or aroma that grabs attention away from the person or thing that deserves to have it all.

When clutter takes over your household, you can often find it difficult to find things and you end up buying replacements for items you already have, but couldn't locate in the mess, only aiding in financial discontent. Cleaning becomes a daunting task as the sheer volume of stuff has made it difficult to access the surfaces that need cleaning. The cluttered environment creates a constant feeling of disorganization and chaos, making it hard to enroll others to assist in the various necessary tasks.

It becomes increasingly challenging to invite friends or family over as we become embarrassed by the state of our homes. Household clutter can have various detrimental effects, excessive possessions, for example, means that you've accumulated more things than you need. The lack of organization in different spaces often leads to a waste of time and the search for items. There is increased stress due to the visual chaos. When it comes to sentimental clutter, or holding onto items that have strong, sentimental value, while appearing to create comfort, the negative impact far outweighs and adds to the lack of functionality. The last cause of clutter in the home is often unfinished projects. Starting home improvements around the house without completing them can clutter the home with evidence of things being unfinished. It is often the disorder of our living space that gives a jolting sign that there is a thunderstorm waiting to rain down on our heads. Implementing systems and products that help facilitate and maintain clean and functional spaces helps you properly display those things that bring you pride and joy, while also justifying the cleansing habit and need to continually declutter and purge.

The final experience with clutter is financial. The grievous impact on a person's overall quality of life can be greatly reduced by their ability to become organized and accountable to the principles that govern their financial future. The following signs of financial clutter such as unpaid bills, past due payments, liens, and loans should be resolved as urgently as possible. A habit of neglecting debt must be resolved. In the mailbox, unopened bills and collection notices may pile up. Purely, the thought of addressing them becomes overwhelming, so they continue to ignore them and hope that somehow, they will magically resolve themselves. One's bank statements are equally chaotic, and transactions are inconsistent, making it challenging to track spending. Credit card balances might be mounting, perpetuating living paycheck to paycheck, constantly feeling the pressure of financial stress. To make matters worse, there may be multiple subscriptions that no one uses but continue to pay for like gym memberships and streaming services, thus throwing money down the drain. Emails are inundated with promotional offers and online shopping receipts. They see no way of getting out of debt or saving for the future and overall have a dread and lack abundance in their planning and faith in the future. The overall mismanagement of your finances can have severe consequences; debt accumulation from ignoring debt, or living beyond your means can clutter your stability with mounting financial obligations and stress. Impulsive spending or frequent purchases and indulgent behavior can clutter your financial resources, hindering savings, and accomplishing long-term financial chaos. The lack of a budget and failing to stick to that budget can clutter your decision-making and lead to financial insecurity while financial procrastination or delaying important financial decisions like investing and retirement planning, cloud your financial future with uncertainty. When these types of decisions manifest in your finances, you may feel constantly anxious about your financial situation, and you may have a hard time having the courage to face it head-on, avoidance of the financial problems will further cause you to accumulate late fees, penalties and growing amounts of debt You may even feel a constant undercurrent of guilt and frustration for not managing your finances better which affects your overall well-being and sense of hope. Financial clutter consumes the average household at alarming rates. This idea of keeping up with the Jones through frivolous spending on fashion, eating out and fast food, and expensive excursions above one's means, has diluted what we once called the land of opportunity. The ability to structure your finances in a holistic way, which reflects a person's true core values often gets lost in the self-soothing feeling and gratification of purchasing something new. The havoc this clutter has reaped on marriages and families can be seen by the number of divorces we hear about, due to fights about money. The relationships are damaged by poor spending habits and the dreams that go unfulfilled.

When clutter appears in any area of our lives, we have to ask how we got here. What came first, the clutter in our mind or the mess that it created? Does the mind become so filled with thoughts, reflections, ambitions, and passions that we simply lose track of the abundance of time we have to actualize things? Harnessing time through the organization of your values maximizes the positive experiences and interactions that create our individual worlds' harmony.

The Art of Brain Dumping

To combat clutter in its various forms, we introduce the concept of 'brain dumping.' This technique allows us to clear the mental fog and make way for a more organized and purposeful life. Through brain dumping, we can bring order to the chaos by transferring our thoughts, ideas, and tasks from our overburdened minds onto paper or a digital medium. This exercise will then allow you to examine all that you are considering, making it easier to identify what should stay and what must go, what deserves more or less attention. We'll explore the numerous benefits that brain dumping offers, and how to create a schedule that allows for flexibility, growth, and prosperity in an ever-changing environment.

In the heart of a lively suburban neighborhood, a dedicated wife and mother, and a driven marketing executive felt the weight of her life's demands pressing down on her. Her mind was a whirlwind of thoughts, a never-ending stream of responsibilities that seemed to pull her in all directions. As the sun cast its warm glow through the windows, she decided it was time for a mental reset and to declutter her mind. She moved throughout her home, from room to room, letting her thoughts flow spontaneously. In the kitchen, she stood at the counter, her pen and notebook in hand. Surrounded by the comforting aroma of her morning coffee, she began to write about her desire for self-care. It was as though the scent of the coffee triggered her longing for more yoga sessions, quiet walks, and moments of meditation. She realized that taking care of herself was a precious investment of time and talent, a means to unlock her true potential. The dining room table became her next point. She gazed at the empty chairs around it, each one representing a cherished relationship in her life. Thoughts about her husband, David, and their children flooded her mind. At that moment, she decided to nurture these connections by scheduling date nights, planning family adventures, and fostering meaningful conversations. She felt an abundance of love and happiness waiting to be cultivated. The household responsibilities echoed from the living room, a space often scattered with toys and laundry called to her next. She realized that transforming her chaotic home into a peaceful sanctuary required better organization and redistribution of tasks. Her writing reflected her determination to efficiently manage her time and to create an environment where her family could thrive. Finally, in her home office, she confronted the financial worries that had long lingered in her mind. She knew she held the power to take control of their finances, to turn their resources into a tool for a better future. She had a mindset of abundance, emphasizing the importance of budgeting, saving, and investing in their family's treasures. As the day went on, her spontaneous brain dump became a journey through her own thoughts, each space in her home triggering ideas and tasks. Her desire for efficient use of her time, talents, and treasures is a recurring theme. The sense of abundance permeated her words, driving her to reshape her priorities, find more time for self-care, nurture relationships, and manage their finances more wisely. The brain dump was not just a release but a destination on a roadmap to a more balanced, fulfilling life, which would allow her to be fulfilled in who she was meant to be.

What Is a Brain Dump?

A brain dump is an activity where you rapidly jot down the thoughts, ideas, and tasks that come to mind without worrying about organization or structure. It's a way to clear your mind and get everything out on paper, making it easier to analyze, prioritize, or organize at a later time. This can be useful for brainstorming, problem-solving, or simply decluttering your thoughts. A brain dump serves as a powerful tool to identify what needs reorganization before implementing new schedules, habits, and routines.

BRAIN DUMP

CLEARING THE CLUTTER

#	IN NO PATICULAR ODER JOT DOWN EVERYTHING THAT HAS/BEEN CLUTTERING YOUR MIND	YQMBWD	FHRS
1			
2			
3			
4			
5			
6			
7			
8			
9			
10			
11			
12			
13			
14			
15			
16			
17			
18			
19			
20			

PATTERNS:

When you perform a brain dump, you empty your mind of its clutter. It allows you to see the full scope of your responsibilities, desires, and concerns. This clarity helps you identify your true priorities, which are essential for effective time management. As you jot down your thoughts, worries, and to-dos, you may uncover hidden stressors or bottlenecks in your life. These could be tasks that have been procrastinated, unresolved issues in your relationships, or financial concerns. Recognizing these stressors is the first step in addressing them. In summary, a brain dump helps you create a comprehensive snapshot of your life, revealing what's cluttering your mind.

Inspiration

Clarity and structure are fundamental in organizing and inspiring individuals to reach their full potential. Categorization serves as a guiding light amidst the chaos of thoughts, bringing about a sense of order. When you segment your brainstormed ideas into categories such as self-care, relationships, household, and finances you create a framework that is both clear and organized. This structure helps you identify which aspects of your life are in need of attention. Balanced prioritization, achieved through categorization, ensures that you maintain equilibrium in your life. It prevents the neglect of any essential facet of your well-being or responsibilities.

ORGANIZE YOUR THOUGHTS

FINDING INSPIRATION

#	HOUSHOLD	RELATIONSHIPS	FINANCES	SELF CARE
1				
2				
3				
4				
5				
6				
7				
8				
9				
10				
11				
12				
13				
14				
15				
16				
17				
18				
19				
20				

Top 3 Desires _____

_____

_____

By having all categories in one place, you can devise a schedule that allocates time and effort equitably among them. Furthermore, categorization offers flexibility, allowing you to adapt to evolving priorities and circumstances. Transferable habits become evident through categorization, revealing habits that can be applied across multiple categories for maximum efficiency. For instance, you may find that effective time management benefits both household chores and self-care routines.

168 Hours of Opportunity a.k.a. Abundance

Scheduled planning becomes more achievable with categorized lists, permitting you to create a structured schedule that designates specific times and days for tasks and habits within each category. This method guarantees that you allocate time for important activities in each area of your life. Moreover, organization empowers you to visualize your aspirations through tools like vision boards or goal charts, offering inspiration and motivation as you see your goals materialize. Additionally, you will notice a well-organized approach can inspire buy-in from those around you, serving as a model of discipline and success for family and friends. When we organize the results of our brain dump to create a coherent schedule, we create a roadmap to declutter our lives.

FIND THE TIME

SEE THE ABUNDANCE

	Monday	Tuesday	Wednesday	Thursday	Friday	Saturday	Sunday
5:00 AM							
5:30 AM							
6:00 AM							
6:30 AM							
7:00 AM							
7:30 AM							
8:00 AM							
8:30 AM							
9:00 AM							
9:30 AM							
10:00 AM							
10:30 AM							
11:00 AM							
11:30 AM							
12:00 PM							
12:30 PM							
1:00 PM							
1:30 PM							
2:00 PM							
2:30 PM							
3:00 PM							
3:30 PM							
4:00 PM							
4:30 PM							
5:00 PM							
5:30 PM							
6:00 PM							
6:30 PM							
7:00 PM							
7:30 PM							
8:00 PM							
8:30 PM							
9:00 PM							
9:30 PM							
10:00 PM							
10:30 PM							
11:00 PM							
11:30 PM							
12:00 PM							

A brain dump can reveal overlaps or conflicts in your daily life. For example, you might find that your work schedule clashes with your desired self-care routine. This insight prompts you to reorganize your work hours or shift your self-care activities to a more suitable time. By examining your brain dump, you can pinpoint time-consuming or unproductive activities. These can be eliminated, streamlined, or delegated, freeing up more time for important tasks. The steps following a brain dump help you recognize where your current routines fall short. Whether it's a lack of time for exercise or inconsistent meal planning, you can identify areas that need to be restructured to accommodate new habits or routines. By assessing how you allocate your resources—time, energy, and attention, you reduce the build-up of clutter in your environment, until it quietly disappears. Organization is a key principle to building a life of abundance. When you create structure, routines, and boundaries, you invite prosperity to enter your world.

Kymberly J. Spears

Kymberly J. Spears, originally from Moreno Valley, Calilfornia, is a distinguished professional with a bachelor's degree in creative writing/ English from CSUSB. With over a decade of experience, she holds licenses as a benefit counselor and retirement planner. Kymberly's passion lies in assisting young women, collegiate athletes, and pre-retirees in navigating the intricacies of long-term savings and financial security. Her expertise is a guiding light for those seeking a secure financial future. In addition to her client-centered work, Kymberly excels as a mentor, trainer, and supporter, aiding fellow agents in their professional development and licensing journeys. Simultaneously, she manages an organizing business, dedicated to helping women and professionals harmonize their home life and finances for a more fulfilling existence. On a personal note, Kymberly enjoys a blissful marriage and the role of a loving stepmother to three wonderful children, with the recent addition of a healthy and beautiful baby girl. Her leisure pursuits include reading, painting, and maintaining an active lifestyle through regular workouts. Kymberly J Spears is a consummate professional who combines financial expertise with a compassionate approach, positively impacting the lives of her clients and peers.

Connect with Kymberly at https://calendly.com/kymberlyspearsshiftinggears/introduction.

CHAPTER 12

Step 6—Move into Action

---

*Stop Living by Default, Get back into the
Driver's Seat of your Life.*
~Patrina Wisdom

The final step in our Anatomy Of Abundance™ Framework is Move. The Move step is where dreams take flight. It's the moment of transition from planning to action, where the blueprint you've meticulously crafted begins to take shape in the real world. This chapter is dedicated to the art of moving forward with accountability, consistency, and the right support system.

The Power of Action

Action is the bridge between your aspirations and their realization. Without action, even the most beautifully designed blueprint remains dormant. The Move step is a call to activate your plans, to breathe life into your vision, and to take that pivotal first step.

The Right Community

Surrounding yourself with the right community is paramount. These are individuals who align with your goals, values, and aspirations. They provide encouragement, motivation, and a sense of belonging. Your community becomes a pillar of support as you embark on your journey. Conversely, the wrong community can be detrimental and hinder your progress.

Accountability and Consistency

Accountability is the compass that keeps you on course. It involves setting clear goals, measuring your progress, and being answerable to yourself and others. Consistency is the engine that propels you forward. It's the commitment to showing up, day in and day out, regardless of obstacles or setbacks.

The Accountability Systems

Having the right accountability systems in place is crucial. These can include regular check-ins with mentors or coaches, joining a mastermind community, progress tracking tools, and/or accountability partners. These systems function as reminders of your commitment and keep you focused on your objectives.

The Role of Coaching

Just as in the Organize step, coaching plays a vital role in the Move step. Coaches offer guidance, feedback, and strategies to help you navigate challenges and stay on track. They hold you accountable to your goals and provide valuable insights to enhance your progress.

Embracing Change and Adaptability

The journey of abundance is not always linear. It may require adaptation and flexibility. The Move step is about embracing change and adjusting your course when necessary. It's a testament to your resilience and determination.

The Courage to Move

Taking action requires courage. It means facing fears, overcoming self-doubt, and venturing into the unknown. But remember, it's in these moments of discomfort that growth occurs. Every step you take brings you closer to your vision of abundance.

A Life in Motion

As you embrace the Move step of the Anatomy Of Abundance™ Framework, envision a life in motion. It's a life where dreams become reality through deliberate action. It's a life where you surround yourself with a supportive community, uphold accountability, and maintain unwavering consistency. With each step forward, you breathe life into your vision, and as you Move with intention and purpose, you reimagine and reinvent your life.

Explore These Questions:

1. Who is holding you accountable to your greatness?
2. Who are the people in your life who are hindering your growth or keeping you from greatness?
3. Now that I've established a clear vision for my life, who can help me formulate the strategy to bring it to fruition?
4. What influences or voices do I need to eliminate or quiet to reach my goals?
5. On a scale of 1-10, with 10 indicating urgency, how ready am I to take action right now?

The Radiant Path: Illuminating the Mind and Spirit Through the Power of Movement

by Dr. Sabrina Nichole Crouch

This chapter is dedicated to my 2nd great-grandfather,
Willie Carlos Brown, who bought 75 acres of land for $500
in 1925. With this action, he created a legacy of believing
in possibilities, no matter the odds.

There is an invisibility to chronic pain. Physically debilitating, but no one can see it. Not just the physical pain, but also the negative mental/emotional and spiritual toll that chronic pain patients experience. If you have ever heard words from the doctor like, There's nothing we can do, then you know the heaviness I am talking about. According to the U.S. Pain Foundation **51.6 million Americans** endure pain every day.

I am one of those people and I found a way to go from managing chronic pain to mastering it. Life experiences shaped me and led me to redefine everything I thought I knew. Pain was my greatest teacher. The first thing I learned is that being still and not moving didn't take away the pain.

Movement is a fundamental component of the healing process, playing a crucial role in both physical and mental well-being. When we are injured or ill, our bodies naturally tend to become immobile, as we instinctively protect the affected area. However, prolonged inactivity can result in muscle weakness, stiffness, and a decrease in overall mobility. To counteract these negative effects, movement becomes essential. Engaging in physical activity not only strengthens muscles and joints but also enhances blood circulation, which promotes the delivery of oxygen and nutrients to the injured or affected areas, aiding in the healing process.

Movement has a profound impact on mental health as well. Exercise and movement release endorphins, often referred to as "feel-good" hormones, which help alleviate stress, anxiety, and depression. Movement can be related to spiritual healing in a few different ways. First, physical movement, such as exercise, walking meditation, or yoga, can help release tension and promote a sense of well-being, which can contribute to spiritual healing. These movements can help individuals connect with their bodies, quiet their minds, and cultivate a sense of inner peace and harmony. Movement can also be a way to express emotions and release energy, which can be beneficial for spiritual healing. When I think of move, movement, and moving, I also think of words like action, activity, flow, and changing direction. Movement is about increasing and shifting awareness and approaching the road ahead with curiosity. It doesn't matter if it is the right direction, but more important is to take that first step.

Movement is a medicine for creating change in a person's physical, emotional and mental states.

~Carol Weich

Journey to Abundance

My definition of abundance has evolved. I had to dismantle and reassemble a new definition. Now it is more fluid, but if you asked the old me, health equaled abundance. It was all or none and to be honest I took it for granted. I was stuck in the loop of Do–Have–Be. I would work more to have more financial abundance with little time just Being present. A chronic pain diagnosis not only affected my physical health but also affected all other aspects of my life. Just recently I had to ask myself, does an illness mean that I no longer have abundance? It depends on how you define abundance. We grow up learning about duality. In school, we learn to compare and categorize. Good vs. bad, right vs. wrong. But is it possible for there to be room for both? What if we did not divide health and illness but looked at it on a continuum knowing that we could flow freely and that each day may be different? Health, illness, disease, injury, diagnosis, and abundance all in one breath. To be able to redefine abundance I had to embrace all of these and shift my focus from being narrowly focused on the pain to widening my focus and seeing pain as a small part of myself.

With new information, a new outcome is possible. For many people including myself, pain equals suffering. Shinzen Young, a meditation teacher, developed a pain-processing algorithm. Suffering = Pain x Resistance. His process of working meditatively with pain involves reducing the perception of suffering due to pain and discovering the taste of purification with pain. This involves letting emotions go through the process or arising, abiding, and dissolving without interference. On

243

the surface, there is nothing we can do about the pain. We can't avoid it, but I believe we can intervene by reducing our perception of suffering by shifting our resistance. It is our resistance to what is happening that is reinforcing the idea of suffering. It is the frustration when realizing we are not getting what we want. A pain-free body. I want you to know our bodies are just one part of the pain. Young has a five-step algorithm to process pain. The first step is seeing subjective reactions to pain and figuring out the triggers. This can be an emotional body sensation, a mental image, an internal dialogue, or some combination. A host of emotions come with resistance like frustration, disappointment, annoyance, anger, and anxiety. What is needed to move away from resistance is a level of acceptance. Accepting that pain is a part of us at the moment, that it doesn't encompass our whole being, and that we can transcend it. There are two things that aren't considered by Western medicine when treating us for chronic pain conditions: the power of our minds and the power of our spirits. By changing our focus and addressing the mental/emotional and spiritual aspects of pain, we can create a new equation. Abundance = Pain x Surrender. This is where I ended up but not how I started.

In one moment, my life changed. My definition of abundance was shattered. In February 2018, I received a diagnosis of cervical stenosis, a chronic pain condition in which the spinal canal is too small for the spinal cord. What does it feel like? Shooting pain through your nerve endings, tingling, numbness, a disturbing crawling sensation all over your body, stiffness, and a crackling sound when you turn your head. In other words: horrendous. I felt uncomfortable in my own skin and couldn't trust my body. When I woke up and couldn't move my hand, I felt powerless. I felt like I was drowning. At each doctor visit, I would ask what else she could do, and she'd shoot me a look of pity and offer the same reply, We can manage it with medication and when it gets worse, you'll be a candidate for surgery. In that room, I felt alone. I felt like the doctor was giving up on me and writing me off. Hopelessness was setting in. I was becoming the diagnosis and didn't see a way out. I dared to continue asking, What else is there? After six months of hearing my doctor say, There's nothing else we can try … I hit a breaking point. I sat silently and there was this dim spark within me that said, This can't be it. F*ck being stuck.

F*ck being stuck became my declaration of liberation.

F*ck the medical professionals who say there's no hope. F*ck the loop of fear, anxiety, and depression inside my own mind, which was holding me back. F*ck being stuck! Determined to shift my life, I dedicated myself to finding relief from pain. I began to challenge the Western view of healing and I began speaking to people who practiced alternative medicine. At first, it seemed like I was grasping straws. I didn't know if acupuncture, EFT, or physical therapy would work, but I tried it anyway, even after my pain management doctor said it wouldn't work. My healing journey took me to places I never imagined. The key place it took me to was within. You see, we often seek answers when we haven't asked the right questions. Luckily, I crossed paths with the person who would put me on the right path to true healing.

His question was simply, "What are you holding onto that you need to let go of?" And I was speechless. Alaa was an Egyptologist, tour guide, and holistic healer. I had met him two years prior, on a trip to Egypt and he solved years of sinus challenges in one moment. I haven't used any medication since. His cure was mint oil. After exhausting other alternatives, I thought maybe Alaa had a cure for the pain I was experiencing. In my naïve mind, I thought I was sure they had an oil for this.

The conversation lasted about five minutes. I was left to sit contemplating the answer to his question. Something about the question resonated with me. Alaa was right. This condition not only settled into my body but my mind and my spirit. With this diagnosis, I was not only dealing with the physical impact, but my worst fears, anxiety, and sadness as well. Would I be debilitated and unable to take care of myself? I believed my life and my body as I knew it were forever changed. It was like I was mourning the loss of my former self and the future was uncertain. That was a scary place to be. But this question was like planting a seed and I didn't know where I was going, but I was determined to explore the answers with a new sense of curiosity. I spent time sitting in silence. I had to learn how to move these emotions I was holding onto. I was trying to recall what resources I had that were consistent with Alaa's direction. Then I remembered that a year prior I had read a book called *Breaking the Habit of Being Yourself* by Dr. Joe Dispenza. Truthfully, this book was a hard read. I had no luck meditating while I was imagining water rising without feeling like I was drowning. Luckily, this wasn't Dr. Joe's only book, so I found one of his other books, *Becoming Supernatural*. This book planted another seed. A belief in possibilities. What attracted me to Dr. Joe Dispenza's work is that he was bold, and he had a personal story of overcoming challenges larger than my own. Also, he didn't just talk about using meditation to relax or relieve stress. He made unbelievable claims that meditation could reverse diseases, cure medical conditions, and change gene expression. A study of advanced meditators found that meditation can enhance resiliency to viral infections and may serve as a supportive therapy in the management of COVID-19 (Zuniga-Hertz, et al, 2023). The beautiful thing is that this was my meditation community that researchers measured. I think it's important to have research in support of methods, but when you are facing something incurable, the willingness to embrace a different approach to healing and take action is the real key.

I heard it said that if you want to hide something from someone, hide it within. They'll never look there. Going inward is not something you learn at home. At home, we are conditioned to focus on our external world and the world of our senses. We then move to the world of work and careers where the focus remains the same. It's rare that you hear someone say they spend time exploring their inner world. I'm talking about the world of the unknown, or subconscious. This is an essential part of the journey. Over time, I dismantled what I thought I knew about meditation. I used to believe the misconceptions that I had to sit still, and that my mind had to be clear. I now know that each attempt at meditation is a victory. I know that I can do it sitting, standing, walking, eating, running, laying down. I can pause right now and turn inward. In a few seconds, my toes are tingling and I can relax my body on demand. The definition of meditation that I follow is To become familiar with. This definition is not attached to a religion, a space, a style of dress, or restricted to a location. It was me getting to know myself in a new way, and becoming curious as I began to uncover a new reality.

Consciousness is only possible through change.
Change is only possible through movement.
~Aldous Huxley

How to create abundance in your life

We can create abundance in our lives by redefining abundance for ourselves. It is going to require you to be forward-thinking and address each aspect of yourself. My process involved movement, attuning my body, and increasing my awareness of my reactions to pain including the internal talk, mental images, and sensations. And then awakening my spirit by connecting with the stories of my ancestors and finding permission to create a new narrative. I didn't learn this from my pain management doctor, I didn't learn this in graduate school or a doctoral program in psychology. These were life lessons that I had to experience and navigate. There are no coincidences.

My unexpected journey up a mountain in Peru happened about a year into my meditation journey. It was a test of my new skills in a way I had never imagined. Although I was planning to travel with my friend Keli, at the airport she wasn't permitted to board the plane. She was in tears and I realized I would be going alone. This hike was my Keli's idea, and she wasn't here. At first, I resisted. Immediately I texted the guide and tried to cancel. He urged me to wait until I arrived. I thought, "Why am I even doing this?" I had only seen a picture of Vinicunca, also known as Rainbow Mountain, and didn't understand the need to go. There I was in a foreign country with a man I just met. Alex was my tour guide and he urged me to continue with the planned tour. Hesitantly, I surrendered. Alex said it would be a 40-minute hike. I thought, "How bad could it be?" It all started in darkness with just a beam of light from a flashlight. We were the first two hikers on the path, and the only other people we passed were the park rangers. I posed for a picture lit by a flash, holding two walking sticks. Let me just say that I am not a hiker. I've walked on some trails before but nothing strenuous and never at an elevation of 15,000 feet. I was dealing with not only the terrain but also the air. Quickly, I realized that my body didn't move as fast as I wanted it to at that altitude.

Alex patiently coached me along the way. I knew right away that I had found the right guide. I could feel his connection, reverence, and respect for the land of his birth. He was familiar and comfortable with the unexpected changes in temperature and terrain. He knew what to do at the right time. At times, he remained silent; other times, he talked to me. When he saw my frustration with the steep inclines as I tried to push forward and then double over to catch my breath, he said, "Walk in a zigzag." He strolled, walking on an angle going one way and then the other. I imitated his movements. At times, when I looked for him, Alex was beside me, behind me, or in front of me, allowing me space to take it all in.

As dawn appeared, I started asking, "Where is the rainbow?" Alex responded, "On the other side." A vague reference to the other side of the large rock formation ahead of us. I refocused my attention on my surroundings and noticed a black dog approaching us. He was friendly; I remember petting him and thinking fondly how much I enjoyed having a dog growing up. Periodically, the dog would disappear and reappear in front of us. He was so relaxed as he walked effortlessly, and I was jealous. He reminded me of the patience and obedience to the process that I needed to embody in this moment. The dog would lie and wait for us to catch up before he continued up the mountain. He led the way to the rainbow.

As the end of the hike neared, I realized I had to stop looking ahead for Alex, the dog, and the rainbow. I thought back to my long-distance cycling days. I reminded myself: *Slow and steady, focusing right in front of me, staying in the present moment.* I could hear Alex's voice in the distance, saying, "You are almost there." His voice sounded closer with each step, but I was not ready to look up until I took that last step and turned to see the rainbow-colored mountain at 16,800 feet. It was cloudy, and the colors weren't as vibrant as I had seen in pictures, but I wasn't at all disappointed. We were the first two to reach the summit that day. At that moment, I felt free and whole, and I realized I was the brightness on the mountain. What I was looking for was within me all along. I just had to surrender to it.

I was amazed by what I had just overcome. It was at that moment that I realized the hike was a meditative experience. Each step of that almost three-hour journey was a walking meditation. I had put the formula I learned into practice without even being conscious of it. The art of settling my body down by regulating my breathing and tuning into my environment was meditation. The feeling of the ground underneath my boots and the changing terrain was a meditation. The feeling of the wind blowing across my face, the chill in my hands, and the warmth from the sun was a meditation. Taking it all in without judgment was meditation. Unconsciously, I began to trust my body again, and in that time of reflection, I felt my heart swell and fill with an overwhelming sense of gratitude and joy. Through the process of being present, accepting the conditions as they were, and surrendering, I had a transformational experience. I looked back on all those times I could not use my left hand, and for the entire hike, I did so without any sensations of pain or limitations in movement. Somehow, amid surrender, I found courage that I didn't realize was within me.

As I sat there, it dawned on me that those feelings were the elevated emotions attached to those intentions that I had set two weeks before in Bogota, at a meditation retreat. I had just accomplished three out of four of those intentions. I could hear the words of Dr. Joe in my head. When you marry an elevated emotion with a clear intention ... What I realized was that the marrying of the two was more of a magnifier, a multiplier. That is how powerful it was for me. Those heavy emotions of fear, anger, and frustration that I used to feel could not have led me to this place. I started out on a hike and what I received was much more than I could have ever imagined. I reconnected with my body, mind, and spirit and reclaimed abundance. This experience reinforced my belief in possibilities past what the doctor believed. It was like another seed of hope was planted. This is not the end, but a new beginning, and I now get to meet each new day with curiosity and wonder. Embracing movement was a vital component of healing. I now feel empowered to take an active role in my own well-being and facilitate a holistic and comprehensive path to recovery and I want you to do the same. I returned home and immediately asked the doctor to wean me off my medication. Each time my dosage was lowered, I'll admit, I was nervous, but I needed to try. I could go back on the medication. It wasn't that the idea that medication was bad but it wasn't the only answer. I had to find a balance between traditional and holistic medicine.

Each day we have a choice, no matter how limited those choices seem. Moving is about action. Action toward a new reality. You get to use your life-changing experience as the initiation into a new life. My mission is to change the lives of 500+ individuals who are living with chronic pain conditions by coaching them into new possibilities. My approach is all about an aware mind, an attuned body, and an awakened spirit. What you'll learn is how to synchronize your body and mind, shift your attention and set new intentions, and honor the power of your ancestors while creating a new reality.

In this life, we can be the person in need of healing or dare to be the healer. What helped me move toward this new role was my spirit being unsettled, a willingness to believe in other possibilities, and approaching this challenge with curiosity. I found success mastering chronic pain. And the journey continues. I have to keep going, even when I'm unsure of the outcome or effectiveness. The data that supports the power of meditation was encouraging, but by itself, this information didn't change me. It was my willingness to move toward a new reality. I urge you to see scientific results as hopeful but hope only transforms into possibilities through action. You get to be the evidence and proof. Through the power of movement, you get to illuminate your mind and spirit. Even my own doctor was amazed and realized the power of what I was doing once I was weaned off the medication. I created a new reality not just for myself, but for those around me. I believe all it takes is one person having a breakthrough for others to believe in possibilities. I want to be that person for you and watch you do the same for those around you. It is important to note that the cost of chronic pain extends beyond the financial aspect and also includes the toll it takes on our relationships, work, and overall life satisfaction, as well as the mental/emotional and spiritual impact. We have much at stake. So, my question for you is: What actions are you willing to take to reclaim your abundance?

I have found that when individuals who are on a similar journey are able to support each other through the process, they can implement changes faster and take the next steps needed to raise their consciousness and move forward with a renewed sense of courage and power.

Movement is the essence of life. ~Anonymous

References

Young, Shinzen (1998-2017). Art Thought Process. Retrieved from https://www.shinzen.orgwp-content/uploads/2016/12/art_thought-process.pdf

Zuniga-Hertz, J. P., Chitteti, R., Dispenza, J., Cuomo, R., Bonds, J. A., Kopp, E. L., Simpson, S., Okerblom, J., Maurya, S., Rana, B. K., Miyonahara, A., Niesman, I. R., Maree, J., Belza, G., Hamilton, H. D., Stanton, C., Gonzalez, D. J., Poirier, M. A., Moeller-Bertram, T., & Patel, H. H. (2023). Meditation-induced bloodborne factors as an adjuvant treatment to COVID-19 disease. Brain, Behavior, & Immunity - Health, 32, 100675. https://doi.org/10.1016/j.bbih.2023.100675

Dr. Sabrina Nichole Crouch

Dr. Sabrina Nichole Crouch is a New York State Licensed Psychologist, speaker, coach, and author. Dr. Crouch has over 25 years of experience working with children and families in New York City and Westchester County.

Dr. Crouch holds a doctorate in School-Clinical Child Psychology from Yeshiva University, a master's and advanced certification in School Psychology from City College of NY, and a bachelor's from Syracuse University. She is also an American Board of School Neuropsychology Diplomate.

Despite all these accomplishments, she is most proud of her own journey from managing to mastering a chronic pain condition and believes in an integrated mind-body-spirit approach as the key to transformation and finding true freedom. Sabrina wrote *Surrendering to Rainbows: The Art and Science of Quieting the Noise of Chronic*

Pain about her unexpected journey to healing that led her to Rainbow Mountain in Peru.

She inspires audiences to believe in possibilities, transform pain into purpose, and live every day to the fullest. Sabrina offers a fresh perspective on the art and science of healing. Her new podcast titled *F**k Being Stuck* is all about sharing stories of how others overcame life's challenges and the badass practitioners that are changing the way we look at health. When Sabrina is not helping others, she can be found meditating, hiking with her dog Phoenix, gardening, and traveling the world with friends and family.

Connect with Dr. Crouch at www.drsabrinanichole.com.

The Eight Energetic Laws of Money

by Micaela Bellopede

---

*I dedicate this chapter to my son for reminding me to play
more and see the miracles everywhere.*

Law #1: The Law of Manifestation ~ Ask For More
Law #2: The Law of Attraction ~ Like Attracts Like
Law #3: The Law of Circulation ~ What You Give Returns
to You Multiplied
Law #4: The Law of Tithing ~ Give 10% Away
Law #5 The Law of Use ~ Use It or Lose It
Law #6: The Law of Focus ~ What You Focus on Expands
Law #7: The Law of Vacuum ~ Make Room for More Money
Law #8 ~ The Law of Affirmation: Your Words
Create Your Future

Law #1 ~ The Law of Manifestation: Ask For More

Manifesting means to create something or turn something from an idea
into a reality.

The Law of Manifestation states: Ask and You Shall Receive.

You may have heard of this Law before, but look at how/if you are putting it into practice.

Whatever you call it God/Source/Creator, there is an energetic force in the universe and IT is the source of our supply. Be clear, you are not the source of your money. That is a fallacy. Your job is to follow your soul's purpose and receive what is yours by Divine Right.

When we think we are the source of our money, we experience a state of lack and stress. We move into a state of chasing money. That is the opposite of manifesting. Manifesting is based on TRUST in a higher power to co-create with us.

Here are the steps I follow to manifest anything:

1. Make a very clear, specific request.
2. Ask for MORE than what feels comfortable.
3. Always add, "This or something better."
4. Follow your intuitive leads (hunches) and **take action.**
5. Trust that the Universe will deliver what you've asked for.
6. Do exercises to practice being open and receptive to the ABUNDANT flow of the universe.
7. Celebrate every time the Universe delivers something you've asked for.
8. Write out a list of all the things you are grateful for every day.

Making clear and specific requests is something you must practice. Don't ask for "a job." Ask for a specific job. How much do you want to earn? What field do you want to work in? How do you want to feel in your job? What kind of boss do you want? Colleagues? What kind of benefits do you want? How many days of vacation? Do you want to work at home or in an office? These are some examples. Follow this rule for everything you want to manifest, be it a partner/home/business/job, etc. The more detail you write, the easier it is for the universe to bring it to you.

Ask for More ~

Most people are trained from a young age to think small. Thousands of years of socialization have taught people to think and act like their parents/grandparents/teachers. If you ask for what your parents had, you will manifest the same level of income. I am giving you the opportunity to think BIGGER. Make bolder requests. Ask for more than feels comfortable for you. Stretch yourself. In my book, *Happiness Is Not a Destination* (see link in bio), I share a poignant story that illustrates this point. When I was traveling in Thailand, I went to the ATM machine to get cash from my Visa card. The machine kept saying, "Transaction declined." I was stuck in Bangkok, alone, with no money. I sat down on the street and cried. I felt desperate and prayed for help. In a city full of thousands of people, at that very moment, a man I knew happened to walk by and see me on the street corner. He offered to loan me some money so I could get to the airport to fly home the next day. (Remember, ask, and you shall receive.) The next morning the bank was open, so I went in to ask the bank teller why my card was being declined. I will never forget her words …

She said, "You didn't ask for enough. You need to ask for MORE money." I did and out flew the bills from the machine.

The universe is filled with an abundant supply of all things. Look around in nature and you will see the bounty everywhere.

Lack is a man-made concept. Free your mind and the money flows like water to the sea.

Law #2 ~ The Law of Attraction: Like Attracts Like

Like energy always attracts to it the same frequency. If you want to be rich, you need to act/think/do as a rich person would act. First, look at who you spend the most time with. Are you surrounded by successful people or people who are stuck in poverty consciousness or victim mentality? They say you become like the five people you spend the most time with, so be very choosy about your friends. I cannot emphasize enough how important this is. It is like smoking, if you want to quit, don't spend all your time with smokers. It is almost impossible to break a bad habit unless you have support from your friends and your network.

Read the autobiographies of successful people and you will see common themes. Many successful people left their towns/cities/families to expand their horizons. My father left his small town in Italy to come to America to create a new life. He taught me that you can start from nothing and become wealthy. This lesson is powerful. There will be people you need to walk away from. And situations you will need to say NO to.

One of my favorite axioms is: Don't settle for good when you can have GREAT.

Like attracts like. So seek out mentors, coaches, and teachers who know more and have more. Look at the results not words. There are some coaches who advertise themselves as money gurus but are actually broke. Learn from people who have manifested what you want.

Another trick I like to use is called "The Benjamins Game."

"Benjamins," are $100 dollar bills. Carry a clean, fresh, new $100 bill with you always. The Benjamins attract the Benjamins. Having $100 in your pocket or wallet will make you feel richer. Go to stores that sell things you want and try them on. Go test-drive that Tesla! Try on those dresses and jewels. It's free to try them on. Feel like you are wealthy.

Have fun with this, and do experiments. I recommend the book: E2 by Pam Grout, it is full of exercises to attract things you desire.

When you act/think/feel rich, you will attract wealth to you. It is an absolute certainty.

Law #3 ~ The Law of Circulation: What You Give Out Returns to You Multiplied

This law stated another way: What comes around, goes around. You get back what you give: Literally. So pay close attention to what you are giving out in the world.

If you give time, you will receive time.
If you give food, you will receive food.
If you give cash, you will receive cash.
If you give kindness, you will receive kindness.
If you give anger, you will receive anger.
If you give fear, you will receive fear.

I have experienced many examples of this law in interesting ways. For example, in 2001, I quit my job and gave away all of my furniture to go backpacking around the world. Some people thought I was crazy to give up a tenured teaching position. But I was so unhappy at my job, it was making me sick. My boyfriend and I set off to 12 countries and manifested a way to pay for the whole trip. We got teaching jobs in Korea for two months with all expenses paid, including our plane tickets. We worked for two months and traveled for 10 months. Upon returning to the USA, I got a better job than the one I had before AND an apartment with NEW furniture. The exact same thing happened in 2021 when I sold my house in California. I gave away all of my furniture again. When I got to Florida, I found the perfect house fully furnished with brand-new furniture. It all came back to me in a UPGRADED form. It doesn't matter what I give away, it always comes back to me. The gifts don't always come back from the same person you give them to, but they always come back. Try it today. Give something away and watch how it returns to you. Be open to receiving it from any source, even finding it on the ground. It will come.

You can't outgive the universe.

Law #4 ~ The Law of Tithing: Give 10% of Your Income Away

You may have heard of this law in the Bible or other spiritual texts. The amount of tithing 10% of one's income has been practiced for thousands of years. There are several reasons why this Law is important. Don't skip over it. You might think it isn't necessary. However, many people have manifested large amounts of money and then lost it all. Tithing helps the world, but it also helps you. It is a PROTECTIVE energy over your assets.

Every time you do something good for others, it comes back to you. Tithing is just an extension of this rule. It helps if you are specific in your giving. For example, one of my businesses is in real estate, therefore, I tithe money to Habitat For Humanity to help people rebuild their homes after floods/hurricanes/fires, etc. Whatever your business is, I encourage you to give money to help others in this same field. It doesn't have to be your only tithe, you can divide your tithing up to various organizations. But do it **consistently**. This is the key. If your giving is consistent, so is your money flow. I do an auto-tithe, which means that it comes out automatically from my bank account each month, so I don't even have to think about it.

When I created The Miraclecatcher Foundation in 2009, I was a teacher with a salary of under 40K per year. It doesn't matter how much you make, what matters is that you give 10% of it. Over the years, the Miraclecatcher Foundation has grown and so have my businesses. What started as one person helping one school for orphans in a small village in Uganda has grown to help thousands of children in over 22 countries. Some people think that being wealthy is bad. Having more money just makes you more of who you already are. If you are generous, you become more generous. If you are greedy, you become more greedy.

My goal is to give away <u>one</u> million dollars to help <u>one</u> million children. And when I reach that goal, I will ask for <u>one</u> billion.

What could you do with <u>one</u> billion dollars?

How many people could you help?

How would the world be different if we all did this?

By helping and protecting people in need, you help and protect yourself.

It's a win-win for everyone.

Law #5 ~ The Law of Use: Use It or Lose It

This Law is self-explanatory. Money is meant to be USED or circulated.

This doesn't mean you can't have a savings or investment account. It means that a portion of your income needs to be spent.

I know many entrepreneurs who are sole proprietors. This means that they work alone. This sounds great, but it doesn't always generate much money. Here's why. When I started my photography business in 2005, I tried to do it all by myself. I printed, edited, framed, and shot all the photos myself. I thought I was saving money, but I was actually blocking my own money flow. Once I took on larger clients, I realized that I couldn't afford to spend hours printing and editing each photo. So I began to outsource jobs to printing companies that had more equipment and more staff to get the job done faster and better.

As my business expanded, I learned to delegate better. Delegating gave me more freedom and more time. Plus it helped others by giving them money to use for their families. I have really come to appreciate the Law of Use. Paying others to help me isn't just good for me and my businesses, it helps my community. Every successful business needs a great team behind it. I have many people I pay to support me now: babysitters, gardeners, accountants, lawyers, plumbers, property managers, etc. Every time I pay my team members, I am circulating money into the economy, and thus, back to myself.

Being a solo act is not only exhausting, but it is actually counterproductive. This law says use it or lose it. In other words, if you don't use your money, the flow will stagnate. Like water in a pipe, it needs to FLOW.

Another key area to look at is how much you are using your money for fun or pleasure. We live in a culture that is focused on GO/GET/HUSTLE but not on enjoying the ride. Some people live for work. However, the truth is that we work so we can live.

How often do you take vacations?

How often do you take a full day off?

How often do you pamper yourself?

What is the point of having money if you aren't going to enjoy it?

Use your wealth to enjoy life. Use it to help others. And use it to help the planet. Money loves fun. Money loves to play, so lighten up and use some of that hard-earned cash on yourself.

You absolutely deserve it.

Law #6 ~ The Law of Focus: What You Focus On Expands

What you focus on expands so start focusing on your money!

Track Your Money.

Track your funnels and create new ones.

Track your spending to see where the money is going.

Track your action steps to see how far you come and where you want to go. Track how much time you are spending on each job/client.

Pay attention! Many people have no idea how much time they are wasting on things that yield no tangible result, like scrolling through social media.

Money is just a number and numbers don't mean anything except the meaning we put into them.

When you track the numbers you get more familiar with them, and you stop resisting them. Think of statistics as your friends. I used to resist keeping track of my earnings and spending because I thought it was tedious. Now, I love seeing all the money coming in from various sources and all the wonderful things I am using it for.

I also love to make lists. I don't add 55 things to my daily list, I add three. Three actions a day consistently over time create massive results. Look at what Michaelangelo accomplished in four years painting the ceiling of The Sistine Chapel.

Life is a marathon, not a sprint. Pace yourself.

What you are focusing on is expanding. So focus on the GOOD.

When I write down all the things I have created over the past year, I am blown away. The results show me that the universe is indeed working in my favor. Moreover, it builds my confidence. Every success allows me to take bigger risks. It is called "The Poker Chip Theory of Success." You take risks in correlation to how many successes you have had in life. Looking at the stats on paper shows me all of my wins. Even if I have momentary doubts, I can look at the numbers and see what is real. The "Monkey Mind," tries to play tricks on our self-esteem, but the numbers don't lie.

Tracking your stats = Tracking your success.

Furthermore, focus on the data with gratitude. Make a list of all of your clients and how grateful you are for them. Focus on the cash flow coming in with joy. Look at how many people you have been able to help by sharing your wealth. Acknowledge yourself for how much you have accomplished.

Another thing I love to track is **UNEXPECTED** income. It is a game I play. Every morning I wake up and ask for unexpected gifts and then track them as they show up. One time I found $100 balled up on the pavement. (Thank you, universe, bring me more of this!) Sometimes unexpected gifts show up as flowers, books, prizes, refunds, upgrades, etc. I write it all down and am grateful for it. You can also pay it forward to give someone else an unexpected gift, such as buying coffee for the person in line next to you, leaving a big tip, or feeding someone's parking meter. It's so much fun!

Also, remember not to put much attention to negative things because they will expand, too. I am not saying to ignore your problems. I am saying don't worry about them. Got a burst pipe? Fix it. Got an employee who is constantly late or disrespectful? Give him/her a consequence. Whatever you do, stay focused on the solution. Make sure that most of your time and energy is going towards things that are moving you forward, not backward.

In my experience, the universe will always bring a solution to a problem if you ask for it and are open to all the possibilities. It might not come in the form you expected, but it will come.

Remember, what you are focusing on is expanding, so focus on what you want more of. Leave the rest for the manager upstairs to handle.

Law #7 ~ The Law of Vacuum: The Universe Will Fill an Empty Space

I like to call this the "Marie Condo Law." Clean out your wallet, your car, your desk, and your house in order to make room for more money to come in.

When I taught in the Business Program at the University of California at San Diego, I used to tell my students on the first day of class, "Take out your wallet and I will tell you about your relationship with money."

How you keep your money is a reflection of how you feel about it.

Is your wallet crammed tight with old receipts?

Is your desk filled with stacks of old papers and bills?

Is your inbox filled with unread emails and incomplete tasks?

The Universe LOVES a clear, clean space where it can CREATE. In fact, the ancient Chinese practice of Feng Shui is based on this Law.

This same principle works for your mind as well. A cluttered mind is not a space for manifesting miracles.

Here are some simple tools to get money FLOWING FREELY into your life.

Right now, pull out your wallet and do the following:

Clear out all receipts and business cards that are not necessary. The only things in my wallet are cash, cards, one photo and one affirmation card.

How big is your wallet? Is it large enough to hold more cash?

If not, buy a new one. What does it look like? Is it old, torn, dirty?

Don't expect wealth to come into a messy or cluttered space

This is true for your home, your car, and your office. All areas must be cleaned out to bring more in. People often report that within minutes of cleaning their desks, they get calls from new clients. No joke!

Law #8 ~ The Law of Affirmation: Your Words Create Your Future

You are what you think and what you say. Your life is an out-picturing of your conscious and subconscious thoughts. In other words, you are creating your own reality, both the good and the bad. This is a bitter pill to swallow. But the faster you accept it, the faster you can create the life you want.

There are several steps when it comes to affirmation.

Always state your affirmation in the positive.

I am. I have. I create.

For example:

I am wealthy beyond measure.

I have a beautiful home near the beach which I can easily afford.

I create multiple streams of income every day.

Always state the reality you desire as if it is already done.

Write it. Say it. Sing it. Dance it over and over again until it overrides any negative subconscious patterns.

My greatest teachers on the power of affirmation are Lousie Hay and Florence Scovel Shinn. They have written countless books on the power of affirmation and how it has changed people's lives.

For me personally, I like to make up affirmations that are easy to remember and repeat, such as:

"I am healthy, wealthy, happy, loved."

"Money comes to me from expected and unexpected sources."

"My income and net worth are constantly increasing."

Write affirmations on your mirror or use post-it notes all over the house. Listen to affirmations in the car or while you are walking or dancing.

Whatever you want to create, say it over and over again.

Don't say: "I want." It just keeps you in a state of wanting.

Don't say: "Maybe or Might." These words create doubt or confusion.

Act as if it is already done.

Make your affirmations clear and specific. It is a prayer for the universe. Just like the *Law of Attraction*, ask for what you want in great detail and add the words, "This or something better."

Don't get too attached to the dates. The universe has its own timing. You can ask for help if you really need to pay a bill by a certain time but be open to how that is going to show up. It may show up in a totally different way than you expect. SMART Goals have a specific date attached, such as, "I will be CEO of my own company by March of 2025." I do recommend setting a date. It helps give the universe clarity. However, not all of my requests have shown up on my schedule. Sometimes the universe has a better plan. I make many requests every day to the Bank of the Universe. I write down 100 requests at a time. This way, I can clearly see all that is manifesting. When one thing appears, I cross it off my list and add another. The mistake I see many people make is that they ask for <u>one</u> big item. If that item doesn't show up right away, they think the Law isn't working. By making more requests, big and small, you will see that the universe is indeed listening to your orders and fulfilling them.

Another tool I have used as a hypnotherapist is to make a recording of my affirmations and play it as I am about to fall asleep when my mind is in a very receptive state. Remember that our subconscious mind is running about 80-90% of the show, so we must get the subconscious on the same page. If you say you're rich, but you are subconsciously afraid of being more successful than your parents, you will sabotage yourself. This takes time and practice. You must do the work to identify what your core beliefs are around money and keep affirming positive outcomes to transform any limiting beliefs. Keep affirming and believing, you will see results. To shift subconscious beliefs around money, I recommend listening to Abraham Hicks or Tony Robbins.

To conclude, I invite you to implement **ALL** of these practices right away. Make it into a game. Money loves fun! These are just some of the energetic laws of money. You can find more exercises and resources in my book: *Happiness Is Not a Destination* (link in bio). I have practiced these laws consistently over many years and they have yielded remarkable results. The key is ***consistency***. Money is like a muscle; it needs to be exercised every day. I am not offering a magical cure. You must do the work and keep at it. Practice makes perfect.

I hope that these suggestions have value for you and that you create a life you love. We all deserve to be happy, healthy, and enjoy an abundant life.

Godspeed on your journey.

Micaela Bellopede

Micaela Bellopede, M.Ed, MIEM, CHt, C.IET, is an international author, philanthropist, entrepreneur eco-designer, and motivational speaker. She holds a master's degree in education and a master's degree in international economics and management. She has lived in 7 countries and speaks 5 languages. Over the past 25 years, Micaela has built several successful businesses, served as a life coach, and created The Miraclecatcher Foundation, a non-profit organization, promoting creativity and building schools around the world. She taught writing and business at the University of California San Diego for 10 years and was nominated for the Who's Who in Education.

Find Micaela's book, "Happiness Is Not A Destination" on Amazon at https://amzn.to/48fyxRy.

CHAPTER 13

Step 7—Embodiment

Success is not the key to happiness. Happiness is the key to success. If you love what you are doing, you will be successful.
~Albert Schweitzer

Embodiment is a celebration of your journey from intention to realization, from aspiration to actualization. It's the culmination of your efforts and the realization of your vision of abundance. In this chapter, we explore what life looks like on the other side, once you've implemented the framework and embraced abundance in its purest form.

The Unburdened Journey

At this stage, you've moved beyond the heavy lifting of creating abundance. The foundational laws, strategies, and practices have become ingrained in your daily life. The sense of struggle and striving has given way to a state of flow and alignment.

Room for Philanthropy

With your own abundance secured, you now have the capacity to extend your blessings to others. Philanthropy becomes a natural extension of your abundant life. You can make a meaningful impact in your community and beyond, contributing to causes that resonate with your values.

Community Building

Abundance is not just about personal gain; it's about creating a thriving ecosystem around you. You have the opportunity to foster a sense of community, to bring together like-minded individuals who share your values and vision. Together, you can create a supportive network that uplifts everyone.

Legacy-Building

Embodiment is also the stage where you begin to contemplate the legacy you want to leave behind. It's about defining the impact you want to have on the world and taking intentional steps to bring that vision to fruition. Legacy-building is a testament to the mark you wish to leave on this world.

The Joy of Abundance

At this point, you're not just living in abundance; you're embodying it. Abundance is not merely a state of material wealth but a state of mind and heart. It's a deep sense of fulfillment, purpose, and joy in everything you do.

A Life of Alignment

Embodiment signifies that your life is in alignment with your true self and your highest values. It's a life where you are unapologetically yourself, where you live with intention and integrity. It's a life of congruence, where your actions mirror your beliefs.

The Continuous Journey

While Embodiment represents a significant milestone, it's essential to remember that the journey of abundance is continuous. Just as a river keeps flowing, your life keeps evolving. Abundance is not a static destination; it's a dynamic, ever-expanding experience.

Your Unique Path

Your path to Embodiment is as unique as you are. It's a path that unfolds with intention, resilience, and unwavering commitment. As you step into the embodiment of abundance, you become a beacon of inspiration and possibility for others. Your journey serves as a testament to the transformative power of intention, commitment, and the Anatomy Of Abundance™ Framework.

May your life be a testament to the boundless potential of the human spirit, and may you continue to inspire and uplift those who walk the path of abundance alongside you.

How to Amplify and Embody Financial Abundance: Practical Steps to Empower You to Live Abundantly

by Carolynn Bottino

What would be possible if you stopped being afraid of not having enough?

Your Money Story

Every single one of us has a money story. The stories you carry around influence just about every thought you have about money. How you earn, receive, spend, manage, save and splurge is a result of your stories. They impact what you think about people who are rich, and people who are poor. Your money stories are a big part of how you experience abundance.

The relationship you have with money is formed by the family you were born into, the neighborhoods you grew up in, friends you hung out with, and your own personality and perceptions that make up how you interpret your experiences with money. Just as siblings can be so alike or so different, each of us has a unique relationship with money that is not necessarily defined by the amount of money we have, the opportunities we have been given or denied, or the financial situations we find ourselves experiencing.

And no matter what your story is…

- you can choose to live an abundant life,
- you can choose to find joy in your relationship with money, and
- you can choose how to interact with money.

When we make an educated choice about how we interact with money and the stories we believe about money, we empower ourselves to open the door to live an abundant life.

Fear and the Lie of Scarcity

Remember the early days of COVID when people were hoarding toilet paper? Everywhere you turned, people were full of fear.

What if I run out?
What if I can't get more?

It was like scarcity on steroids.

But think about this for a moment: There was just as much toilet paper in the world in April of 2020 as there was in January before the pandemic began. The actual need for toilet paper had not increased, and the ability for the toilet paper manufacturers to produce more toilet paper hadn't changed either.

So, why did it feel so different? The toilet paper was sitting in someone's storage room rather than on the grocery store shelf.

Toilet paper is a lot like money. Money didn't disappear, the flow just temporarily slowed because people were afraid to spend. People began holding on to their money for fear they were going to run out and they wouldn't be able to get more, but there was just as much money out there as there was before. Our ability to make and have money didn't go away – it just shifted.

Sometimes fear blocks us from seeing the truth about money. Fear is what keeps us from experiencing abundance because we feed into the lie of scarcity, feeling like there won't be enough. But the truth is *there is always enough*. We always have the ability to make more money. The Universe is constantly expanding, and so is our ability to generate money.

When we make the choice to live abundantly, we are choosing to see life through the lens of possibility and plenty. In order to live an abundant life, we have to let go of fear and scarcity and unlearn the stories that are holding us back.

My Money Story: Lessons in Unlearning and Leaning Into What's Possible

As a bookkeeper, I have the honor and privilege of witnessing hundreds of people and their intimate relationships with money. Believe me, I've seen every single emotion possible around money. Fear. Guilt. Shame. I've also witnessed money to be joyful, empowering, and full of possibility.

I've felt ALL of these emotions around money as well. **But** it wasn't until I was willing to dig into my own money story that I saw how fear blinded me from what's possible.

I was born in middle America to a middle-class family in the middle of the 1970s. We weren't rich; we weren't poor. Both of my parents were entrepreneurs and I learned at a very young age about **working really hard**.

The last "real" job I had before I started my business was running an event center that was operated by a non-profit. We had about 130 events per year, with 75% of those being weddings. And no surprise - I worked really hard, just as I had learned from my parents.

Around year four of running the event center, I was given a second building to manage. I was working HARDER than ever. My workload had essentially doubled, although my pay remained the same.

It took me a *year* before I got the courage to ask my boss for a much-deserved raise. It felt so awkward, greedy, and shameful to ask for more money, but I simply couldn't keep working at that pace without being fairly compensated.

I outlined my case with all that I had accomplished to date. I held back what I *really* wanted to ask for, and suggested a 25% increase, although I knew there was three times that amount in the budget. My boss came back and offered me a *FOUR* percent raise.

As you can imagine, I was shocked, hurt, and furious all at the same time.

After a few agonizing and sleepless nights, I decided to stand up for myself and drew the line in the sand.

"I'm not willing to work for free," I courageously told my boss.

The next day he walked into my office and fired me.

OH MY GOD!

What am I going to do without a paycheck and health insurance?

I worked so hard, doesn't that mean anything?

What happened in the next couple of days was life-changing. Instead of looking for a "stable" job where another boss could underappreciate my work, I started asking myself soul-searching questions.

The simple question, "What should I do?," opened up so much space and possibility. That question turned into many more over the following weeks.

- What do I love to do?
- What skill sets do I have that I would like to share with the world?

- If I could spend my day doing anything and get paid for doing it, what would I choose?
- What does an ideal day look like for me?
- What would l like to be paid?
- If money were no object, what would I do with my time?

Those questions gave me my first glimpse of what I like to call **The Land of Plenty** - a world where I can **choose** what is possible for my future instead of being afraid of not having enough.

Within a week of getting fired, I made the decision to open my own bookkeeping and event planning business, All The Details Consulting.

Ten years later, I now have a *life I love*. My husband and I moved to San Diego which I had dreamed about for over a decade. I'm making a LOT more money, and I'm not working as hard.

Although... it took a lot of soul searching and more hard work to get to this place. It's not like the day I got fired and decided to become an entrepreneur, I *magically* left behind my belief that I had to work really hard to make money. If anything, that story only amplified.

As a new business owner, my hard work paid off at first. I quickly grew my business to 40 plus clients, and made more money than I ever had before. It felt like amazing success!

There was *just* one problem – I didn't have any time to enjoy the life I was creating! I was just repeating the same patterns as an entrepreneur that I had as an employee. Nothing had changed. I was still working REALLY HARD to earn money.

I would get up at 5:00 am and get right to work. I was working nights and weekends to get it all done. I loved hiking in the hills behind my house, but was I getting out? NO! My clients' needs *always* came first.

I was operating in a state of fear, feeling if I didn't work really hard, I wouldn't have enough clients and, therefore, I wouldn't have enough money. To make sure that didn't happen, I underpriced my services and over delivered.

Eventually, this led to another problem. I ended up with more clients than I could handle. Sounds like a great problem, but I didn't have the systems in place to support the number of clients I was attracting. I just worked even harder.

I was living in the Land of Scarcity and Lack. For me my lack-of-money story was amplified by my lack-of-time story.

I was hovering just below that *elusive 6-figure mark*. No matter how hard I tried, it always seemed just out of my reach. The thought of taking on even more clients to reach this goal was exhausting.

*How could I **possibly** fit one more client into my busy workload?*

So I raised my prices just a bit, without being "too greedy" hoping clients would self-select and fall away. One big problem — *No one* left.

I knew the only way to increase my income was to hire someone to help with the workload, but I didn't want to complicate my business model, and I didn't want to take the time to train and manage someone. I was *afraid* of giving up control.

I was exhausted and overwhelmed but didn't see any other way to run my business.

The truth? I was self-sabotaging my success. The belief I had to work really hard was running the show. I feared no one else could do it like me.

My money story stopped me from moving forward. I stopped networking and seeking out new opportunities because I simply didn't have the bandwidth.

Something had to change.

In spring of 2017, I was cleaning out my inbox and the word "Soulpreneur" caught my eye. My client's colleague was hosting a three-day event called Ignite. Somehow I knew I had to be there.

At the time, I was very apprehensive about spending three days working on my business. How would I ever take the time out of my busy schedule? But I followed my intuition and signed up.

What happened over those three days was nothing short of magical. While the event's main focus was on marketing, it really was about possibility and **asking questions that opened up space for transformation**.

It was in that space of possibility that I met a business coach that combined *systems, strategy and soul* by working in the Akashic records. Honestly, I did not go to Ignite looking for a business coach, let alone a business coach with woo. Up until that point, I had never thought I needed a coach. After all, I was successfully bringing in clients left and right. Why would I pay for a coach to help me expand this ever-growing problem?

But this somehow felt different. I followed my intuition and hired her.

Over the next six months, we worked to lay out the foundations of my future and I transformed into a *soulpreneur* **and I FOUND my Land of Plenty.**

- I unlearned my belief that I had to work really hard and I hired a team to support me.
- I unlearned putting my clients' needs before my own and restructured my business so I could GO on my daily hikes and have time to enjoy my life.
- I worked on my money mindset and invested in myself and my business through coaching and courses.
- I let go of clients who were no longer a good fit and didn't bring me joy.
- But most importantly, I STOPPED being afraid of not having enough - enough time, enough clients, enough money. I left scarcity at the door and **walked into The Land of Plenty**.

You see, it wasn't just about making money – I discovered my soul's calling to inspire women to rise up and embrace their money power.

My leader within emerged and I gave birth to a movement. I opened a second business, The Money Empowerment Project, to help others transform and find their own Land of Plenty.

Amazing things happen when we stop being afraid.

When I finally reached my six-figure goal, to my surprise and delight, it didn't happen by working hard. It was a direct result of unlearning the stories that no longer served me, leaning into possibilities and letting go of fear.

What's so crazy was the more I stopped working hard and being afraid of not having enough, the easier it became to make money. It was only through letting go of fear and unlearning that I was able to embody abundance.

Since that year, my business has flourished, growing over 20% each year. The last 45 days of 2020 I brought in more income than I made in an entire year when I was managing the event center. And in 2021, I officially became a multi-six figure business owner.

I'm sharing the details of my success because it's time we *change* the conversation about how much we make – no matter the dollar amount – from one of secrecy and shame to one of *celebration*. I want to celebrate not only my success, but ***all my fellow soulpreneurs'*** success as well. When you live abundantly, celebration of yourself and others comes naturally.

My success is a direct result of **embodying abundance**. I follow my intuition in *everything* I do. How I invest in my business, the clients I choose to work with, the vendors I hire - it is all done from a place of standing in my power and asking what is possible. I no longer allow fear to make the decisions. I know there's always enough. I now live in The Land of Plenty.

The Flow of Money

One of the most important lessons in how to embody and amplify abundance is understanding the flow of money.

"Money is a lot like water. It flows in and out of our lives. It can gush like a raging river or come through our lives like a tiny little trickle."

These wise words were spoken by a woman named Gertrude, a housekeeper from Harlem. Her story comes from *The Soul of Money* by Lynne Twist, one of my all-time favorite money books. While Gertrude didn't have much money and would be considered poor by most people's standards, she knew she had the power to let money flow into her life and pass it on in a way that made the world a better place. The night Lynne Twist met Gertrude, she generously let the $50 she made that day washing clothes flow through her as a donation to end world hunger.

I've thought a lot about Gertrude's story over the past couple of years, and I have to agree. Money *is* a lot like water. When we spend money, it doesn't disappear. It moves and flows like water to the next person who is receiving it and, eventually, it flows back to us.

What would be possible if we were more conscious about the flow of our money?

Instead of waiting for it to flow in, and unconsciously letting it flow out, how would our world be different if we all spent and received money in a way that made the world a better place?

One of the most important acknowledgments we can make with our money is knowing we have the power to use money for good. We each have a choice about how we interact with money, and when we spend in a way that supports people and causes we care about, we change the world. I know this sounds big, but follow the flow of money with me for just a moment.

Say I have $100 and I pay my hairdresser to cut my hair. If I lived in a world of scarcity, I would think the money is gone. But there is so much more to the story!

- My hairdresser takes the $100 and buys flowers for her mom.
- The flower shop owner uses the $100 to buy concert tickets.
- The concert venue spends $100 to advertise in a local magazine, that just so happens to be my client.
- The magazine spends the $100 on bookkeeping services so the $100 returns to me.

The coolest thing about the flow of money is that the same $100 has multiplied five times and has turned into $500 of income for five different people, and each person has received something in return.

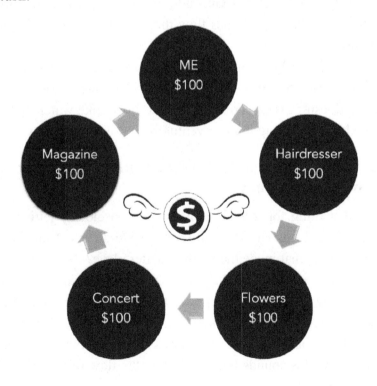

This is an example of what I call a micro-community and illustrates how quickly and easily money can regenerate, multiply, and flow. It is the most simplistic way to look at the energy behind money. You see, money is simply a tool that allows us to barter and trade. Money is a piece of paper that symbolizes the energy you expend providing a service, or the gratitude you feel for the service someone provides to you.

The truth is, our economy is built on all of us generating service for one another. The flow of money relies on all of us spending and receiving.

The more money I spend with my clients, the more money my clients have to spend with me.

I love to think of this like reimbursements from the Universe. When I spend money deliberately, I know it will eventually flow back to me.

Knowing that money can quickly and easily regenerate and multiply *empowers* me. I know my ability to generate money no longer lives outside of me. It is no longer a source of fear.

I'm also not afraid to spend money because I know it's just a matter of time before the money I spend comes back to me.

So how do we embody and amplify abundance? Take deliberate action to make the money in our lives flow.

We *all* have the power to create more money.

I see the power of money flowing every single day as a bookkeeper. Each month as I am going through my clients' transactions, I see mutual clients spending money with one another. My event planner client is spending money with my florist client. My massage therapist client is spending money with my magazine client. And all of these clients are paying me to do their bookkeeping. And so the circle continues.

We all spend.

We all receive.

We all create more money.

We are all part of this circle.

It's incredibly powerful and empowering.

When we embody abundance, we understand how money multiplies and regenerates.

As a business owner in the Land of Scarcity and Lack, you may have a perception that people aren't willing or able to spend money. As a bookkeeper, I can assure you this is not true - I see first-hand how people spend their money.

When we are conscious and deliberate about how and where we spend our money, we can create our own micro-communities, which allows money to quickly and easily regenerate and multiply.

I used to have a strict rule of no trade. As the whirlwind of the pandemic unfolded, I was feeling the fear and uncertainty that every business owner was experiencing. I realized I needed coaching services to help me navigate the changes that were happening. But I was scared to spend the money. *What if I didn't have enough?*

Then I remembered that my coach mentioned she really wanted to go through my money mentoring program but needed to wait until she had the money.

So, we decided to purchase each other's services. We exchanged $3,333, which created $3,333 income for each of us, *and* we both received services we wanted and needed. How does it get better than that?

This has now become one of my favorite ways to do business. I love supporting other business owners by purchasing services I need, and I love having business owners purchase services from me.

Micro-communities can be as small as two people if you both need each other's services, or as big as a town or city. It may be five, ten, or

100 people. The magic happens when you are intentional about how you spend and receive.

Micro-communities can be a powerful way for you to generate and multiply money.

When we are scared to spend and live in fear that there will never be enough, we stop the natural flow of money. I am not saying it is irresponsible to save money, or to frivolously spend. Quite the contrary. I believe that conscious spending and receiving is one of the most empowering and transformative actions we can take to change the world. This is amplified, embodied, abundant living at its finest.

What can you do right now to embody and amplify the flow of money? Here are a few ideas to get you started.

- Hire a friend or someone in your network for services you need
- Ask yourself how you can be of service to others (paid and not paid) and take action!
- Buy from your local farmers markets and shop owners
- Seek out and encourage micro-communities that support you and your needs
- Bank at a local credit union or community bank

Money is always expanding. Because our ability to create and be of service is limitless, so is money. Money is infinite. Money loves to flow.

One of my favorite emojis on my phone is the money with angel wings. I love to think of money coming in and going out like a feather happily dancing in the wind.

If you trust in the flow and realize how money regenerates, it is simply a matter of time, and making some deliberate choices before the money you "spent" comes back to you.

Carolynn Bottino

Carolynn Bottino is the founder of the Money Empowerment Project and author of *The Land of Plenty: A Soulpreneur's Guide to Finding Joy, Possibility and Abundance through Money Empowerment*. After working with more than 100 bookkeeping clients, Carolynn realized that she was so much more than a bookkeeper and discovered her soul's calling to empower soulpreneurs to find joy in their relationship with money.

Carolynn is a truth guide for money. She walks her talk and serves as an example of how to live in The Land of Plenty, leading with her soul, and using her intuition to guide her business decisions. She loves to inspire others to find joy, possibility, and abundance in their lives and businesses.

Carolynn continues to follow her dreams and now lives in sunny San Diego with her husband and two cats. Her happy place is anywhere near water, and she believes she was a mermaid in a past life.

Connect with Carolynn at www.all-details.com.

EMBODIMENT — FOUNDATIONAL LAW

Money is Non-monogamous!

by Sunny De Leon

I dedicate this chapter to all of the educators, advisors, counselors, activists, and healers who paved the way for me to live in my truth today. I am eternally grateful for my family (both biological and chosen) who have supported me even when my wild ideas terrified you, I'm just getting started so buckle up! To my angel and north star, Maddy, who protects and guides me and still gives me that sisterly sass all the way from heaven, thank you for being you. Most importantly, to all the past versions of me who had no idea what would be on the other side of any scary leap you took, and yet you fiercely did it anyway, y'all the baddest bitches out there!

If you were to talk about money as if it were your partner, how would you describe your partnership? Are you happily married in a loving and secure relationship where money flows to you with ease and you trust that it is always there for you? Or maybe you're in a situationship where the two of you don't really communicate much, you're not putting in a whole lot of effort and you're receiving that same kind of energy in return. Maybe you're a needy partner who always worries that money is leaving you even though they show up for you consistently and you just spent a whole romantic, sexy weekend getaway together. Or worse, you might be in a toxic relationship where you mistreat and talk shit about this partner and you experience major conflict in ways that are detrimental to your wellbeing.

These are some of the thoughts I found myself exploring after having experienced a financial downturn that left me questioning my role in that relationship. Your relationship with money is just that, a relationship. Because it is a relationship, we actually approach it very similarly to the way we form close relationships. This happens in part because of our attachment styles (more on that) which lead us to replicate the same patterns in all of our relationships.

I have been in the mental health field for over a decade. I have served many roles including suicide hotline counselor, peer advisor, harm reduction facilitator, and social work therapist for BIPOC and Queer and Trans people. A lot of my work has centered on helping clients navigate interpersonal and intrapersonal relationships.

As I write this chapter, some of my most salient identities are Black, Latinx, first gen Dominican immigrant, Queer, Trans non-binary, non-monogamous, kinkster, neurodivergent, and mental health warrior. These identities and the process of owning them have informed my practice and tie into the transformative work I do to empower my clients to embody unapologetic self-love.

Before repairing your relationship with money, you need to understand your attachment patterns.

What is attachment theory?

Attachment theory is a psychological concept that helps us understand how our early relationships with caregivers shape all of our relationships.

Think of it as the blueprint for how we connect with others. Attachment styles fall under two main categories, secure and insecure. Folks with secure attachments feel comfortable with emotional intimacy and independence. They trust others and themselves, making it easier to build healthy relationships. I will focus on insecure attachments as they are the most common and typically where we experience the most relational challenges including with money.

There are 3 forms of insecure attachment:

Anxious Attachment: People here often worry about losing their partner's love and approval, and thus, seek constant reassurance. They may fear abandonment and can be overly dependent. During conflict, they might be described as clingy, or needy.

Some examples of how they communicate in conflict:
- "Do you still love me?"
- "Why haven't you texted me back? Are you mad at me?"
- "I can't handle this uncertainty; we need to talk right now."

Avoidant Attachment: These individuals tend to downplay the importance of emotional connection and independence. They tend to pride themselves on not needing anyone or asking for very little in relationships. During a conflict, they may be described as cold and uncaring.

Some examples of how they communicate in conflict:
- "You're smothering me, give me some space!"
- "Emotions are overrated; let's just move on and forget about it."
- "I don't see why this is such a big deal; you're so dramatic."

Disorganized Attachment: This comes with a mixture of anxiety, avoidance, and unpredictability. People in this category may want closeness but fear getting hurt, leading to unpredictable and sometimes chaotic behaviors in relationships. They tend to have push/pull dynamics with partners and give mixed messages. They might be skeptical when there are no active issues in the relationship and may be more inclined to create conflict in relationships.

Some examples of how they communicate in conflict:

- "I can't trust anyone to stay in my life, so I keep testing you to see if you'll leave me too."
- "I want to be close to you, but I also need my space. It's like I can't decide whether I want to be with you or not."
- "I need some time to think about us and figure things out. I just don't know about this relationship anymore."

These are just a few examples. Your attachment style does not define you, so don't get caught up in these definitions. Understanding your attachment style can help you improve your relationships overall and personal growth by recognizing patterns and making conscious choices to develop healthier connections.

Below are some of the ways these attachment patterns likely show up in your relationship to money.

Anxious Attachment with Money Can Look Like ...

- Excessive worry about money, even when there is no immediate financial threat.
- Tendency to overspend or engage in impulsive buying to soothe emotional distress.
- Difficulty setting boundaries with others, leading to financial exploitation.
- Inability to enjoy the present moment due to constant preoccupation with financial concerns.

Avoidant Attachment with Money Can Look Like ...

- Aversion to discussing or acknowledging financial issues, leading to avoidance and denial.

- Reluctance to seek help or support from others, even when facing financial difficulties.
- Difficulty trusting others with joint financial decisions or pooling resources.
- Emotionally distancing oneself from the impact of financial decisions or consequences.

Disorganized Attachment with Money Can Look Like ...

- Difficulty with consistency in managing money, alternating between impulsive and avoidant behaviors.
- Engaging in self-sabotaging behaviors that undermine financial stability, like excessive gambling or overspending.
- Chaotic financial patterns, such as frequent borrowing, accumulating debt, or inconsistent income streams.
- Experiencing intense shame or guilt around financial mistakes, making it challenging to learn from past behaviors.

These don't include every single behavior and you might feel like you fall into multiple categories, but that's okay. Below are some ways you can manage these.

Ways to Manage Anxious Attachment with Money

- Practice mindfulness to develop awareness of anxious thoughts and emotions around money.
- Engage in self-reflection and explore the underlying emotional triggers related to money anxiety.
- Practice gratitude and focus on what is currently going well financially.

Ways to Manage Avoidant Attachment with Money

- Practice open and honest communication about money with trusted individuals.

- Gradually increase trust in others by involving them in financial decisions and joint planning.
- Develop a deeper understanding of the emotional and psychological aspects of money.
- Reflect on the role of avoidance in other areas of life and explore ways to address it holistically.

Ways to Manage Disorganized Attachment with Money

- Develop a structured financial routine that provides stability and reduces impulsive behaviors.
- Build a support network of trusted individuals who can offer guidance and support in managing finances.
- Establish clear boundaries in financial relationships to prevent exploitation or enabling behaviors.
- Consider working with a financial planner or coach experienced in addressing disorganized attachment and money-related issues.

There is no shame in having an insecure attachment, it is quite common. In my case, I grew up with a disorganized attachment style. This looked like gravitating towards co-dependent relationships that were toxic and volatile. When things were calm, I felt destabilized and found ways to re-create chaos. With many years of therapy, self-development books, and applying the information, I have been able to repair this dynamic and form healthier relationships with others.

All forms of insecure attachment stem from the same issue; at some point in your childhood, you learned that your primary caregivers could not meet your needs usually due to some form of absence. Whether it's because you had a parent who worked extra-long hours, or they struggled with mental health conditions, incarceration, or you had a sibling with more needs, etc., you were not able to get your needs met. While you cannot change your attachment style, you can certainly repair it and form healthy relationships.

In addition to understanding your relationship with money from a relational perspective, it is important to acknowledge how shame, trauma and early messaging around money create and reinforce your narratives. I grew up with many of the stories that centered on hardship and struggle growing up in a low-income, immigrant family system. In addition to those challenges, I had the added layer of navigating the shame around my sexuality and gender, though it would take me years before I could allow myself to truly explore those identities.

In 2017, after ten years of dreaming about going to grad school for my MSW, I was accepted into NYU's School of Social Work program. The ten years leading up to that acceptance were a rollercoaster. I had graduated from an Ivy League institution where I had struggled as I managed newly diagnosed mental health conditions, learning disabilities, and unexplored trauma. After graduating, I became enmeshed in a co-dependent, emotionally and financially abusive partnership. It left me with fucked up credit, garnished wages, and a huge mess to fix that would take years to repair.

After leaving that partnership, I moved back in with my mom and committed to a path of unapologetic self-love to ensure that I would never find myself in that kind of relationship again. I wanted to embrace my identities unapologetically and show up fully for myself. I set long-term goals of going to graduate school and repairing my credit in order to eventually buy a home. I was done dimming my light and playing small. During this period, I threw myself in the fire. I worked with financial counselors to repair my credit and immersed myself in therapy, holistic care, and everything that would bring me joy, pleasure, and healing.

I came out as Queer and non-monogamous to my family which was no small feat especially as I was living with my mother who had many homophobic embedded ideals. Having grown up in the church where I learned it was a sin to be queer, let alone being a woman who wanted to

293

experience multiple partners and sexual freedom, it was really hard to openly own those parts of my identity and shed the shame around it. I was almost 30 and it felt like it was "too late" to come out and start my life over but it was an act of self-love to allow myself to fully explore what these identities meant for me (also it's actually never too late). I dove into books about non-monogamy, attended more queer-centered events personally and professionally, and started widening my circles to more affirming spaces. I became more vocal about these parts of my identities because I knew I wasn't alone and it felt important to affirm others.

So by the time I was accepted into graduate school, I felt like I had climbed mountains to get there, but as life does, it threw me another curveball. Six weeks after starting my MSW program, my 30-year-old sister Maddy, was diagnosed with a rare type of cancer that had spread throughout her body and she eventually passed two years later. It was an earth-shattering loss.

It was during that time, I truly realized that life would never stop throwing curve balls. It was crucial to cultivate joy and continue choosing myself every day. I managed to repair my credit, travel the world, discover the kink community, and experience pleasure beyond my wildest dreams all while experiencing continuous loss and grief. Living in the duality of pleasure and grief became a way of life for me. Intentionally prioritizing my pleasure became paramount to my self-care and my overall well-being.

I finished my degree at the start of the pandemic and became a therapist for BIPOC and Queer and Trans people the week after George Floyd was murdered. It was a hard time to be human let alone a therapist. During that time, I bought a home and moved into my own space. I became super intentional about creating a peaceful, joyful, and nourishing home in order to heal, grieve, and ground myself amidst the chaos of the world.

Working with queer and trans people as a therapist turned into one of the most transformational roles I've served. I saw the impact it had on my clients for me to show up as my full self. Being a queer, non-monogamous therapist who curses, jokes around, and promotes sexual liberation gave my clients the permission they were seeking to also embrace their full selves.

Affirming trans clients in navigating their gender identities allowed me to see the stark difference between how I affirmed my clients' gender explorations versus how I denied my own. So I leaned into my own exploration of gender and again saw how valuable it was to clients to see me doing my own work. I changed my pronouns and had conversations with clients who were curious about that change. I was honest about being in a space of exploration and confusion because that is completely normal. It is self-love to allow yourself to embrace not having all the answers.

While the work was transformative, money and access to resources for me and clients alike were still major barriers. I felt powerless about the harmful legislature threatening trans lives every day, fear about our livelihood, getting proper healthcare, not having enough money to live comfortably, and an overarching theme of needing to work harder to survive.

I thought earning my degree after ten years in the field would mean making more money and feeling more accomplished but instead, I found myself devalued, burnt out, and angry. I had dedicated my life to a field that did not value me and saw me as replaceable. I remember sitting next to my sister Maddy (who was actually a social worker) while she was on her deathbed and seeing a job listing that her workplace had posted to seek her replacement. She wasn't even dead yet and they were already looking for her replacement! It became important for me to never tie my identity to any job and to never put their needs above my own. I simply refused to let any job decide my value and worth anymore.

I decided to bet on myself and start a coaching business. I had to believe that I could make good money by being 100 percent myself. I wanted to prove to myself that I could do it because I wanted to show others what was possible, especially those of similar identities. I needed to free myself from the toxicity of hustle culture and the belief that I needed to work harder to make more money.

I quit my job with no other prospects to fall back on. I depleted my emergency fund and paid a scary ass amount of money to an amazing business coach. What happened next was pure magic! Within the first ten days of launching my business, I made $10,000 in revenue. A social worker making $10,000 in ten days?!? My mind was blown. I continued learning and investing right back into my business. I attended business retreats, started networking, and showing up on socials. I began teaching my clients what I had learned and encouraged a few of them to start their own businesses. A few of them did and went on to have some amazing results.

Within a couple of months, I was embodying the wildest dream version of myself. I changed my name to Sunny which is 100 percent aligned with me. I changed my entire look from clothing to hair to gender expression. Everything changed and I couldn't believe what I had accomplished in such a short time. Within six months, I made $50,000 in revenue and my whole belief system about money was shattered. I absolutely could make good money being 100 percent myself.

I was ecstatic and yet I was also enraged that as social workers and activists, we perpetuate this narrative that it is not possible for us. So while the success felt huge and exciting, it came with so much grief. What people don't tell you about success (especially "rapid" success) is that you will experience a lot of grief. I had essentially let go of an identity that no longer served me but gave me a sense of safety.

In letting it go to make space for my new identity, I was completely destabilized.

Every experience that I had pushed through in the years leading up to that moment caught up with me including the grief, depression, and PTSD of experiencing so much loss. It led me to create chaos and struggle in my business and with money. I had essentially replicated the same financial mess I was in after leaving that abusive relationship. Except I had a business now and owned a home, so I had much more to lose.

If you recall from the attachment section, I mentioned having a disorganized attachment. So naturally when I experienced making thousands of dollars with ease and found myself receiving what I had been wanting, I recreated the chaos and volatility that came with all of my previous successes. If you have found yourself in similar patterns know this, you were doing what was familiar and your body was trying to keep you safe. It is time you shed your shame around that. Self-love isn't just about the massages, vacations, or the treat yo' self-moments! Self-love is about loving yourself through the darkest moments. It's about forgiving yourself and giving yourself the chance to do a little better next time.

As I started resurfacing from my depressive and self-destructive episode, I reflected on the mess I had created and the calm confidence I felt about repairing it. I knew that I could repair that mess because I had repaired many messes before. It was clear then that I believed I *had* to lose everything in order to succeed to the next level. So I began questioning my overall relationship with money (instead of focusing just on that episode) and why I only felt good about it when I was actively repairing it.

So that's when I asked myself, if money was my partner, what kind of relationship are we in? And that's when I realized, OMG, I was a toxic partner! So I decided right then and there that I would heal my relationship with money. It was time to go to couple's therapy with my money!

To make the experience pleasurable, empowering, and more practical, I gave my money a persona. I named my money Monae and gave her a whole identity. She looks like Janelle Monae. She's fine as hell and is supportive, loving, and abundant. Her love knows no limits. She is non-monogamous and has infinite love to give to all! She is meant to be shared lovingly with others who want her and it comes at no cost to me. That is what non-monogamy is all about. Non-monogamy rejects the idea that we can only love one partner at a time and that if they love anyone else we somehow lose out or that there's less for us. Love is abundant just like money and pleasure. There's plenty to go around for us all.

When I started reflecting on our relationship I realized, Monae has actually always been there, even though I didn't see it that way. So I decided to commit to becoming a healthy partner to Monae. It became so fun to start talking about money in this way. A piece of advice, always incorporate pleasure into your life, especially in areas that feel more challenging. Who said you can't have fun in the repair process?

As I started sharing this perspective with other entrepreneurs, I saw them experience some major breakthroughs and immediately knew that I could not keep this information to myself. I didn't need to wait until I was at a certain point of "success" to share this. It was crucial to help other badass entrepreneurs (especially queer and trans ones) heal their relationship with money. This is important so that collectively, we can gain economic power and make major shifts in our system.

After this mental shift, my energy around money changed. I began to be more outspoken about my desires for wealth and economic justice. I embraced unapologetic self-love when it came to money. To put it simply, to love money is to love yourself. Blocking yourself off from money keeps you in scarcity mode and keeps you from receiving the blessings that are all around you, not just financially but energetically too. Having an abundant, pleasurable relationship with money is self-love. You deserve to make the kind of money that allows you to live comfortably and creates systemic change. One does not have to come at the expense of the other.

This shift in perspective started changing things in my life pretty immediately. Suddenly opportunities for new business ventures were opening up, folks were reaching out to hire me, and money was flowing to my business from clients and external sources. I was finding money in unexpected places. It started flowing to me in small and large quantities. I began celebrating every penny like it was a million dollars. I'm not suggesting that everything is all good now. I'm repairing my relationship with money every day and feel very trusting of where I'm headed, but it is not an overnight fix. As I write this chapter, I have actually started exploring the process of filing for bankruptcy. I am dissolving my business in its current iteration and will be starting anew with more clarity and a wealth of knowledge.

The fact is, I outgrew my business shortly after starting it. I mean for starters, I changed my whole ass name and look! And don't even get me started on the administrative nightmare it is to change your name legally (especially your first name) which a lot of trans folks do in order to align with their identity. So I deserve a fresh start and there is no shame in giving myself the opportunity to build back better. Letting myself "fail" without shame is self-love.

I am not suggesting that mindset or this relational analogy is the only key to wealth. It is by systemic design that historically excluded groups are living in poverty at disproportionate rates and have strained relationships with money. Many of us will continue believing that we don't have money because we haven't worked hard enough. This is what white supremacy was built off of, the exploitative labor of Black folks. We are taught that we have to work hard for our money and if we don't have money, it's because we haven't worked enough. It is complete bullshit. I saw my mom work long hours and multiple jobs for years to the point of becoming disabled and experiencing long-term health conditions. So with all that work, shouldn't she be rich by now? I reject the idea that I need to sacrifice my body, health, and pleasure in order to make money. It is time you rejected this harmful narrative too.

I'm on a mission to empower Queer and Trans entrepreneurs to build wealth by being their full authentic selves. We need economic power to combat the legislature that becomes more oppressive towards our identities every day. The fact is, when people of historically excluded groups build wealth, they contribute directly towards their communities in major ways and that is where we have the largest impact. Having economic power is the only way we can actually uplift our communities without depleting ourselves in the process. If you leave with anything from this chapter take this; If you care about societal change, **you must heal your relationship with money**. Money is non-monogamous! Your version of Monae is waiting for you. So let's get to work!

Sunny De Leon

Sunny De Leon (She/They) is an entrepreneur, social worker, and activist, who is dedicated to the liberation of Queer and Trans people of color through economic justice.

With over a decade of experience in the mental health field, Sunny uses a strengths-based and trauma-informed framework to care for clients in their transformations in ways that play on their strengths while acknowledging their trauma. Sunny shares their lived experiences and identities as an Afro-Latinx, queer, trans, non-binary, and non-monogamous person to empower clients to embody their full authentic selves.

After achieving rapid milestones in their business and experiencing significant mental blocks afterward, Sunny is dedicated to ending the cycle of centering struggle in their work by healing their relationship with money and helping other Queer and Trans entrepreneurs do the same.

Sunny shows up with unfiltered realness and brings in a fun and refreshing approach by empowering clients to center pleasure and joy in their healing journeys.

They provide a nurturing and inviting space for clients to explore their identities, break free from oppressive structures, and create lifestyles rooted in unapologetic self-love. Sunny focuses on guiding entrepreneurs toward embracing their authentic selves, reclaiming their power, and achieving success on their own terms.

Sunny holds a Bachelor of Science degree from Cornell University and a Master of Social Work from New York University.

Connect with Sunny at www.sunnydeleon.com.

CHAPTER 14

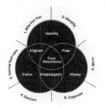

Integrating Abundance, Continue the Journey

In the journey of abundance, the final destination is not a place; it's a state of being. Embrace each moment, live in gratitude, and watch as your life becomes a masterpiece of abundance.

~Patrina Wisdom

As we draw this transformative journey to a close, I want to express my profound gratitude for the time we've spent together exploring the Anatomy Of Abundance™. It's been a voyage of self-discovery, growth, and empowerment, and I hope you now carry with you the seeds of a more abundant life.

Throughout this book, we've delved into the myriad of dimensions of abundance: the power of mindset, the impact of gratitude, the role of self-love, and the importance of setting intentions. We've navigated the waters of financial empowerment and harnessed the strength of resilience. You've learned that abundance isn't a destination; it's a dynamic journey that flows through your life.

Here's the key takeaway: abundance isn't a destination; it's a journey. It's not a static state you arrive at and remain in perpetuity. Abundance is a dynamic, ever-evolving force that flows through your life. It's not about material wealth alone; it's about a wealth of experiences, connections, and fulfillment in all aspects of life. Your journey to abundance is an ongoing story, and it's one best shared and nurtured within a supportive community.

Continuing the Conversation:

The wisdom you've gained within these pages is the beginning, not the end. To continue your exploration, I invite you to take part in the ongoing conversation about abundance, personal development, and growth. Whether you choose to revisit this book, engage in meaningful discussions, or practice the exercises with friends, family, or colleagues in a self-led book club, remember that your personal journey to abundance is a living, ever-evolving process.

The Power of Community:

Community plays a pivotal role in nurturing your journey. Surrounding yourself with like-minded individuals who share your passion for personal development can be a source of inspiration, encouragement, and accountability. Seek out or create spaces where you can explore abundance, exchange insights, and celebrate one another's growth.

Specialized Support:

At times, your journey may require specialized guidance or support. You may encounter challenges that seem insurmountable or areas of growth that demand more focused attention. In such moments, don't hesitate to seek specialized support from our mentors, coaches, or experts who can provide tailored guidance on your path to abundance.

To make the most of the wisdom you've gained, consider continuing your exploration in one of two ways.

1. **Self-Led Book Club:** Consider gathering a group of like-minded individuals, perhaps some of your friends, family, or colleagues, and forming a self-led book club. Create a space where you can revisit the book, discuss its concepts, and share your experiences with one another. Challenge each other to implement the ideas and exercises from each chapter, and celebrate your growth together. The Anatomy Of Abundance™ is designed to be a living, breathing guide, so make it an ongoing part of your personal development.

2. **Join Our Ongoing Book Club with the Authors:** For a deeper dive into the Anatomy of Abundance™, I'm thrilled to invite you to join our book club. This club is hosted by the co-authors who have contributed to this book. Together we provide a unique opportunity to engage in discussions, workshops, and practices that bring the pages of this book to life. You'll have the chance to interact with the authors themselves, be guided in the implementation of the framework, and gain even more insight into their perspectives.

JOIN OUR BOOK CLUB HERE:
https://go.patrinawisdom.com/abundance-book-club

We are here to help you every step of the way. The authors who have contributed to this book are not just names on a page; we are a community dedicated to supporting you in your quest for abundance.

The journey is continuous, and the possibilities are endless. Keep exploring, keep growing, and continue to embrace the abundance that resides within you. Let this book be the beginning of a profound, lifelong conversation about abundance and personal development.

With gratitude and excitement for the adventures ahead, Patrina Wisdom

Made in the USA
Las Vegas, NV
11 January 2024

84232927R00184